Fear Not

For You Are Redeemed

A One-Year Journey Pursuing Your Healing Through Christ

STEFANIE JANE MARTINO

R/L

Fear Not For You Are Redeemed

© Copyright 2022 Stefanie Jane Martino

ISBN: 978-1-7358089-9-4

Published by:
Roaring Lambs Publishing
17110 Dallas Parkway, Suite 260; Dallas, TX 75248

Published in the United States of America.

Contents

Introduction

Born into a family of abuse, I was conditioned to live in fear at a young age. Even as a preschooler, I had already constructed my walls of fear high and strong, built of pain and violence, insults and cruelty, maltreatment and neglect—all summed up as sexual, physical, and verbal abuse. I was only three years old when the sexual abuse started.

Growing up, I didn't see every day as a bad day, but every day I lived in fear. As punishment in our home could be extremely brutal, even for committing a little childish blunder, I was terrified of getting in trouble; I did not feel free to learn and grow through mistakes. Raised in a home with alcoholics, I realized that what worked yesterday might not work today. I questioned everything about decisions as I saw myself through eyes of criticism; fear has a way of distorting our view.

With all the abuse and in a constant state of fear, I could have written a horror novel. In fact, as a teen I found it fun to captivate an audience through crafting dark, disturbing poems. I felt a thrill in seeing people moved by my deep, dark emotions. But the harsh, ominous writing did not give God glory and kept my mind caged in the horrific world I so desperately wanted to forget.

Saturated in fear and negative thinking, my brain could not comprehend how to love myself or how to stop talking down to myself. The abuse left me filled with hate . . . but I wanted to live differently.

At thirteen years old, I read the Bible cover to cover, and on October 21, 1990, I prayed to ask Jesus to come into my heart. Miraculous, yes? It certainly was. Yet, fear did not lose its grip on me, and life did not get any easier. The harsh environment started to spill over into the neighborhood where I lived.

The next year proved to be the beginning of my downward spiral. I couldn't comprehend why I had to endure all the suffering. I felt hated at school. And I became a victim of sexual abuse by "Mr. Popularity"—seeing myself hurled into another pit of shame. And if all that misery were not enough, I was then jumped and beat up, leaving my emotions completely shattered. That beating was so brutal that it left me not only physically damaged but with emotional scars that lingered for decades. As a fourteen-year-old, having my front tooth broken in half and the family unable to pay for a dentist proved deeply humiliating. To me, it offered yet another reason not to smile, but it did not stop me from reading the Bible.

"Why me?" became my constant question to God, and life continued to run its collision course. Reaching a new bottom at seventeen, I was homeless and extremely suicidal. Not valuing my life, I wanted nothing more than to stop the pain. Maybe through my death, I thought, my soul could find the rest that my shattered heart needed.

I begged God to let me die, but instead He wrapped His love around me like a blanket swaddled tightly around my body. The glory of the Lord completely surrounded me. Everything in that moment felt perfect. I had questioned God's love over and over, yet in a split second, all my doubt was gone. All the constant questioning, "God, why me?" disappeared. Before this moment, I thought my death would bring relief from pain, yet I found there is life, choosing to believe God.

God breathed Jeremiah 29:11 into my life: "For I know the plans I have for you, plans to prosper you and not to harm you,

12

plans to give you a hope and a future." So, this was the second time I truly had faith in His promises, and I began taking Him at His word over my earthly life. Slowly, I began to see things differently, with a new understanding that perfect Love is found only in the glory of God.

Choosing to walk out the truths of the Bible daily, I had to stop making excuses about how I was living. Thankfully, the Holy Spirit surrounded me, and as I practiced, I learned to be accountable to myself and to God. The Holy Spirit also reminded me to ask God into every moment of every day, yet in my young faith, I thought I was doing it through my own persistence. I needed God to show me how to live for Christ, and now throughout the years, Jesus has been an awesome teacher.

Our hands are never too dirty to open the Word of God; I am living proof. God will clean us up if we are willing to open our Bible, regardless of the surroundings. In my teens, I was running with pagans, completely wasted, yet still reading my Bible and praying. The horrible circumstances I found myself in did not seem to matter; I simply had a desire to read the Word of God. However, wanting to live in the Light, I felt stuck in the dark. Thank God, He gives us the desires of our heart.

Having no idea how God was going to make His plans for my life prosper, I had the faith that He would accomplish what He said He would do. God taught me to open my journal and write to Him. He showed me how to write for a better purpose. Before my glorious visit from Father God when I felt enwrapped in His love, I liked to write heavy, depressing work to connect with people on a "deeper" level, but in reality, the darkness was keeping my mind clouded. Yet after His visit that ignited my faith, I wanted to write Him to find relief from the pain. I wanted to deal with my past and my aching heart instead of trying to mask them with catchy melodies. And soon, I stopped fixating on the pain and started to write to God to heal me from the inside out.

One of the greatest treasures God has given me is the ability to be completely honest with Him. God asks me *hard* questions all the time. My healing in Christ has been so authentic and far-reaching because, through writing and prayer, I consider the questions He places on my heart and I answer Him. I find clarity in my writing as I talk to the Lord. In my teen years, I was blinded by fear, asking for clarity so many times I thought it was impossible to find, but He gives abundantly to those who ask. Staying connected to God, following the leading of our Good Shepherd, proves critical.

I am still blinded to many realizations about myself and the world, but day by day, God gives me new clarity. He opens my eyes to see His traits and views. Needing His mercy every day, I am so thankful He sanctifies my mind, enlightening me with His perspective. Each day I gain more clarity on how to live a life free from the bondage of fear. It was Satan who lied to me, so I have nothing to fear but God Himself.

With God's help and leading, lean into His love for you and find the desire to reach into yourself and heal down into the depths of your soul. Everyone is broken, fragmented and hurting, which God's power can mend. God allowed my severe brokenness in order for me to learn, through my healing, how to live a courageous life for Christ. And if God can do it for me, He wants to do it for you as well. We are made whole in Christ alone.

Learning God's Word, reading your Bible, is the key to unlock the bondage of fear. God wants to teach you how to live courageously for His good purpose. Your future hope depends on it.

How to Use This Book

I have been praying for you to come alongside the Lord and make a commitment to Him. This book is designed for you to find healing in the name of Jesus, and healing is not easy; but as you read daily, considering each message thoughtfully, you will at a certain point find yourself talking honestly with God and your commitment to Him and this journey growing. That's my prayer. If you want to live a life free from the bondage of fear, you must take an honest, persistent approach with the pages you find here.

Read one daily devotional *every morning*. You'll find that two great benefits come with doing so. Matthew 6:33 says, "Seek first His kingdom and His righteousness and all these things will be given to you." What things will be given to you? Freedom from worry, and provision for your needs. God deserves to be first in every area of your life. You forgo the blessings of God when you do not seek Him first. Freedom from fear takes you putting God first in all your circumstances, and then the blessings flow. Which leads us to our second benefit. When you choose to spend your time with God first, you can walk out your day with Him, pondering what you have read and learned. This will give you an unlimited number of blessings throughout your entire day. Plus, it helps you get in the habit of thinking things through with God.

Prayer is not complicated, and anyone can do it, but how often you communicate with God does matter. Each morning before you start reading the devotional, ask God to join you. It does not need to be long-winded; just pause and say, "Jesus, please join me." Then once you have invited Him into your devotional time, He can help bring to mind the things that can help you find freedom from fear. God will whisper into your heart the areas that need to be mended by His loving touch.

Each day has a *question* or set of questions. Prayerfully, you should answer those. Some questions will cut you to the core when you read them. Other questions may not be easy to answer; perhaps you have believed a lie for so long that the truth is not easy to process. But God brought you to difficult questions so you can face the truth and do things differently. God wants to change you into the person He created you to be. He is not intimidated by your heart that sits behind a formidable wall. In fact, He will soften your heart if you allow these questions to sink into your core and you internalize them with Christ.

I highly suggest you start this devotional with a brand-new *spiral notebook*. I understand not everyone likes to journal, but I firmly believe that you will have more success if you choose to answer each question of the devotional in a notebook. This will help you distinguish your true, honest answers. Clarity can happen when you put your thoughts on paper. Plus, this notebook will become a mile-marker for you. Down the road you can go back and look at your answers and see how God is moving you away from fear into His love. If you like to journal, this could be a great tool to get you in the habit of thinking things through with God while writing out your thoughts. I know the power of journaling with Christ, and this devotional gives proof of that.

There is no perfect road map to healing. Perhaps that's why God did not want me to set a rigid number of consecutive days for you to stay on a specific *subject* matter as you read through these devotions. You will, however, flow through the days' topics and the truths you will discover, building upon what you have already learned. As you gain knowledge from God, you will gain insight into your own fears that are keeping you from being courageous for Christ. God wants to expose your fears, doubts, and misguided perspectives so you can find the freedom in doing things God's way.

If at any time during your healing journey you are curious about a subject matter, there is a guide in the back of the book to help you locate that subject.

This devotional was constructed in a way that takes you on a journey of healing. Each day you go a little deeper with the Lord, and every day you will see things in a new light. You do not need to know how God will heal you; you just have to believe He will. It is not His design for you to live in fear. He chose you to be His child, and He gave you all the power in the Holy Spirit you need to find your complete healing in the name of Christ.

Day 1

Fear Not For You Are Redeemed

Fear not for I have redeemed you;
I have called you by name, you are Mine.
When you pass through the waters, I will be with you;
and through the rivers, they shall not overwhelm you;
when you walk through fire you shall not be burned,
and the flame shall not consume you.
For I AM the LORD your God, the Holy One of Israel, your Savior.
Because you are precious in My eyes, and honored, and I love you."
Isaiah 43:1b-2, 4 (ESV)

Your Savior finds you precious. He loves you and knows your time on earth can be difficult and sometimes painful, filled with great sorrow and loss, injustice and heartbreak. Yet while God does not promise an easy life, He promises to be with you when life is hard; He will not abandon you. Very importantly, all those who seek God, find God. Everything you have endured, all you have suffered, has brought you here today to this place—the perfect time to ask God to shine a light on all the terrible circumstances in your world . . . and to change, restore, and redeem each one.

Will you ask God to begin to reveal how you are allowing fear to control your life instead of living in the redemption you already have? If you have accepted Jesus as your Lord and Savior, God promises He has already redeemed you. You are already a new creation; now you need to walk out that new life and let Jesus redeem you daily.

Are you listening when He calls you by name and directs you to walk by His side? He wants to walk with you through the fire. He wants you to know that your flood of emotions need not overwhelm you. God is not pleased with Satan or the sin in this world, but He is calling you to His side so you can learn to lean in and trust Him amidst the world's sins. Your reward will be great when you learn to trust His daily redemption—where the freedom from fear is found.

Day 2

Safe Boundaries

*The serpent was more crafty than any other beast of the field
that the LORD God had made.
He said to the woman, "Did God actually say,
'You shall not eat of any tree in the garden?'"
The woman said God instructed her to not eat from one tree in the garden.
But the serpent said, "You will not surely die.
For God knows that when you eat of it your eyes will be opened,
and you will be like God, knowing good and evil."
When the woman saw that the fruit was good for food
and that it was a delight to the eyes,
and that the tree was to be desired to make one wise,
she took of its fruit and ate, and she also gave some to her husband
who was with her, and he ate it. Then the eyes of both were opened
and they knew they were naked
and hid themselves from the presence of the LORD.*
Genesis 3:1-8 (ESV, paraphrased)

Because Eve disobeyed God, sin entered the world. Everyone born of flesh, every person on this earth, has a natural tendency to sin—to think, speak, or act in ways that go against trust and faith in God and His Word. Satan often comes to people and plants seeds of doubt and deception, thus kindling half-truths in their hearts and minds. Adam and Eve's eyes were opened, just like the serpent stated, opening their eyes to sin, shame, and fear. While God had given them safe boundaries for their protection, they did not take Him at His Word; instead, they listened to the doubt of the serpent and allowed their pride, their appetite for wisdom, to rule their desire—and thus failed to follow the direct instructions of God.

Have you seen God place boundaries in your life to keep you from slipping over the edge? Are you listening to the doubts Satan is using to try to deceive you? Anytime you do not believe God, when you do not believe every Word of the Bible, you separate yourself from Him. And this sin always has a price tag dangling in the darkness. If you call to God in the ditch, Jesus will meet you there, but you must repent of the sin of doing things your way. Your cry of repentance often leads to a repentant outpouring and the cleansing of your heart, bringing you to a place where you rely on Him each step of the way. Through the power of the cross, you will soon realize that sin no longer has its grip on you. Then, oh, what a relief and a joy!

Day 3

Righteous Living Through Belief

The LORD came to Abram in a vision: "Fear not, I AM your shield;
your reward shall be great."
But Abram said, "O Lord GOD, what will You give me,
for I continue childless? . . . Behold You have given me no offspring."
The Word of the LORD came to him and He brought him outside and said,
"Look toward heaven and, number the stars,
if you are able to number them." Then He said to him,
"So shall your offspring be."
And he believed the LORD, and He counted it to him as righteousness.
Genesis 15:1-6 (ESV, paraphrased)

Some rich theology lies wrapped in these verses. Here, the first "fear not" verse in the Bible resounds. It's also the first time the word "believe" shows up, as well as the first I AM statement. Do not fear, believe God's Word above all, and you will be righteous. The great I Am is your shield and worthy of your trust. He keeps your feet steady when you believe Him; He shows you how to live a righteous life.

And who are the righteous? Those who have faith, a sincere trust, in our loving God. It sounds so simple: believe God above all the other influences around you. With certainty, God will empower you to live a life free from fear; all you have to do is believe it. *What influences is God asking you to remove from your life so you can listen to His voice more closely?*

God is Love

21

Day 4

Obedience Brings Blessings

*If you follow My decree and are careful to obey My commands,
I will send you rain in the season, and the ground will yield its crops
and the trees of the field their fruit.
You will eat all the food you want and live in safety in your land.
I will grant peace in the land, and you will lie down,
and no one will make you afraid.*
Leviticus 26:3-4, 5b-6 (NIV)

If you follow God's commandments, God will bless you. Sometimes those blessings mean more joy, a happy heart. Or maybe they mean a great sense of peace flooding your soul. Blessings could come in whatever shape or form He thinks is best in order for your faith to grow, for you to become more like Jesus.

Jesus said the most important commandment is to "love the Lord with all your heart, soul, mind, and all your strength." Plus, you are to love your neighbor as you love yourself (Mark 12:28-31). Put God first and humble yourself because you are on the same playing field as everyone else.

You are a sinner, living in a fallen world. Therefore, you can never live a sinless life. But God will bless those who seek Him first—in the situations and puzzles of life. His presence in the darkness will be a blessing, but you must put your strength in God instead of wasting your strength on worry, doubt, lack of trust, and being fearful of the "what ifs" and what might have been. You will not find peace there; trusting Jesus is the only answer to living in peace.

Trusting Jesus means you depend on His atonement for your sins. He paid the price you could never pay.

In much the same way, the Law is perfect; we are not. We needed a Savior who could live a perfect life so He could be the sacrifice for our sin problem. Jesus fulfilled the Law perfectly so He could meet you right where you are. *Have you been honoring the commandments of the Lord?* He is waiting to bless you through your obedience.

Day 5

God Loves You

*"For God so loved you that He gave His one and only Son,
that whoever believes in Him shall not perish but have eternal life.
For God did not send His Son into this world to condemn the world,
but to save the world through Him.
Whoever believes Him is not condemned,
but whoever does not believe stands condemned already
because he has not believed in the name of God's one and only Son.
This is the verdict: Light has come into the world,
but men loved darkness instead of light
because their deeds were evil.
Everyone who does evil hates the light
and will not come into the light for fear that his deeds will be exposed.
But whoever lives by the truth comes into the light,
so that it may be seen plainly
that what he has done has been done through God."*
John 3:16-21 (NIV)

Have you accepted Jesus' work on the cross for your sins? Have you prayed to ask Jesus for a personal relationship with Him? Jesus died on the cross for the sins of the world, for the sins you have committed. Accepting this truth is the beginning of your personal redemption story in Christ.

Jesus is the only way to freedom. There is no Plan B. "Jesus is the Way, the Truth, and the Life, and no one gets to the Father except through Him" (John 14:16).

If you do not know if you have a personal relationship with Jesus, you can pray a simple prayer like this:

"Jesus, I am a sinner, and I need a Savior. Thank You for taking my place on the cross. For only You could pay the penalty for my sins. Thank You for Your grace. Please help me walk in the ways that You want me to walk. Jesus, please come into my life and rule over me. In Jesus' name, Amen."

If you prayed this prayer just now, if you prayed with faith that God exists and hears you, with a desire to turn to Him and give Him your heart and your future, then hallelujah! The angels in heaven are celebrating. It's time to rejoice. You are part of His family, your eternity is secure in heaven, and He will never let you go.

23

Day 6

Love Above All

"You shall love the LORD your God with all your heart
and will all your soul and with all your mind.
This is the greatest and the first commandment and the second is like it;
you should love your neighbor as yourself."
Matthew 22:37-38 (ESV)

Jesus loves the people He created; He loves you. He does not want to see any of us perish. And our stories of hardship should be an opportunity to have God fill in the gaps, the broken places, in our lives.

Remember, God's love is perfect; people are not. He calls us to forgive, but we must learn to heal in the way He intends; He is not pleased when we choose anger or rebellion. He wants to give us something better, something more, something amazing . . . by the power of the Cross.

Jesus' work on the cross was final; He completely overcame death, sin, and fear. Nothing is outside His power. Nothing is too hard for God, but He wants you to believe in the power of the cross—all the way down to the smallest areas of your life and into the excruciating pain that left you feeling crushed and defeated.

When you have been shattered by the people who were supposed to love you, it can be extremely difficult to trust your heart to anyone. The fear of being wounded again can make a person's heart calloused, but God calls us to have a tender, loving heart. God is asking you to look deep inside yourself and see where the love of Christ needs to be the focus of your affection.

Toward what are you affectionate? Your mind will shift its attitudes to where the affection of your heart lies. God deserves your whole affection, which in turn will lead you to a place where you can forgive people who wounded you. You can remove the hate in your heart. You can be free from fear when you choose to keep your heart, soul, and mind centered on the love of Christ. *Are you ready to live out your daily salvation waiting for you?*

Day 7

Good News of Great Joy

The angel said to them, "Do not be afraid,
I bring you good news of great joy that will be for all the people.
Today in the town of David a Savior has been born to you;
He is Christ the LORD."
Luke 2:10-11 (NIV)

Jesus did not have to leave heaven. He was not forced to come to earth and die on a cross for you, but He did. He humbled Himself and came to earth as a little, helpless baby. And during His entire time on earth, Jesus had complete confidence that Father God would do exactly as He said; Jesus knew His whole life He was headed toward the cross.

Jesus knows what it is like to be tempted by sin, as He was tempted in the desert (Matthew 4:1-11). He understands what it's like when our heart hurts and feels ripped and torn because a loved one has stepped into heaven and left us alone here (John 11:35). He was a "man of sorrows, despised and rejected by men" (Isaiah 53:3), so He is completely aware of how it feels to be insulted and beaten.

We do not have a far-off God who does not relate to our pain and grief. Jesus understands because He did walk a mile in your shoes. Jesus did not just experience the world of sin we live in; He was also abused by this world. Yet Jesus overcame the sin of this world to give you the hope and power of God through the Holy Spirit—and with the Holy Spirit, we are not left alone to fend for ourselves.

God graciously gave us the Holy Spirit, who will direct your steps toward healing the way God wants you to heal. By Jesus' stripes we are healed; nothing is done on our own. We can accomplish every good work in the Lord through the power of the Holy Spirit. *Have you asked God to ignite the Holy Spirit that dwells within you?* God can burn away all that is not of Him so you can burn for the Gospel message of Christ.

Day 8

Listen to Jesus

*"This is my beloved Son, with whom I AM well pleased;
listen to Him."*
*When the disciples heard this, they fell on their faces and were terrified.
But Jesus came and touched them, saying. "Rise, and have no fear."*
Matthew 17:5-7 (ESV)

Do you want to live a life free from the fears of life? Are your intentions good but your follow-through or actions speak otherwise? Do you feel your downward spiral is making you dizzy with grief? Have you found the end of yourself?

When you do, you will find that Jesus is waiting there . . . and He wants to fill you, just as you want to be filled with Him. You will not merely stumble into a holy life filled with the goodness of God. You must seek Jesus and learn how to depend on how He wants you to live. Jesus is speaking to His people, but He is doing so with outstretched arms, not screaming in your face to get you to change your ways.

God's voice is calm and brings peace. God's voice will convict your heart; He declares that sin in your life needs removing. He lovingly wants to have a pure relationship with you, right where you are. Satan is the one trying to make you feel condemned by your sin. But your sin is not your end; you are not doomed. You have freedom from sin because of Jesus' work on the cross. *Do you believe with your whole heart that Jesus died on the cross for every sin committed?*

Shame has no place in your life. Satan wants to remind you of your sin, but Jesus cancelled the entire debt of your sin. *Do you have the confidence to claim it?* If not, pray to God and ask Him to help you with your unbelief.

Day 9

It Is Finished

Jesus said, "It is finished," and He bowed
His head and gave up His spirit.
John 19:30 (ESV)

All debt was paid, all sins nailed to the cross. Jesus was the perfect sacrifice. He came to earth to redeem you from your sins—past, present, and future. *Jesus gave the free gift of grace . . . have you accepted it?* Sin separates us from a holy God. "For we all sin and fall short of the glory of God" (Romans 3:23). You cannot work your way to God; you must ask God to forgive you of your sins. *Have you asked Jesus into your heart so He can rule your heart as only He can do?* Jesus is the Bridge you need in order to walk and live a life courageous for Christ. The only way to be healed is to accept that Jesus died for your sins, but God did even more than cancel your sin debt. He wants you to walk in newness of life! He wants you to be saved from the schemes of the devil every day.

Throughout this devotional I will have you ask yourself this same question. You only have to pray this prayer once and then it is finished. You are sealed by the blood of the Lamb and nothing can separate you from the love of Christ. *Have you asked Jesus to be your personal Savior?* If not, and you would like to do so, then pray a prayer like this:

Dear Heavenly Father, I know I am a sinner, and You sent Your only Son Jesus to redeem my life. I accept the free gift of grace through Jesus Christ. Please come into my heart and make me into the person You want me to be. Thank You for the sacrifice. In Jesus' holy name. AMEN!

When you accept God's free gift of eternal life, you will be changed, from the inside out. That doesn't mean you will be free from pain, suffering, or the temptation to sin. But you will be living with Jesus at your side, bringing you His strength to live for Him, and comfort and peace as He carries you. And that makes all the difference.

Day 10

Victory Because He Lives

The angel said to them, "Do not be alarmed.
You seek Jesus of Nazareth, who was crucified. He has risen; He is not here.
See the place where they laid Him. But go, tell His disciples and Peter
that He is going before you to Galilee.
There you will see Him, just as He told you."
Mark 16:6-7 (ESV)

We have victory in all He has told us. We know the end of the story. We know Satan will be bound in Hell forever after the last soul God created, for His purpose, has lived his or her life on earth. Very significantly, God designed us for a purpose—a purpose that is both eternal and helpful for Him here and now.

You will see Jesus, just as He told you, if you believe. There is nothing complicated about the Gospel message. Satan wants to complicate your life by taking your simple faith and illuminating your failures. But you do not live in failure; you live in victory over the dark places in your life. You have victory over the lies you have believed. You can turn your life around. You can do things differently. Believe that Jesus has risen, and you have nothing to fear. God will equip you for the victory.

Do you believe every word Jesus has told you? You cannot prove God wrong. God is always right, God is always just, and He always has your best interest at heart. Do not be alarmed. Keep seeking after Jesus, and He will show you how He is going before you, every step of the way. Jesus can clear your path. Claim the victory!

Day 11

He Destroyed the Devil

Since the children, as He calls them, are people of flesh and blood,
Jesus Himself became like them and shared their human nature.
He did this so that through His death He might destroy the devil,
who has the power over death,
and in this way set free those who were slaves all their lives
because of their fear of death.
For it is clear that it is not the angels that He helps.
Instead, He helps the descendants of Abraham.
This means that He had to become like His people in every way,
in order to be their faithful and merciful High Priest
in His service to God, so that the people's sins would be forgiven.
Hebrews 2:14-17 (GNT)

Jesus destroyed death. Therefore, no longer do Christians have to live in death's shadow; they need not fear death.

Precious friend, nothing can separate you from Christ forevermore. You have victory eternally and in your daily life. Sin does bring death, which does separate you from God; but you have been justified in Christ, and you were made holy. Father God sent a Savior so you can have a relationship with Him. You are made new because of Jesus and Jesus alone. You are no longer a slave to sin. With the power of the Holy Spirit, you are more than a conquer in Christ. *You can overcome and become whole.*

Following Jesus is putting all your trust in Him alone; He wants you to be bold for Him without fear—trusting and believing His sovereign plan for your life. When fear comes knocking, remember Jesus destroyed fear so that you can live in confidence. You are right where God wants you to be. Satan wants to distract you from the glory of God, but God is merciful; His plans do come through.

Have you given yourself mercy over the poor choices you have made? God destroyed those past mistakes, your past life; remember His faithfulness to you. He let it go. *Why can you not let it go?*

29

Day 12

There Is Freedom

Whenever anyone turns to the Lord, the veil is taken away.
Now the Lord is the Spirit, and where the Spirit of the Lord is,
there is freedom.
And we, who with unveiled faces all reflect the Lord's glory,
are being transformed into His likeness with ever-increasing glory,
which comes from the Lord, who is the Spirit.
2 Corinthians 3:16-18 (NIV)

How often do you turn to the Lord? Do you seek His wisdom or resort to your fleshly ways like fear, pride, and lack of self-control?

When we turn to The Lord, He is faithful. Jesus left us His Holy Spirit so that we have the power of God living inside us.

Do you claim it? Do you believe and receive the Holy Spirit? That is our freedom: living in Christ Jesus whom we glorify as we abide in Him. When we live our lives dependent on His direction, wisdom, and power, He sanctifies us to be more and more like Jesus. We learn how to respond to life the way God wants us to, and this brings an ever-increasing glory.

Satan and the world will try to keep you from seeking Jesus any moment they can, but Jesus left His followers His Spirit so that we can have confidence and freedom in Him. Daily, God is changing you to become an image-bearer for Christ. *Why not reflect on that thought throughout your day?* And as you do, talk to Jesus, asking Him to help you bear His image—in freedom and without fear.

Day 13

Strengthened by His Salvation

*"Behold, God is my salvation; I will trust and will not be afraid;
For the Lord God is my strength and my song and
He has become my salvation."*
Isaiah 12:2 (ESV)

God is your salvation *every day* when you lean in and trust Him. Fear has no place when you fully trust Him, when you confidently know He is sovereign overall.

Certainly, this world can be abusive and harsh. The world asks us to toughen up, to grow a thick skin . . . but this often leads us to wall off areas of our heart, areas of our life, leaving us far from tender or gentle like God calls us to be. So, what can we do?

Rely on God's strength, for His strength is interwoven with compassion and love. For us, it takes much more strength to be tender and compassionate, acting in love at all times, than it does to be hard hearted and short tempered. In fact, He is our song as we are blessed to be called children of God, and we can praise Jesus because He is our salvation.

What areas in your heart have you walled off because of the past? Ask God to help you soften up so He can mold and shape you for His good purpose. Because He is your salvation, He *will* give you the strength—and put His song in your heart.

Day 14

Prayerfully, Mountains Move

Jesus said, "Have faith in God. Truly I say to you,
whoever says to this mountain, 'Be taken up and thrown into the sea,'
and does not doubt in his heart,
but believes that what he says will come to pass, it will be done for him.
Therefore, whatever you ask in prayer,
believe that you have received it and it will be yours."
Mark 11:22-24 (ESV)

For each person, God has a good and perfect plan. You can stand on His promises; He will never leave you nor forsake you. So, today, ask yourself . . .

"Do I have the faith to believe Jesus died on a cross for my sins? Do I have the faith to believe all of my sins—past, present and future—were nailed to the cross?"

Each and every time you cursed, when you allowed sinful and prideful thoughts to fill your mind, whatever your sins may have been, have you prayerfully recognized them and left them at the foot of the cross? These are just some of the mountains that will move, that will be cast into the sea, as you believe and stand on God's every word. Ask, believe, and receive your sanctification. One cannot live a life in doubt. Belief is of utmost importance with God. Abraham believed God and it was counted to him as righteousness (Romans 4:3).

Do you believe His every word, trusting and relying on Him? Or do you doubt you can do it? Does your self-esteem tell you that you cannot take risk and make a change? Or are you praying to God for a solution, believing you can change, being confident in who God created you to be, and knowing that, in love, He has eternal plans for you? The mountains in everyone's lives look different . . . cancer, a divorce, a childhood of abuse, the loss of a loved one, an unfaithful spouse.

Come to God with an open heart in prayer and believe it will be done. You do not have to stay in your situation. Sometimes the mountains do not need to move, but you do. *Do you receive it?*

Day 15

The Spirit Empowers His Children

For all who are led by the Spirit of God are sons/daughters of God.
For you did not receive the spirit of slavery to fall back into fear,
but you have received the Spirit of adoptions as sons/daughters,
by whom we cry "Abba! Father!"
The Spirit Himself bears witness with our spirit
that we are children of God.
Romans 8:14-16 (NIV)

Are you allowing yourself to be led by the Spirit? Are you listening for Father God's voice? If God is for you, nothing can stand against you (Romans 8:31).

This world is full of vile terrors and complete annoyances. Christians are affected by many evils, but we do not live like the rest of the world. We have a hope and a confidence that is in Christ, and believing Christ allows us to become children of God by the power of the cross. Jesus left His Holy Spirit with those who follow Him, to direct us in our walk on earth. Fear has no place in the heart of a Christian. God's Spirit is powerful, holy, loving, clean, and the opposite of fear.

We lack trust in God's sovereign plan when we live in fear instead of the freedom that is ours in Christ. *Will you cry out to Him today, ask Him to free you from fear and bind it far from you, and know beyond a shadow of doubt that you are His child?* There's nothing else like it in all the world.

Identity

Day 16
Seek and Obey Our Merciful God

If you seek the Lord your God, you will find Him
if you look for Him with all your heart and with all your soul.
When you are in distress and all these things have happened to you,
then in later day you will return to the Lord your God and obey Him.
For the Lord, your God, is a merciful God;
He will not abandon or destroy you or
forget the covenant with your forefathers;
which He confirmed to them by oath [the oath in Gen. 22:16]
Deuteronomy 4:29-31 (NIV)

No matter where you are in life. No matter your place of despair. No matter how far from God you may have wandered . . . you can always find Him if you seek Him. This is a promise you can count on.

As a Christian, we should find ourselves living in a state of repentance. We are not perfect, but in seeking God, He often sheds light on areas where we need to change course. Little by little, God changes your heart to be in line with His ways. His mercy is where your identity can rest.

He knows what happened to you. He understands the things that have put you in distress. He comprehends how you arrived at a horrific place in your life. And He has not overlooked you. He sees you right where you are. And He still loves you and has mercy for your poor choices, but you do not have to live in regret and guilt for your bad decisions.

Are you learning from your past mistakes, or are you making them over and over again? God's mercies are new every single day. Regardless of what you did yesterday, you can change the direction of your today if and when you seek Him with your whole heart. The power to do so comes from Him.

God is not interested in your half-hearted, self-sufficient attempts to be a better person. You cannot self-help yourself to treat others with kindness, to deny a temptation, to cast off a sin. All you can do is seek Him for His direction, and He will grant you mercy.

Day 17

Fret Not, Trust and Be Still

"Fret not yourself because of evildoers; be not envious of wrongdoers!
For they will soon fade like the grass and wither like the green herb.
Trust in the Lord and do good;
dwell in the land and befriend faithfulness.
Delight yourself in the Lord,
and He will give you the desires of your heart.
Commit your ways to the Lord; trust in Him and He will act.
He will bring forth your righteousness as the light,
and your justice as the noonday.
Be still before the Lord and wait patiently for Him;
fret not yourself over the one who prospers in his way,
over the man who carries out evil devices!
Refrain from anger and forsake wrath!
Fret not yourself; it tends only to evil."
Psalm 37:1-8 (ESV)

You can ask yourself a lot of questions from this passage. Questions that can change your environment, change your perspective, and change your way of thinking. For example, *"Am I ready to have the mindset of Christ? What am I focusing on . . . the good or the bad of a situation? Am I upset because the liars keep lying, the thieves keep stealing, and they seem to be getting away with it?"*

God will judge them; you can be certain of that. It's not your place to fret over their mistakes, and it might not be your business to be in the middle of their mess. When we fully trust God, knowing He is sovereign and that He loves and protects us, then we can be still and rest in the peace that Jesus gives us through the Holy Spirit.

What are you fretting about? Have you asked God to take over the situation? Have you asked God for His strength so you do not fall into your old patterns? Befriend faithfulness, delight in the Lord, trust Him—for God is perfectly faithful and gives you the desires of your heart.

What desires do you long for? Have you brought them to God? You might not ever be able to trust certain people, but you can trust that God has them in your life for a reason. You may be the only Jesus they ever see in this world. It's an honor that God finds you faithful enough to carry out His mission of love.

Day 18

Wisdom Is Found in God

The fear of the Lord is the beginning of knowledge.
The fear of the Lord is the beginning of wisdom,
and the knowledge of the Holy One is insight.
Proverbs 1:7, 9:10 (ESV)

God alone should be feared. He holds the keys to every person's eternal future. He alone judges each person after they die. Regardless of where you spend eternity, God will judge your life on earth. What is done on earth matters because it will affect your Judgment Day.

But also know that Jesus paid for your sins; you have nothing left to feel shame about. Jesus justified you so you can confidently stand before the throne of God and boldly speak to Him.

Also remember that God is loving, a merciful Father. Satan distorts and confuses you to think otherwise. God is only good; no evil exists in Him. He is perfect and holy. And the fear of Him is the beginning of knowledge and wisdom.

When you spend time with God, His insight gives you the wisdom you need to live the way He wants you to. When you know Him as the One who loves you, as your Lord and your Savior, then your fear of the Lord should not be one of fright for your soul or trembling for your eternal destination; it should be one of awe and reverence.

If you are justified by Christ, you have nothing to be scared of, nothing to fear. If you have not accepted the redemption of the cross, you have everything to fear. Thanks be to God, Jesus liberated you on the cross. *Do you live afraid of God, or are you confident in your Savior, who rescued you from all the fears of Satan and the world?*

Day 19

Walk with Humility and Gentleness

Walk in a manner worthy of the calling to which you have been called,
with all humility and gentleness, with patience,
bearing with one another in love,
eager to maintain the unity of the Spirit in the bond of peace.
Ephesians 4:1b-3 (ESV)

Sanctification means to be set apart, made holy, purified, free from sin. This verse offers an example of how Christians are to live in unity as ones being sanctified. But you cannot live in unity in your own strength, only by being dependent on God and His strength.

John 14:27 says that Jesus left you His peace, but it's not a worldly peace. His peace allows you to have peace and be content no matter the circumstances so you can process and handle what life throws your way. *(Note: This mindset does not apply to an abusive situation.* If you are being abused, this is *not* what God intends for you. Please seek help immediately!)

God is not a God of confusion, but of clarity. Satan loves to confuse a situation and bring chaos to your life, but Jesus wants peace for you. This verse is a great one to memorize and store in your heart. Believe it and receive it so God can work through you. God's plans are peaceful, and they bring unity, not division.

Are you walking in a manner worthy of the calling that Christ has made available to you? How is your attitude toward agape love (doing what is best for another person, regardless of how they have wronged you)*?* Bearing with one another in the love of Jesus, with humility, gentleness, and patience, can bring unity and peace to your life and relationships.

Day 20

Scripture Equips You

*All scripture is breathed out by God and profitable for teaching,
for reproof, for correction, and for training in righteousness,
that the man of God may be complete, equipped for every good work.*
2 Timothy 3:16-17 (ESV)

Jesus tells us in Matthew 24:35, "Heaven and earth will pass away, but My words will not pass away." *Do you believe with your whole heart that every Word of the Bible is from God?* The work of the Holy Spirit is the breath, the life of God. The God who spoke the world into existence can certainly write a book and protect this sacred Book.

Moses penned the Pentateuch, the first five books of the Bible, several millennia ago—between 1500 and 1300 BC. Yet no other book has been able to stand the test of time like the Bible. The Bible has not been nor will ever be discredited. Lee Strobel, the author of *The Case for Grace,* wanted to discredit the Bible and ended up finding faith in Jesus Christ.

God knows living in a sin-soaked world is difficult, which can leave you fearful if you do not learn how to release your fears to God. God's Word sparks your Spirit, giving you an understanding in your life through the lives of the people you are reading about.

God's Word has power; it is not just a book. The Bible is the only Truth to live by. He left you the Bible so you can be complete in Him and in His Word. The Bible is the standard for living in truth and freedom. *Will you ask God today to give you a thirst for His Word and a faith that each verse is written by Him, personally for you?* God is waiting for you to learn to live out His Word—for your strength will be built up in the Word of God. This is the easiest way to find your courageous path next to Jesus.

Day 21

Jesus Is the Word

*In the beginning was the Word, and the Word was with God,
and the Word was God. He was in the beginning with God.
All things were made through Him,
and without Him was not anything made that was made.
In Him was life, and the life was the light of men.
The light shines in the darkness, and the darkness has not overcome it.
And the Word became flesh and dwelt among us,
and we have seen His glory, glory as of the only Son from the Father,
full of grace and truth.*
John 1:1-5 and 14 (ESV)

Jesus is the Word. He has always been with God, and through Jesus all things have been made, including you. Being in Jesus gives you a light that penetrates the darkest areas of your heart and soul. Your deepest hurts and darkest hours do not define you; Jesus does. When you enter into His healing, He exposes the dark areas. His gentle touch can bind your heart in ways you will know it is Him. Jesus is your Healer.

Jesus, the Word, loves to hear the words of His children. He created you in such a way that you must rely on Him.

Have you learned how to be honest with yourself in prayer with God? He gives you everything you need for an open, honest relationship with Him. He loves you where you are right now, and He is cheering you on. You have the Spirit of His strength. Talk it all through with Jesus. Only Jesus can bring you exactly what you need.

Day 22

Center Your Life

Sanctify them in truth, Your Word is truth.
John 17:17 (ESV)

Perhaps ask yourself, "What lies at the center of my healing?" The answer: God's Word.

In your healing, everything is dependent on your complete belief in God's every Word. That means trusting God with everything, down to your every breath. He gives His breath to you—and the breath of God gives life and moves freely.

In your healing, everything is dependent on God's Word . . . and that means your complete surrender to God's perfect plan. For only God holds the future and only God can change another man's heart.

Have you discovered the need you have to be sanctified in the truth of God's Word? God has given you an instruction manual on how to live your life in this chaotic world, but you forgo the blessing when you choose not to open your Bible and choose not to follow God's instructions.

You cannot out dig the Bible. You can learn from the Bible till the day you step into Heaven. God's Word is the plumb line for your life, and you can set everything else in your life around it. Consider it a blessing to put God's Word at the center of your life . . . and then watch and wait patiently to see the blessings that follow.

Day 23

Confidence in His Promises

God is not man, that He should lie; or a son of man,
that He should change His mind. Has He said, and will He not do it?
Or has He spoken, and will He not fulfill it?
Numbers 23:19 (ESV)

God's promises are true; His Word is true. God is faithful, trustworthy, holy, merciful, kind. He is love and peace, ever present, a Strong Tower, the Cornerstone, sovereign. He is our salvation and strength. He is good. He is the great I AM.

To live courageous for Christ, you must live out your life faithful to Him for He has been faithful to you. The only way to heal your fears is to faithfully follow Jesus. He will ask you to do things or stop doing things, but He is trustworthy. Satan wants you to lose faith in God; he knows this can affect you living courageously in Christ.

Our world is corrupt with so much evil and dishonesty that many have become numb or hardened to it. But God called you out of the darkness and into the light. You are to fight with honesty and the love of God. You need to make a change, both personally and in the world you live in.

Are you living in fear of doing what God has called you to do? Or are you being faithful in knowing you have nothing to fear when you do life God's way? When fear comes, be certain that God is faithful, and He will help you overcome.

Day 24

You Have Authority

*Behold, I (Jesus) have given you authority to tread on
serpents and scorpions, and over all the power of the enemy,
and nothing shall hurt you. Nevertheless, do not rejoice in this,
that the spirits are subject to you,
but rejoice that your names are written in heaven.*
Luke 10:19-20 (ESV)

God gave you the Holy Spirit, which is the power of God. *Do you have faith in this power within? Do you trust it? You have authority over everything evil; do you claim it?*

Once Jesus enters into your heart, nothing can separate you from Christ. The bond is eternal. *Are you rejoicing in that?* Satan knows he cannot touch you in heaven, but here on earth he will certainly try, and he has been doing it so long he is good at it. He sees how you react.

Relying on God and trusting the Holy Spirit will bring you victory against Satan. Jesus gave you the authority.

Are you acting in authority or are you acting like you are weak? Whatever disaster you have endured, it has made you stronger, not weaker. Whatever you are experiencing, whatever your blistering trial may be, it can be an opportunity for you to draw closer to God . . . but Satan wants to pull you from God. So, what can you do? Have complete faith in the authority you have over all the powers of the enemy, and proclaim with great rejoicing that your name is written in heaven.

Day 25

Content to Face the Battle

God says to you, "Do not be terrified; do not be afraid of them.
The Lord your God, who is going before you, will fight for you,
as He did for you in Egypt and in the desert."
Deuteronomy 1:29-30 (NIV)

Israel did not believe God; they did not take Him at His Word. Instead, they doubted; they murmured and complained. They were so close to the Promised Land but lost faith in God's promises. They went and spied on the people of the land and discovered that these inhabitants were big and strong. They felt too small and weak to stand up against them.

But God told them He would fight for them; all they had do was have faith—faith that He does what He says He will do. Yet, they were confused in their weakness, and instead of clearly seeing that God did miracles in the past, just like He will certainly do in the future, they began quaking in their sandals. Certainly, God did not intend for them to fear, and likewise, He does not intend it for you.

Yet, the Israelites were not content with His plan or His path. In turn, this sent them into the wilderness, a place God did not intend for them to go.

Are you content with God's direction for your life? Sometimes attitudes need to change more than the situation. Trusting and having faith in God often leads to contentment. *Are you serving Him faithfully? Or are you too terrified of making a change?* God is by your side, wanting to grow your faith and waiting for you to see that your desert place can lie behind you.

Day 26

Devotion Brings Strength

*If you devote your heart to Him and stretch out your hands to Him,
if you put away the sin that is in your hand and
allow no evil to dwell in your tent,
then you will lift up your face without shame;
you will stand firm and without fear.*
Job 11:13-15 (NIV)

Repenting is a daily act when we walk with God. His mercy is new every morning. He knows we are human. So, do not let guilt and shame hold you captive. Some things take longer to get past, but you are not meant to camp out on any obstacle, sin, or circumstance too long. God has created a time and season for everything.

However, just like Job, not everything bad that happens is a consequence of some sin you committed. God has a plan and a purpose for it all. In Job's case, God was in control of what Satan was allowed to inflict on him. And through all the deep pain, Job had faith in God, even when he wanted to die. Certainly, Job lost everything: his family, his wealth, and his health. But Job remained faithful and relied on who God says He is. While not understanding why God allowed him to endure such distress, Job's heart was devoted to a faithful God, regardless of the despair of his circumstances.

To what is your heart devoted? Are you spending your time asking God, "Why me?" or are your eyes open to God testing your faith to make you stronger in and through Christ? God is there to help and bless you in your faith walk. Job is our example of how to face trials and heartache while leaning into who God says He is. God healed Job and blessed him with more in his second half of life than all he had before. What Satan meant for evil, God meant for good.

44

Day 27

God Gives Discernment

Come to Me, all you who are weary and burdened,
and I will give you rest.
Take My yoke upon you and learn from Me,
for I am gentle and humble in heart,
and you will find rest for your souls.
For My yoke is easy and My burden is light.
Matthew 11:28-30 (NIV)

God wants you to bring all your burdens to Him. He wants you to express to Him all that makes you weary. *Do you want the power of God to flow through it all—everything that drains your energy, drags you down, and tires your soul?* God gives discernment when you seek His solution for your burdens. God is not trying to complicate your life; Satan brings you confusion, but Jesus brings us His shalom.

Shalom is not only peace, but also the essence of God's glory; it's pure wholeness and prosperity. *Are you worried and fretting, or are you handing your burdens to the One in control of the universe? When you see no answer or solution, will you pray and have faith that God will guide you through?* Sometimes it's a huge storm, while more often than not, it's the subtle things that bind you—the little worries or nagging, negative thoughts.

Are you running around but not going anywhere? Scurrying on the hamster wheel doesn't define rest, and it's not productive. Talk to Jesus more and He will answer your prayers. In time, you will have complete faith in the One who is sovereign.

Day 28

He Can Carry Your Load

Cast all your anxieties on Him, because He cares for you.
1 Peter 5:7 (NIV)

God knows we get anxious. He is not blind to the troubles you face in this world. *In your flesh, do you feel you need to have a game plan, an itinerary, or a spreadsheet for everything God is calling you to do?* God may not give you the road map to your healing because, just maybe, the road might look so difficult or daunting that you may end up avoiding His plan altogether.

It proves extremely important to set goals, to have a vision of what God wants you to accomplish, but He does not want you anxious about how you spend your time. And He does not want you anxious when He sends your day on a detour. Instead, He wants us to cast our cares on Him—to literally throw your anxiety onto Him, and He won't throw it back.

He is not the one making you wallow in self-pity or feel downtrodden but wants to lift your spirits. He wants you to have joy amidst your circumstances—to see your blessings and respond with happiness. One of the translations for the Greek word "blessed" is happy. John 13:17 (KJV) states, "If ye know these things, happy are ye if ye do them." Why? because He cares, and He wants you to completely rely on His way and His Word. He wants you to have faith that He can carry your load; He will help you through this mess.

God's care for His children is not harsh, critical, or abusive. If you grew up in a home with abusive parents, it can be harder to trust or have faith in something new. Satan would certainly like to keep your view of God's nature distorted and not see that He genuinely loves and cares for you. Gaining confidence in Jesus will lessen the fears Satan tries to throw your way.

Day 29

His Plan Is Perfect

*Trust in the Lord with all your heart
and lean not on your own understanding;
in all your ways acknowledge Him,
and He will make your paths straight.*
Proverbs 3:5-6 (NIV)

Do you really trust God's plans and purpose for you? Do you live in your victory, accepting Christ with complete faith that God is sovereign and wiser than you? God put you right where you are now for a purpose. He directs your steps, whether you give Him credit or not. You can fight Him, or you can accept His sovereign plan and purpose.

He put you here on earth in this exact time and place. You could have been born in any era, but He wanted you here *now* in the outline of *HIS*tory. Before anyone was born on earth, He had a specific place in time and space just for you.

In Exodus, chapters 7–11, God made Pharaoh's heart hard repeatedly to show His glory through spectacular plagues. God was writing *HIS*tory for us to read today—so we can learn from others' experiences and see God's never-changing character. He is not swayed by emotions and fear.

Are you trying to do things your way and in your time? God's ways are higher and wider than ours. *He knows better than you; can you humbly accept it? Are you acknowledging God within the plans you make?* Your time is best spent when you seek the Lord wholeheartedly, asking Him to direct your path. Then you can have success and share in *HIS*tory. *Are you willing to have faith in His plans for you today?*

Day 30

God Is Pursuing You

Jonah prayed, "In my distress I called to the Lord, and He answered me.
From the depths of the grave I called for help,
and You listened to my cry.
You hurled me into the deep, into the very heart of the seas,
and the currents swirled about me;
all Your waves and breakers swept over me.
I said, 'I have been banished from Your sight;
yet I will look again toward Your holy temple.'
The engulfing waters threatened me, the deep surrounded me;
seaweed was wrapped around my head.
To the roots of the mountains, I sank down;
the earth beneath barred me in forever.
But You brought my life up from the pit, O LORD my God.
When my life was ebbing away, I remembered you, Lord,
and my prayer rose to You, to Your holy temple.
Those who cling to worthless idols forfeit the grace that could be theirs.
But I, with a song of thanksgiving, will sacrifice to You.
What I have vowed I will make good. Salvation comes from the Lord."
Jonah 2:2-9 NIV

How far are you willing to run away from the life Christ wants for you? Freedom in Christ is not really free; you must relinquish who you are in the flesh. You must die to self. When you want to go back to your old habits and actions, only through surrender and submission will you see the salvation of the Lord, over all areas of your life.

Praise the Lord; He is pursuing you. His Holy Spirit speaks into our hearts. *Are you listening?* No matter how deep you have sunk, Jesus can raise you out of the pit, or He can spit you out of the belly of a huge fish. Your weapon against the spiritual realm is prayer, and you simply cannot abide in Christ every step on earth without a constant dialogue with God. A prayerful life is a contented life—and that's the best place to be.

Day 31

Enjoy Where God Has You

Be happy, young man [woman], while you are young,
and let your heart give you joy in the days of your youth.
Follow the ways of your heart and whatever your eye sees,
but know that for all these things God will bring you to judgment.
So then banish anxiety from your heart and
cast off the troubles of your body, for youth and vigor are meaningless.
Ecclesiastes 11:9-10 (NIV)

God wants your joy to abound; blessed means "be happy." He wants you to enjoy what you do here and now. While He knows this world is challenging, He does not want His children depressed.

What lies is the spirit of depression telling you? How are you allowing this deception to shape your thoughts and reactions? God, not your situation, is your hope, and He wants your sorrow to turn to joy. Your trials and hardships should bring you to a place of perseverance so you are not short-tempered but patient. God wants to build your character so your character matches His. He is faithful at molding you into the image of Christ.

God may give you what you cannot handle in your own strength; He may allow what you can face only through the power of the Holy Spirit. And therefore, as you have the seal of the Holy Spirit, you may visit heavy-hearted places for a season but cannot take up residence there. Instead, you are righteous, seated in heavenly places, as Jesus cleansed you from your sin and circumcised your heart. Your identity lies in Christ, not your situation, lifestyle, or work, so cast off your troubles and banish anxiety; you are whole in Christ. You have victory! Live in the victory of Christ—He is your Comfort and Joy.

Day 32

Jesus Sympathizes, so Draw Near

For we do not have a high priest who is unable to sympathize with our weaknesses, but we have one who has been tempted in every way, just as we are—yet without sin. Let us then approach the throne of grace with confidence, so that we may receive mercy and find grace to help us in our time of need.
Hebrews 4:15-16 (NIV)

By His grace, you have unmerited favor. He gave you the Holy Spirit so that you can have His power live inside you—the power you can and should rely on. Jesus came to earth so you can have a relationship with Him. He understands what it's like to have fleshly desires; He was fully God and fully man. In Matthew 4, Jesus was tempted by Satan, just one example of how Jesus can relate to your temptations.

Does your soul long for someone to understand who you really are, and why you are the way you are? God is not far off; He sees and knows every detail about you—who you are and why. Have faith that He is with you in both the difficult times and the times of blessing.

By His grace, you have the power to do what you cannot on your own, including the ability to overcome evil and our fleshly battles. You live in His grace and by His power working through you. So, please give yourself the same grace as He gives you; He sees past all the rebellion, all the lying to yourself, and all the walling off of your emotions. Forgive yourself as God forgave you. When we're in Christ, when we give our lives to Him, none of us gets what we deserve. Praise God joyfully that we receive mercy and find grace for our every time of need.

Day 33

Claim It

*I write to you because you are strong,
and the word of God abides in you, and you have overcome the evil one.*
1 John 2:14b (ESV)

You have overcome. Although Satan tries to keep you thinking you are in a losing battle, in Christ you have won. So, claim it! As Satan comes to steal, kill, and destroy (John10:10), do not let him destroy your faith in God. Remember, you have already overcome Satan by accepting Jesus as your Savior, and He is your Savior moment-by-moment. By His Spirit you are strong.

Have you asked God to fill you with His strength? "The Word of God is alive and active, sharper than any double-edged sword; it penetrates even to dividing soul and spirit, joints and marrow; it judges the thoughts and attitudes of the heart" (Hebrews 4:12). Remember that Jesus, the Word, became flesh. And He abides in you. When you read the Bible diligently, seeking His truth, He will give you strength, direct your steps, and lead you to overcome all evil and any obstacles in your path.

Day 34

Fight With God on Your Side

Submit yourself therefore to God.
Resist the devil and he will flee from you.
Draw near to God and He will draw near to you.
Cleanse your hands, you sinners, and purify your hearts,
you double-minded.
James 4:7-8 (ESV)

Are you completely submissive before God at all times? Or, are you proud, saying "I've got this"? It's extremely difficult to resist the devil without submitting to God; indeed, God wants you to worship Him and Him alone.

Fear can easily become an idol. You bow to fear; you may chart your course based on the anxieties and worries that shackle your heart. In fact, fear can keep you from doing many of the things God is calling you to do. Reconciling a relationship, making that phone call, putting aside all regret and shame ... these can all be scary places. Just as missionaries might say they must trust God's plan and sovereignty over the fear of dangers that could arrive, you can choose to draw near to God, trust Him, and let Him purify your heart.

When your fears arise, and they will, *do you choose to stand firm in the faith of Christ?* God can change any situation if you are where He wants you to be. Do not let Satan second guess your destiny; you are not destined to be double-minded but to be made whole.

Faith

Day 35

Help My Unbelief

"If You can do anything, have compassion on us and help us."
Jesus said to him, "If I can! All things are possible
for one who believes."
Immediately the father of the child cried out and said,
"I believe; help my unbelief!"
Mark 9:22-24 (ESV)

Do you believe or have faith that God can make you whole? Do you believe that Jesus can heal your sick heart? You should. In the Bible, Abraham believed God and His promises, and this faith was counted to him as righteousness.

You do not have to know how God will heal you; you just have to believe He will. You do not have to make the same mistakes; learn and move on. This path or journey with God is called a "walk" for a reason. You walk out your faith with God beside you, every step. Do not camp out on what you lack; God makes all things possible. In the grace of God, you lack nothing, including the strength to live a righteous life. Ask God to shed light on the areas where you lack belief so you rely completely on Him.

Day 36

God Is the Reward

*Without faith it is impossible to please Him,
for whoever would draw near to God must believe that He exists
and that He rewards those who seek Him.*
Hebrews 11:6 (ESV)

Do you have an adoration for God? Do you trust God over all? Do you worship Him with your whole heart? Is He worth dying for? Could you walk away from your fears for Him?

Lots of questions, but through faith, they all have the same answer: you can say "yes!" And I pray you can say "yes" right now. I pray that God becomes so real in your life that you will wonder how you ever survived without complete dependence on Jesus.

God knows our hearts, our intentions, our motives . . . He knows everything about you. Nothing you have ever done or were forced to do is too dirty for Jesus. He took the world's sin upon that cross; and that means anything that has darkened your soul or trampled your heart. That means anything and everything. Have faith to believe that drawing near to God will make you clean; you no long need to feel despair or shame. He will reward you for seeking Him—with a clean heart, a new future, and renewed hope and peace.

Day 37
God's Way Is Righteous

Thus says the Lord God, "Behold, I am the one
who has laid as a foundation in Zion, a stone, a trusted stone,
a precious cornerstone, of a sure foundation:
'Whoever believes will not be in haste.'
And I will make justice the line, and righteousness the plumb line."
Isaiah 28:16-17a (ESV)

Jesus is our trusted stone, our precious cornerstone. He remained faithful to God every moment on earth. And everything in your life should be built on Him: your attitudes, your integrity, and your love toward yourself and others. And when you believe in Him, you need not worry, panic, or make rash decisions; "haste" in your life will be thwarted. Righteousness, as the plumb line, means it all depends on your belief and your confidence in God during all circumstances of life.

Do you know in your heart that you personally want to be different? Do you want to be completely free to be who God created you to be? Self-confidence does not come from within; it comes from believing God, taking Him at His Word. You are loved by God, His precious child filled with His goodness.

Day 38

Doubt Destroys Possibilities

*Jesus answered them, "I assure you; If you have faith and do not doubt,
you will not only do what was done to the fig tree,
but if you tell this mountain, 'Be lifted up and thrown into the sea,'
it will be done.
And if you believe, you will receive whatever you ask for in prayer."*
Matthew 21:21-22 (HCSB).

We do not have to know how God can let us take part in His miracles, but He can and He will if we believe Him in faith.

Are you in a situation that has mounted so high that you feel blocked . . . stuck . . . unable to go around, over, or past it? Has your mountain of problems led to despair? God has a path planned for you so that you *will* conquer the mountain. You can move ahead sure-footed in the salvation and provision of God.

Do not become like the fig tree, which symbolized Israel's moral state. Christians are to live in faith that God is watching over everything. He is in control, and He never worries and never fails. He alone is trustworthy, and His power can allow you to do the humanly impossible in response to prayer. When you believe things can truly change, when you desire in faith what He desires as you pray, then the "mountain" before you can be cast aside to make way for His will and purpose in your life.

Day 39

Be still and know I AM God.
The Lord is good to those who wait for Him, to the soul who seeks Him.
Psalm 46:10, Lamentations 3:25 (ESV)

"Be still" in the original Hebrew means "let it go." The saying "Let go and let God" is literally what it means to "be still and know" that He is God. He is in control of life, even when life seems out of control, messy and disheveled.

Prayer is the key that releases you from the shackles and chains in your life. *Perhaps you don't know what to say to God?* Simply think things out with Him; tell Him what's on your heart, and ask Him for His guidance.

"How do You want me to handle this difficult person or situation, God?"

"I'm afraid to confront this person, Jesus. Please help me to plan my words carefully."

"I will mostly likely lose my temper if they bring up _____ again. God, I need you to guide me."

And you still might blow up when they bring up that hurtful, hateful, or prickly topic, but when you choose to go back to God and seek a different solution, not all is lost. An initial setback is not always failure; it's how you learn what does not work, and you press on. God often teaches how to let go of resentment, unforgiveness, and anger through trials and testing. The more mercy you ask for, the more mercy you will extend to others. He is a God who is merciful (Psalm 116:5).

Day 40
God of Justice

This is what the Sovereign Lord, the Holy One of Israel says:
"In repentance and rest is your salvation,
in quietness and trust is your strength . . .
The Lord longs to be gracious to you; He rises to show you compassion.
For the Lord is a God of Justice. Blessed are all who wait for Him!
O people of Zion, you will weep no more.
How gracious He will be when you cry for help!
As soon as He hears, He will answer you.
Although the Lord gives you the bread of adversity
and the water of affliction, your Teacher will be hidden no more;
with your own eyes you will see them.
Whether you turn to the right or to the left,
your ears will hear a voice behind you saying, "This is the way; walk in it."
Isaiah 30:15; 18-21 (NIV)

Are you returning to God? Are you repenting? Or are you taking care of things yourself? Do you trust God's justice to prevail on everyone? The people that have hurt you, God knows. He will judge each person one day. *Is that enough for you?*

God wants to mold you to be like Jesus. He wants you to be completely dependent on Him. Israel wanted to fight a battle that God did not want them to fight; therefore, it was the consequence of their actions that caused adversity and affliction.

When you listen to the Holy Spirit, you are protected in a way that you cannot comprehend, and your faith pleases God. In other words, on this side of heaven, sometimes protection does not look like protection. You won't know the "what could haves" or the" what ifs," but God does.

Are there places in your life that God does not want you to go, but you do anyway? Open your Bible and read all of Isaiah 30. This passage provides a huge warning from God. He wants faithfulness from you, in every area of your life. Even a white lie is still a lie. Sometimes we have bought into Satan's lies for so long that we cannot recognize them, but God can reveal each one.

58

Day 41

In the Storm, Jesus Comes to You

*When evening came, His disciples went to the sea, got into a boat,
and started across the sea to Capernaum.
It was now dark, and Jesus had not yet come to them.
The sea became rough because a strong wind was blowing.
When they rowed about three or four miles,
they saw Jesus walking in the sea and coming near the boat,
and they were frightened.
But He said to them, "It is I; do not be afraid."
Then they were glad to take Him into the boat,
and immediately the boat was at the land to which they were going.*
John 6: 16-21 (ESV)

When the storms of your life become rough; do you know how to find rest, peace, and security in Jesus? Can you trust His sovereignty, knowing He sent you into a storm? He did not do this to make your faith shaky, but to strengthen your faith. He wants you to bring Him glory in the storm.

Jesus displayed His power and sovereignty over everything He created when He walked on water. Jesus knew the disciples were heading into a storm—one He chose to let them experience, but He also knew that His power and sovereignty would be displayed there among them.

As you know, storms of life occur all around us. Many of them you cannot escape as you live in a broken world. In and through these storms, Jesus needs you to carry His message. He is with you, and He wants you not to fear getting wet; He won't let you drown. He is reaching His hands toward you, guiding you to your destination. This experience of learning to trust Jesus amidst the gales and tempests of life, seeing His love and power at work, will stretch and grow your faith in supernatural ways. Don't run from the storms and miss your calling; instead, grow your faith as you lean into your loving Savior.

Day 42

Miracles Through Faith

Elijah said to her, "Do not fear; go and do as you have said.
But first make me a little cake of it and bring it to me,
and afterward make something for yourself and your son.
For thus says the Lord, 'The jar of flour shall not be spent,
and the jug of oil shall not be empty, until the day that
the Lord sends rain upon the earth.'"
And she went and did as Elijah said.
And she and he and her household ate for many days.
The jar of flour was not spent, neither did the jug of oil become empty,
according to the word of the Lord that He spoke by Elijah.
1 King 17:13-16 (ESV)

When Elijah meets this mother in 1 King 17, she is gathering sticks to make a fire, trying to feed herself and her son with their last bit of food. With a famine in the region, food is scarce. She is a widow, the lowest in the social hierarchy back then, and also a Gentile. In those days, Jews and Gentiles do not get along. So, all these factors make her conversation with Elisha, a Jewish prophet, out of the ordinary. As it turns out, Elisha is the first prophet to bring the glory of God into a pagan nation.

But Sidon is not just any pagan nation. The people of Sidon worship the god Baal, and moreover, Elijah's arch enemy, Jezebel, is from Sidon. Jezebel has search parties looking for Elijah as she does not want him proclaiming God's Word; God is pronouncing their destruction. Although much is stacked against this desperate mother and Elijah, this is when God can shine the brightest.

God can take the little you have and turn it into a miracle. Fear and faith cannot stand together for long. One will always overtake the other. What Elijah is asking of this mother sounds crazy. Her mother's instinct must have had all kinds of bells going off, but God says, "Do not fear; go and do." Then the miracle can happen. *Do you have faith to go and do what God is asking of you?*

Day 43

Seeking God Extinguishes Worry

Jesus said to his disciples: "Therefore I tell you,
do not worry about your life, what you will eat;
or about your body, what you will wear.
For life is more than food, and the body more than clothes.
Consider the ravens: They do not sow or reap;
they have no storeroom or barn; yet God feeds them.
And how much more valuable you are than birds!
Who of you by worrying can add a single hour to your life?
Since you cannot do this very little thing,
why do you worry about the rest?
Consider how the wildflowers grow. They do not labor or spin.
Yet I tell you, not even Solomon in all his splendor
was dressed like one of these.
If that is how God clothes the grass of the field, which is here today,
and tomorrow is thrown into the fire, how much more will he clothe you—
you of little faith!
And do not set your heart on what you will eat or drink;
do not worry about it. For the pagan world runs after all such things,
and your Father knows that you need them.
But seek His kingdom, and these things will be given to you as well."
Luke 12:22-31 (NIV)

Not being able to put food on your family's table is a huge concern for those who cannot. Yet God knows you need food, clothing, and shelter. *Do you fully trust He will provide? Or do you fall into a fearful pity party? Are you seeking His Word to guide and comfort you? Are you praying and listening to His voice?* God expects you to work. Sometimes He pushes you along by closing one door so another will open. *Are you faithful while waiting in the hallways?*

In these verses Jesus said, "Adding a single hour to someone's life is easy for Him but impossible for us." When you worry, your mind is not where God wants it to be. He wants your mind trained in the Word of truth. Seek God's truth first before the worry sets in because God is your provider. All good things come from above.

Sovereign

Day 44

Remember His Goodness

The Lord said to Moses "Is the Lord's arm too short?
You will now see whether or not what I say will come true for you."
Numbers 11:23 (NIV)

Moses was burdened by the people's complaints. Although God was providing in a miraculous way, the people complained. God had taken this generation out of slavery and had plans to take them to the Promised Land. Yet, they complained, not liking God's provision. They were ungrateful, forgetting that God had rescued them from an excruciating life of endless toil. Greed, ingratitude, and pride can send anyone off God's intended path. Yet, we serve a merciful God, so He gave them exactly what they wanted: meat. Even Moses doubted God. But God controls all living creatures. Sending quail to the Israelites was not difficult for Him.

Do you remind yourself of how God has taken you out of a place of slavery? Do you remind yourself of the chains He has unlocked for you? Do you remember how His Word has become true for you? God does not want you to forget about how far He has taken you. You might not think your provisions from God are glamorous, but be careful what you complain about. When you doubt God, it will send you to places you are not intended to go. An unthankful heart will complain while a thankful heart will find the joy in the mundane.

Day 45

Courage and Perfect Timing

*Who knows whether you have not come to the kingdom
for such a time as this?*
Esther 4:14b (ESV)

overeign

God's providence was written all over Esther's life. He had given her great beauty mixed with compassion; both her parents had died, so Esther knew the sting of deep pain and loss. By God's providence, the king found Esther favorable and eventually made her queen, a role allowing her to learn that one of the king's servants wanted to kill the Jews. While she was scared to face the king, she found her courage, acted, and managed to save her Jewish people.

Even so, Esther was not a superhero; she had simply followed God's leading. When Esther eventually showed her heart to the king, his compassion grew, and he sought justice for the Jewish people. God works through people from all walks of life, with all backgrounds, with pain as the canvas of their hearts.

God had Esther right where He needed her to be. He designed her steps, giving her what many today have called "An Esther Moment" . . . for such a time as this. Many Christians cannot understand why God orchestrates their steps the way He does—until they look at situations in hindsight. Sometimes nothing makes sense . . . until that one defining moment.

Perhaps you have stood in front of a court of law or in front of your co-workers and friends, exposing the evil plans of people trying to dismantle the ways of God. If so, *have you recognized that God has sovereignly put you where you are to speak up about the things in your world that are evil, in God's perspective? Can you accept that God has groomed you for a defining moment in your life?* It's your choice to speak up or stay silent. Only God will know where you really stand. Ask God to help you cast off all fear and speak with the boldness of Christ.

3

Day 46

Understand Whom to Fear

Do not be afraid of any man, for judgment belongs to God.
Deuteronomy 1:17b (NIV)

Who are you afraid of? Which man instilled fear, so deep, that it overrides your knowledge of God? God alone is to be feared. Only God holds your eternal destiny in His hands. Only God has control over everything in the cosmos. Only God knows the hearts of people. Only Jesus died on a cross for your sins. Only God is to be fully trusted because He is without sin; He is holy, He is perfect, and He knows the beginning and the end.

You are stuck in time, not God. You must be committed to God and serve Him alone. Yet, when you are faithless, He is still faithful. He does not change with your moods and emotions. But when you trust God completely, He reassures you.

Are you trying to do the work only God can do? It's His job to pass judgment. It's your job to trust that He is perfectly just and will faithfully carry out justice, not matter what. Romans 14:13 says, "Let us stop passing judgment on one another. Instead make up your mind not to put any stumbling block or obstacles in the way of a brother or sister." You cannot control how others will judge you, but you can allow God His rightful place, as judge, over everyone you encounter.

Day 47

Welcome the Light

Since the day I, the author, started writing to you,
I have not stopped praying for you and asking God to fill you
with the knowledge of His will through
all spiritual wisdom and understanding.
And I pray this in order that you may live a life worthy of the Lord
and may please Him in every way: bearing fruit in every good work,
growing in the knowledge of God, being strengthened with all power
according to His glorious might so that you may have
great endurance and patience, and joyfully giving thanks to the Father,
who has qualified you to share in the inheritance of the saints
in the kingdom of light.
For He rescued us from the dominion of darkness
and brought us into the kingdom of the Son He loves
in whom we have redemption, the forgiveness of sins. Amen.
Colossians 1:9-14 (NIV)

Prayer is such a vital part of your healing process. If you genuinely want to be healed, you must do it through open discussion with Christ. Prayer will open the door to your soul. Jesus said, "I stand at the door and knock. If anyone hears My voice and opens the door, I will come in and eat with him, and he with Me" (Revelation 3:20).

Are you allowing yourself to hear His voice? Are you regularly asking God to shed His light on your darkness? Are you open to His spiritual wisdom and understanding? Are you willing to let it change you? Darkness can feel comfortable when you are used to living there, but trust Him; His light is warm and tender.

Day 48

Strengthened Through His Spirit

I bow my knees before the Father,
from whom every family in heaven and on earth is named,
that according to the riches of His glory He may grant you
to be strengthened with power through His Spirit, in your inner being,
so that Christ may dwell in your hearts through faith.
And ---that you, being rooted and grounded in love,
may have strength, to comprehend with all the saints
what is the breadth and length and height and depth ,
and to know the love of Christ that surpasses knowledge
that you may be filled with all the fullness of God.
Now, to Him who is able to do far more abundantly
than all that we ask or think, according to the power at work within us,
to Him be glory in the church and in Christ Jesus
throughout all generations, forever and ever. Amen.
Ephesians 3:14-21 ESV

Are you asking God daily to fill you completely with His Spirit? For God alone can strengthen you so that His glory flows freely through you. When you accepted Christ as your personal Savior, He deposited His Spirit within you. His Spirit cannot be taken from you, but your sinful ways can grieve the Holy Spirit within you.

When you grieve the Holy Spirit, you are not being ignited by the Spirit; you are being led into captivity by your desires that are not of God. Your spiritual health depends upon you asking God to empty your heart and mind of the things that are not of Him—so He can fill you with the Holy Fire that sets your soul ablaze for following Jesus. Remember, God is your daily bread. *Why not ask Him daily to help you seek Him and fill you with His Spirit to live and walk with Him?*

Day 49

Jesus Has the Best Advice

First seek the counsel of the Lord.
2 Chronicles 18:4 (NIV)

Where do you turn when your fleshly fears become a reality? Do you seek a friend for advice, a substance to numb the pain, or Jesus? What are your tendencies? What is your attitude? In the next week, keep a notepad somewhere easily accessible and track to where or to whom you turn when your fears try to besiege you.

What did you run to when you were faced with adversity and stress? God wants to be first in every aspect of your life. Nothing is too small for Him. Many people are comfortable running to God when the big stuff happens, but what about the small stuff? The stresses add up if you choose not to bring them to God first.

You can find peace in the stresses of life if you choose to seek Him first. God wants to have fellowship with you—the kind of relationship you have with your best friend, the one with whom you talk about everything. God wants to be first in every area of your life. *Whom or what do you serve first? . . . God? Or your fleshly desires and reactions?* You choose moment by moment what or whom you serve. If you serve your own interests, there is no promise that God will bless your efforts. If you serve God, He will make "your cup overflow" (Psalm 23:5).

Day 50

Throw Off Your Burdens

Listen to my prayer, O God, do not ignore my plea.
Hear me and answer me. My thoughts trouble me
and I am distraught at the voice of the enemy,
at the stares of the wicked, for they bring down suffering upon me,
and revile me in their anger . . .
Cast your cares on the Lord and He will sustain you;
He will never let the righteous fall.
Psalm 55:1, 22 (NIV)

Have you been violated, raped, or abused? Have things been done to you that left you wounded and scarred? Have you felt like God is not listening to your prayers? This world is full of injustice and hate. That hate often falls on the people of God, and many people question why the pagans seem to be so happy and successful in this life.

Satan can lead you to believe that God just might be like the world, but in John 17:14 (NIV) Jesus states the exact opposite: "I have given them your word and the world has hated them, for they are not of the world any more than I am of the world." Jesus and Christians are not of this world; we are seated with Christ in the heavens. Satan is afraid of you finding the power of a praying Christian, but he is unafraid of the people who choose to deny God. They do not have a testimony to tarnish, but you do.

God is so gracious, and He loves all the people He created. The ones who deny Him only get to find happiness here on earth as their eternity will be brutal. Those who follow Christ have to deal with the pain of this world only for a moment, and they will be in glory for eternity.

Satan is afraid of your prayers. God wants you to cast all your cares on Him; nothing is too dark, too shameful, or too small. Your soul is safe with Him. Only God can give you real protection, and often, during your prayer time, you will find that faithful, supernatural protection that you direly need.

Day 51

Keep It Up

Those who were my enemies without cause, hunted me like a bird.
They tried to end my life in a pit and threw stones at me;
the waters closed over my head, and I thought I was about to perish.
I called on Your name, LORD, from the depths of the pit.
You heard my plea: "Do not close Your ears to my cry for relief."
You came near when I called You, and You said, "Do not fear."
You, Lord, took up my case; You redeemed my life. LORD,
You have seen the wrong done to me. Uphold my cause!
You have seen the depth of their vengeance, all their plots against me.
LORD, You have heard their insults, all their plots against me . . .
Look at them! Sitting or standing, they mock me in their songs.
Pay them back what they deserve LORD . . . Put a veil over their hearts,
and may Your curse be on them! Pursue them in anger
and destroy them from under the heavens of the Lord.
Lamentations 3:52-66 (NIV)

This heavy prayer in Lamentations presents an honest, heartfelt cry to the Lord. This prayer offers an example to you. You can ask God to punish the people that have hurt you. Your torment can be spilled into the lap of Jesus. It's your responsibility to hand them over to Jesus and leave them there, in His hands. He will judge everyone justly.

Have you been the object of someone's gossip, jealousy, rage, or abuse? Day in and day out they just will not stop. *Are you in that place where others can be so cruel that remaining patient seems exceptionally harsh? Have you cried out with your whole heart to God? Do you prayerfully trust His judgment and mercy?* God wants you to bring Him your troubles, to pour out your heart to Him. He will not be offended unless you try and twist His character. You can honestly bring Him your anger and pain. He will not shun you for being honest with Him but will give you needed comfort.

Day 52

Keep It Up

An angel said, "Don't be afraid, Daniel.
Since the first day that you set your mind to gain understanding
and to humble yourself before your God, your prayers were heard,
and I have come in response to them."
Daniel 10:12(NIV)

What is the one prayer you keep asking God to answer? Do you think, just maybe, Satan is opposing your God-given answer to this prayer? If you were to read the rest of chapter 10 in Daniel, you would learn that it took twenty-one days for the angel to get to Daniel because of opposition from an evil spirit.

Life is so much more than what you can see and hear. There is a spiritual realm at work to both help and oppose you. God sent His angel to Daniel, and Satan sent his fallen angel to stop God's angel. However, God always wins. Do not stop praying just because your request has been said over and over again to God. He hears and is working on your behalf. Do not give up on the hope of God; your answer to prayer could be tomorrow.

Day 53

Trust the Power

Put no trust in a neighbor; have no confidence in a friend;
guard the doors of your mouth from her who lies in your arms;
for the son treats the father with contempt,
the daughter rises up against her mother,
the daughter-in-law against her mother-in-law;
a man's enemies are the men of his own house.
But as for me, I will look to the LORD;
I will wait for the God of my salvation; my God will hear me.
Micah 7:5-7 (ESV)

Romans 3:23 attests, "We all fall short of the glory of God." Not one of us is perfect; in fact, it is safe to say that everyone sins daily. Whether it be in thoughts or actions, our sin, which was poured out on Calvary, is known by God. Our sin separates us from a holy God, but Christ came to unify us. When all the redeemed in Christ pray to God, they find His will. And when Christians find the will of God, they learn how to be unified in Christ. All things of earth are born to die, but our prayers have an eternal place in the incense bowls of heaven (Revelation 5:8). Your prayer life is dependable, and your relationship with God is dependable.

In other words, while we cannot rely on people, things, or circumstances, God is always dependable. We live in a world where people place their hope in the wrong things. Dependence on the wrong things means we are gambling on the unreliable and the foolhardy. God takes away the trust in man, weapons, or things and blesses our trust in His name alone. For God can turn a person's heart cold, or He can make a person feel compassion. He has dominion overall. *Are you putting your trust in your bank account, your job, or your name? Or are you putting your trust in the power of prayer? Is your confidence in what is seen, or in what is unseen?* Through prayer and faith, the unseen will become the seen. Your vision will be cleared as you sit with Him in prayer.

71

Rescue

Day 54

It Takes Time

When they were oppressed, they cried out to You.
From heaven You heard them, and in Your great compassion
You gave them deliverers, who rescued them from the hands
of their enemies . . . When they cried out to You again,
You heard them from heaven and in Your compassion
You delivered them time after time.
Nehemiah 9:27b, 28b (NIV)

I can think of only one way to describe the speed of spiritual life change: markedly slow. Most people do not go from "depression and loneliness" to "sanctified in the image of Christ" overnight. Sanctification is a lifelong process. Repentance is a daily event. You will not be perfect on earth, but when you arrive in Heaven, you will be. God gives you more mercy than you know.

So, do not get lazy in your Christian walk. Get involved with people at church, and allow other Christians to keep you accountable. Consider this: *Are you spending daily time with God, in prayer; are you a student of His Word?* God will continue to show you mercy, *but will it be a mercy that brings you to an intimate relationship with Jesus, or a mercy that keeps you in survival mode?* God rescues you so you can learn to lean into Him and become more like Jesus. *Do you want a deep transformation of your life, one that grows deeper with time and brings Him glory?* Then don't give up or turn back. Let Him finish His work in you over time. As you keep pressing into His Word, you will see more clearly how He delivers on His promises!

Day 55

His Word Heals

Then they cried to the LORD in their trouble,
and He saved them from their distress.
He sent out His Word and healed them;
He rescued them from the grave. Let them give thanks to the LORD
for His unfailing love and His wonderful deeds for mankind.
Let them sacrifice thank offerings
and tell of His works with songs of joy.
Psalm 107:19-22 (NIV)

Are you praising God? Are you lifting up your voice and heart to Him? He alone can sovereignly rescue you. *How are you at thanking Him for what you have? Do you pray before you eat? Do you pray as you go about your day?* All the confidence you need to be rescued by Jesus is written in the Word of God. Your Bible breathes life into you that will rescue you in many situations.

Yet Satan does not want you to know about a rescue plan. *Why do you keep letting him distract you?* God inhabits the praises of His people. When you praise and give thanks, you keep the Holy Spirit near to you. When discontent, you tend to grumble alone. Grumbling kept Israel out of the Promised Land for forty years. In this Psalm, verses 26 and 27 go on to say, "Don't let your courage melt away. Don't let yourself reach your wit's end." *Are you at your wit's end and in need of rescue?* God is waiting.

Day 56

You Have No Excuse

"Before I formed you in the womb, I knew you, and before you were born,
I consecrated you; I appointed you a prophet to the nations."
Then I said, "Ah, Lord GOD! Behold, I do not know how to speak,
for I am only a youth." But the LORD said to me,
"Do not say, 'I am only a youth'; for to all to whom I send you,
you shall go, and whatever I command you, you shall speak.
Do not be afraid of them,
for I AM with you to deliver you, declares the LORD."
Jeremiah 1:5-8 (ESV)

In our flesh, we can feel just like Jeremiah when he said ". . . for I am only . . ." We look at the tools we have in our toolbox and say, "Well, I cannot make this work; I do not have what it takes to fix this brokenness." Thankfully, our redemption does not depend on our own abilities.

In verse eight, God promises Jeremiah that He will rescue him. God does not promise to keep Jeremiah away from trouble, but says He will be with him during the trouble. *Do you have the faith that God will rescue you from letting the troubles of the world consume you?* Before God even formed you, He knew you; He set you apart. You are significant and important to God. And God does not make mistakes.

Your life has value in God. You can fear your consequences of not listening to God, or you can obey His instructions. A sovereign God created you, and a sovereign God will rescue you. *Are you willing to go into the troubles of this world with God, not fearing the outcome?* I promise you, not everyone will like what you have to say. The Gospel is the power of life and death, but some choose not to be rescued. You can choose God's way today—and He will walk each step of your life with You, dispelling your fears.

Day 57

Focus on Your Lane

*The Lord knows how to rescue the godly from trials,
and to keep the unrighteous under punishment
until the day of judgment.*
2 Peter 2:9 (ESV)

Sadly, you may encounter people in the Christian community who do not represent God's ways at all. The Christian community is not exempt from people still living and acting in their sin natures, and thus they may hurt you, lie to you, steal from you, and even use God against you. But God and only God knows each person's heart. The people who distort the truth, God knows, as He has put His truth in place.

None of this reality gives you an excuse to run away from all churches. Not all churches are good and filled with the Holy Spirit. Corruption is everywhere, but God wants to give you discernment. *Are you contemplating the things of God?*

You must keep yourself in your own lane. People are acting with injustice all over the place. God knows. In His sovereignty, He will not put you in trials that will overtake you. He wants to test your faithfulness. He wants to teach you that He is a reliable God. *Will you trust His rescue plan?*

Day 58

The Lord Is Good

I will bless the Lord at all times;
His praise shall continually be in my mouth.
My soul makes its boast in the Lord; let the humble hear and be glad.
Oh, magnify the Lord with me, and let us exalt His name together!
I sought the Lord, and He answered me and delivered me
from all my fears. Those who look to Him are radiant,
and their faces shall never be ashamed.
This poor man cried, and the Lord heard him and saved him
out of all his troubles. The angel of the Lord encamps around those
who fear Him and delivers them.
Oh, taste and see that the Lord is good!
Blessed is the man who takes refuge in Him!
Oh, fear the Lord, you His saints, for those who fear Him have no lack!
The young lions suffer want and hunger;
but those who seek the Lord lack no good thing.
Come, O children, listen to me; I will teach you the fear of the Lord.
What man is there who desires life and loves many days,
that he may see good?
Keep your tongue from evil and your lips from speaking deceit.
Turn away from evil and do good; seek peace and pursue it.
The eyes of the Lord are toward the righteous
and His ears toward their cry.
Psalm 34: 1-15 (ESV)

What are you pursuing? Does it keep your conscious clear? You cannot find peace when your conscious is telling you to change direction, to choose differently, or to stop your actions. The fear of the Lord will rescue you from making sinful choices—ones that lead you down the wrong path. The fear of the Lord will keep you on the straight and narrow path—the one headed to heaven. *Are you allowing fear to control you, your thoughts and your actions?* If so, you are not trusting God's protection and deliverance. *Why not submit to His holiness and allow Him to rescue you?*

Day 59

God Sustains You

Even to your old age and grey hairs I AM He,
I AM He who will sustain you. I have made you and I will carry you;
I will sustain you and I will rescue you.
Isaiah 46:4 (NIV)

Do you live your life with purpose? Do you see the value of your purpose? Do you need God to sustain you while you work out your purpose? God has a purpose for you every day you live on earth, from birth and infancy to the day you take your last breath.

But, your mind is often focused on the here and now—the pain you have endured and your emotions that assail you. You see with your eyes all that is earthly, not often the spiritual realm. You cannot touch God, angels, or evil spirits, but they are all around you. One day you will see into that realm, but not this side of heaven.

Satan wants to steal, kill, and destroy the purpose of your godly, righteous, and holy living. In Christ, you are a new creation, perfected in Christ with a divine plan—even until the last day of your life. God has something He needs you to do, and He will sustain you so you can accomplish it.

Will you ask God today to help you stop listening to the negative voices, including your thoughts, and tune your mind and perspective to Him instead? Why not ask Him right now to carry, sustain, and rescue you once more, to help you live out His plan for you? The time is always right for sharing your fears, your hopes, and your heart with your Savior.

Day 60

Not What It Seems

He sent from on high, He took me; He drew me out of many waters.
He rescued me from my strong enemy, from those who hated me,
for they were too mighty for me.
They confronted me in the day of my calamity,
but the LORD was my support. He brought me out into a broad place;
He rescued me because He delighted in me.
2 Samuel 22:17-20 (ESV)

Sometimes God will allow scary situations in your life to prevent something worse in the future. God knows the "what if?" He knows how your decisions will affect situations.

Take, for instance, a lady who is robbed. Of course, she is scared and loses some money, but perhaps she is not injured physically. And through it all, she realizes God protects her from physical harm. Down the road, she learns how to act more cautiously and how to protect herself. Not living in fear, she is learning how to take care of herself in this evil world.

In much the same way, God rescues you in ways you cannot comprehend. So, openly look at situations in life that you experience. Talk to God about them, learn from them, and then move on. God wants you to share your testimony of His handprint on your life. He does not want you to forget your past; He wants you to forgive it.

Are there certain areas in your life where God wants you to learn how to be more cautious? Do you need to take steps to learn how you can protect yourself instead of throwing caution to the wind? Why not start today? While we may still experience some loss and heartache on earth, He will guide your steps. He will support you, never leave you, and rescue you from eternal calamity because He delights in you!

Day 61

Teach Me Your Ways

*"Incline Your ear, O LORD, and answer me, for I am poor and needy.
Preserve my life, for I am godly; save Your servant, who trusts in You—
You are my God. Be gracious to me, O Lord, for to You do I cry
all the day. Gladden the soul of Your servant,
for to You, O Lord, do I lift up my soul.
For You, O Lord, are good and forgiving, abounding in steadfast love
to all who call upon You. Give ear, O LORD, to my prayer;
listen to my plea for grace. In the day of my trouble, I call upon You,
for You answer me. There is none like You among the gods, O Lord,
nor are there any works like Yours . . .
Teach me Your way, O LORD, that I may walk in Your truth;
unite my heart to fear Your name. I give thanks to You, O Lord my God,
with my whole heart, and I will glorify Your name forever.
For great is Your steadfast love toward me;
You have delivered my soul from the depths of Sheol.
O God, insolent men have risen up against me;
a band of ruthless men seeks my life,
and they do not set You before them. But You, O Lord,
are a God merciful and gracious, slow to anger
and abounding in steadfast love and faithfulness.
Turn to me and be gracious to me; give Your strength to Your servant
and save the son of Your maidservant.
Show me a sign of Your favor,
that those who hate me may see and be put to shame because You,
LORD, have helped me and comforted me." Amen.*
Psalm 86 (ESV)

Have you cried so long and hard that your soul feels deeply depressed? You try and catch your breath, but you find it so difficult to trust anything around you. God alone can be trusted in these moments. *Can you give God the sacrifice of worship when you feel this way? He wants to teach you in this time, but are you listening? Are you looking for His help?* He is waiting to show you favor, but you must ask.

79

Day 62

In the Moment

*Seek first His kingdom and His righteousness,
and all these things will be given to you as well.
Therefore, do not worry about tomorrow,
for tomorrow will worry about itself.
Each day has enough trouble of its own.*
Matthew 6:33-34 (NIV)

What do you seek first when things get frantic or challenging? Where do you place your trust when you feel angst toward your world or the people in it?

Seek Him first; in every situation, God expects to be first in your life—the first reaction and the first thought. God is stronger than your fleshly desires and temptations. When anger is arising in your heart, pause and seek God first. When you want to reach for a substance to dull the pain, seek God first.

You lack nothing in Christ; you are clothed in His righteousness. You can be the person God wants you to be. *Do you believe in His righteousness through your situation, that you will overcome the obstacle facing you?* You can and you should. Do not jump ahead of today. God wants you to deal with the problems of today, properly and lovingly. When you worry, you are telling God that you do not trust His sovereignty, protection, or provision. I remember a sticker in my grandmother's Bible that said, "Worry slanders every word of the Bible." That's a great reminder to me. You can trust God's Word and be content right where He has you . . . today.

Day 63

You Are Valued

Are not five sparrows sold for two pennies?
And not one of them is forgotten before God.
Why, even the hairs of your head are all numbered.
Fear not; you are of more value than many sparrows.
Luke 12:6-7 (ESV)

God is holding everything together. He knows every detail of the cosmos and the earth. He knows how many birds He has on earth right now. He knows about every animal headed toward extinction. He knows every detail about you. No one knows you like God does. Since God knows your heart, He understands your intentions. He sees your flaws, and He still loves you. His Son, Jesus, set you free so you could live a life of value. A life free from fear.

Where do you find your confidence and self-worth? Is your identity in Christ, wearing the full armor of God (Ephesians 6:11)? Are you confident in who God created you to be? Yes, God purposely created you with some flaws, some rough spots, each designed to keep you running toward Jesus so you can learn to rely on Him. Yet your flaws are not meant to make you callous toward your God-given design. You are perfect in the eyes of the Lord. *Why not close your eyes right now and thank Him for how He has created you?* Ask Him to help you trust Him, just like the sparrows do.

Day 64

Planted by the Water

*Blessed is the man who trusts in the LORD, whose trust is the LORD.
He is like a tree planted by water, that sends out its roots by the stream
and does not fear when heat comes, for its leaves remain green
and is not anxious in the year of drought, for it does not cease
to bear fruit. The heart is deceitful above all things,
and desperately sick; who can understand it?
I, the LORD, search the heart and test the mind,
to give every man according to his ways,
according to the fruit of his deeds.*
Jeremiah 17:7-10 (ESV)

Satan plants lies in our minds, but only God knows our hearts, our motives and thoughts. And He knows the lies Satan is telling you. Searing heat is sure to come your way. *When it does, where are your feet planted (Ephesians 6:15b)? Are they planted in the Gospel of peace?*

Jesus is our peace. You will not find true peace in your circumstances, lifestyles, friends, or substances; peace lies in Jesus, and in Jesus alone. Nothing in this world can satisfy, so trust in Him alone. People will fail you, but God never will.

Three negative forces often rise against us; Satan, our flesh, and the world. But blessed is the man who trusts in the Lord. If your feet our not firmly planted in who God says you are, then you could easily believe Satan's lies. No one is good enough or smart enough to overcome, but Jesus fills in the gap. The only way to unlock the power of Jesus is to pray and ask for God's direction, believing He will answer.

Why not ask God for courage today? Ask Him to reveal the deceitfulness of your heart. Merciful and just, God wants you to recognize the type of fruit you bear and repent. He wants to heal you and reward you when you fully trust His will.

Day 65

Eternal Safety

Fear of man will prove to be a snare,
but whoever trusts in the Lord is kept safe.
Proverbs 29:25 (NIV)

Not fearing people can be extremely difficult, especially those that are abusive and cruel. It's a fearful atrocity to be raped, kidnapped, jumped by thugs, or robbed at gun point. All are horrible crimes, and if any brutality has happened to you, please know that it does not have to define who you are.

God should define your life and eternity. *Can you trust God, knowing He allowed the fear of man to overtake you momentarily?* And only momentarily did the fear confront you; you are not created to live in that place. God sees you and will not let the evil of this world overtake you. He wants you to feel safe in His love. When you walk in His path, you will encounter all kinds of trials and scares, but eternally you will always be safe with Him. You have a heavenly place awaiting you someday. *Can you trust God, regardless of where His path may lead you?*

Day 66

Sing Praises

Let all who take refuge in You be glad; let them ever sing for joy.
Spread Your protection over them, that those who love Your name
may rejoice in You. For surely, O Lord, You bless the righteous;
You surround them with Your favor as with a shield.
Psalm 5:11-12 (NIV)

Have you found the blessings of singing to God? Unexplainable revelations happen when a person submits to their God, losses their pride, and finds joy in worshiping God in Spirit and truth. He revitalizes your spirit as it unites with His Spirit.

Your spirit should be on fire for Christ's redemption. His redemption should set your heart ablaze. Music is a gift from God, and He wants us to sing praises. We can face huge battles and still see all the blessings of the day—for His mercy is new every morning.

Music is the only activity that uses your whole brain. So, turn up the music and belt it out to the Lord. You do not have to do so with others; you can be alone, singing with the Lord. Just you, Jesus, and worship music. If you make it a habit, you can be doubly blessed. God will move in your heart in ways that will reassure you, knowing for certain that He is with you. God inhabits the praises of His people. If you learn to submit your whole heart to God in worship, you will also learn how to submit to God in other areas of your life. *Will you sing His praises today?*

Day 67

Set Your Mind on His Peace

Open the gates, that the righteous nation that keeps faith may enter in.
You keep him in perfect peace whose mind is stayed on you,
because he trusts in You.
Trust in the LORD forever, for the LORD GOD is an everlasting rock.
Isaiah 26:2-4 (ESV)

The righteous keep the faith. *Are you being faithful to God in your whole relationship with Him? Can you be fully faithful in trusting Him?* Satan wants to distract you in any way he can, but the Word says perfect peace is found in a mind focused on God. You can go about your day doing what needs to be done and have conversations with God through the Spirit.

Do you want to know how to get your mind off the broken record repeating in your mind? When in doubt, pull out a Bible verse. Memorizing Scripture will bring a new clarity and sharpness to your focus. Meditating on the Word simply means contemplating the Word of God—a great way to build trust in the Lord. Focus your mind on Him and His truth—and discover the perfect peace that only He provides.

Day 68

Live Holy

To fear the Lord is to hate evil.
I hate pride and arrogance, evil behavior, and perverse speech.
Proverbs 8:13 (NIV)

We are called to live holy lives, but how do we do so? God gives us the motivation to seek out practical ways that are genuine and true. In other words, it's our responsibility to live out our calling, for we are saints, pure and holy, because of Christ.

Where in your life are you displaying arrogance or pride? Do you have an evil intent to hurt or cheat someone? Do you speak with perversion? God knows each time you do, and these are the things God hates. Sin is sin, and it always produces some form of death, some type of separation from your Heavenly Father.

Hyper-grace, the idea that God will forgive you no matter how dark your sin, has no place in the Christian walk. The cross is not your ticket to keep on sinning. When people claim God paid their debt on the cross, yet they feel comfortable with their sin so they keep on sinning, they are relying on hyper-grace. Those who tend to think this way do not have the correct perspective of Christ.

Give your best to Christ as He gave you a perfect sacrifice. He demonstrated perfect love. He died on a cross because of all sin, and He paid a high price for yours personally as well. Our holy, heavenly Father can take His holy hand of protection from you when you chose to sin, and this exemplifies where the real fear stands: in your consequence of sin. Fear entered the world through sin, and you are inviting fear into your life when you choose to sin. If you want to live a courageous life for Christ, you must strive to put your sins behind you.

Day 69

Pray for Clarity

May the Lord grant you discretion and understanding,
that when He gives you charge over Israel you may keep
the Law of the Lord your God.
Then you will prosper if you are careful to observe the statutes
and the rules that the Lord commanded Moses for Israel.
Be strong and courageous. Fear not; do not be dismayed . . .
Set your mind and heart to seek the Lord your God.
1 Chronicles 22:11-13, 19 (NIV)

God created David to be a strong warrior dependent on God. In return, David wanted to build God a temple. However, because David had too much blood on his hands, God did not want him to do so. Yet, God answered the desire of David's heart through his son Solomon. Sometimes God answers your prayers in ways that look different from your expectations.

Are you asking God for understanding each day, for discretion over the situations and challenges you face? When God calls you to a task, He is certainly with you. He equips you for the job. When you pray and ask for discretion and understanding, He gives it to you. He teaches you to pray for miracles in your life so you can accomplish what He has planned for you. And He will test your faith along the way so you can learn to stretch your spiritual muscles for a kingdom purpose.

Today's verse says, ". . . you will prosper if . . . " As a critical step, you must remain careful to learn and follow God's law. His law is not burdensome; it is freeing. Which is why Jesus left us the commandment to love (Mark 12:30-31). Bitterness can keep you in a holding pattern if you refuse to let forgiveness reign. Ask Him today to help you let go of the strongholds. Jesus is the cornerstone, and He should be the only *strong hold* in your life.

Day 70

The Fountain of Life

In the fear of the Lord, one has a strong confidence,
and His children will have a refuge.
The fear of the Lord is a fountain of life
that one may turn away from the snares of death.
Proverbs 14:26-27 (ESV)

Are you respecting the Fountain of Life by being cleansed by the baptism of Jesus? Or are you running back to your old ways? You have complete security in Christ. Living in the world as a child of God, you will learn how to live a life worthy of your calling. You will experience a learning process to stand up to the wrongs of the world—to do so not with an evil intent but with a loving intent.

Are you allowing the process to flow, or are you getting frustrated with your lack of perfection? Only God can make things perfect, and He will make you perfect; it is a process. Gaining tenderness and compassion is part of the process, and these traits are a blessing, but they are also more challenging to develop, much harder to display, than showing hostility. When you choose to make a difference in people's lives, you can change the world around you. Hostility will not get you far.

Day 71
Blessed Love Forever

Let those who fear the LORD say, "His steadfast love endures forever."
Out of my distress I called on the LORD; the LORD answered me
and set me free. The LORD is on my side; I will not fear.
What can man do to me? The LORD is on my side as my helper;
I shall look in triumph on those who hate me.
It is better to take refuge in the LORD than to trust in man.
Psalm 118:4-8 (ESV)

His love endures forever. If you are in Christ, His love for you will never stop; it is eternal. Our situations on earth are not going to last forever, praise God. Nothing can separate you from the love of Christ. Man can take your physical life, but only God has the power to save your spiritual life.

God helps us on earth, but nothing compares to what is to come. *Have you given your whole heart to God, or are you holding something back from Him?* If you have not given your whole heart to Jesus, then perhaps you should rightly fear eternity, a fear you cannot outrun. Hell will be the absence of all of God's glory—not the fun party that many may imagine.

Day 72

Your Duty to Follow

*Fear God and keep His commandments,
for this is the whole duty of man.
For God will bring every deed into judgment,
with every secret thing, whether good or evil.*
Ecclesiastes 12:13-14 (ESV)

Are you taking your duty seriously? Are you trying to keep secrets from God? God is omnipresent; He is present everywhere and sees everything. God is omniscience; He knows your heart and your thoughts. Indeed, God loves you and redeems your life when you place your faith in Him, when you believe that His Son died for you and ask for His forgiveness and grace. But this is God's world, and He brought people into His world for His own pleasure and glory.

God wants His children to love above all. He wants your intentions to be good. He wants your mind clear of negative talk. He wants us to fellowship and break bread together. He wants unity, not division. One day, God will hold you accountable for everything you did and everything you said. When you think you are doing something in secret, you are not; God is watching. *He is a merciful God, filled with loving-kindness, but do you really want to explain to Him why you did not do the right thing when you had the opportunity?* God desires integrity of the heart.

Day 73

The Key to This Treasure

The Lord is exalted, for He dwells on high;
He will fill Zion with justice and righteousness.
He will be the sure foundation for your times;
a rich store of salvation and wisdom and knowledge;
the fear of the Lord is the key to this treasure.
Isaiah 33:5-6 (NIV)

See now that I, even I, AM He, and there is no god beside Me;
I kill and make alive, I wound and heal,
and there is none that can deliver out of My hand.
Deuteronomy 32:39 (ESV)

Are you living your life with confidence that God will have justice over everything that has happened to you? Every lie you were told, every form of abuse you endured, God will bring to justice, and He will give you the knowledge of how to face the torment within your mind. His salvation brings clarity when you are honest with Him.

Only God has the power over life and death. Only God has the power to heal, restore, and destroy. Certainly, He wounds by allowing consequences to fall. He can destroy whole towns like Sodom and Gomorrah because of sin. He is holy, and only He knows how to keep everything held together.

We sin against God, and His righteousness paid for those sins. He alone knows how to judge with complete justice and righteousness. God alone is a sure foundation.

Obedient

Day 74

Have Faith in Doing Right

Have I not commanded you? Be strong and courageous.
Do not be terrified; do not be discouraged,
for the Lord your God is with you wherever you go.
Joshua 1:9 (NIV)

God is commanding you to be strong and courageous. It's a sin to live in fear and disobey this commandment. *Where do you lack the courage to stand up for the things of God? What event keeps happening that is discouraging you from doing what God has called you to do?* God has told us over and over again to not fear doing what is right.

God's way is found in Scripture. Therefore, stand up and fight for love and do what is right in the eyes of Jesus. God wants His lessons to spill over from one area of your life to other areas of your life. When you let go of anger, you can walk in peace. When you stop hardening your heart, you become tender and compassionate toward the things of God. One must be strong and courageous to be willing to be compassionate and tender. Do not fear showing courage for Christ, for He is with you. Obey Him in faithfulness, and you will build trust with the Lord.

Day 75

Jesus Teaches You

Many nations shall come, and say:
'Come, let us go up to the mountain of the LORD,
to the house of the God of Jacob,
that He may teach us His ways and that we may walk in His paths.'
For out of Zion shall go forth the law,
and the word of the LORD from Jerusalem.
He shall judge between many peoples,
and shall decide disputes for strong nations far away;
and they shall beat their swords into plowshares,
and their spears into pruning hooks;
nation shall not lift up sword against nation,
neither shall they learn war anymore;
but they shall sit every man under his vine and under his fig tree,
and no one shall make them afraid,
for the mouth of the LORD of hosts has spoken.
Micah 4:2-4 (ESV)

Many Christians wonder if they are doing the will of God, but the will of God is simple. Matthew 22:37 says, "Love the Lord with all your heart, soul, and mind," and Matthew 22:39 says, "Love your neighbor as yourself. 1 Thessalonians 5:18 says, "Give thanks." 1 Timothy 2:3-4 tells us, "Come to know the knowledge of truth: the Word." Proverbs 3:5 says to "trust the Lord." We read in 1 John 1:9 that we are to "confess our sins." Hebrews 10:36 says that we are to "persevere." *This* is the will of God in your life.

God's will is not a complicated walk with Jesus. *Not* doing the will of God will complicate your life, which is why learning the Word is so critical for you. When you come to know your Bible and seek out His understanding, His path becomes clearer—not necessarily easier, but clearer.

In today's verse we read about Jesus. *Do you find your confidence in Jesus being the supreme Judge over all?* I hope you do. God's people are a chosen nation, and He decides who enters in. Those who are a part of His chosen nation have a peace that is eternal.

Day 76

Biblical Values Create Stability

*Take care that you are not carried away
with the error of lawless people and lose your own stability.
But grow in grace and knowledge of your Lord and Savior Jesus Christ.
To Him be the glory both now and to the day of eternity.*
2 Peter 3:17-18 (ESV)

Without you being aware or even noticing, our culture can swerve you into sin. Girls and women today have a hard time finding modest clothes that do not look outdated. Blue jeans are extremely tight, and undergarments like tights are now considered acceptable in public. Profane words are becoming mainstream. Lying seems to be normal—in the workplace, in politics, in schools and colleges, etc. Divorce is now commonplace. Scenarios once frowned upon are now happening everywhere—unmarried couples living together, sex outside of marriage, homosexuality, and abortions.

Where is your morality on these issues? What are you tolerating that you probably should not? What are your core values? Biblical values do not change with the culture. Take care you do not lose your stability. The only way to stand firm is to stand with Christ in His morals and values. Sin separates you from Christ, and ignorance of sin does not mean you are not sinning. But it does mean you are not focused on God's values; you are not growing to your fullest potential in His grace, knowledge, and glory. God wants you to reevaluate your moral values. Ask Him to open your eyes to your cultural sins.

Day 77

The Company You Keep

Rise up; this matter is on your hands.
We will support you, so take courage and do it.
Ezra 10:4 (NIV)

God's law states that we are not to intermarry with pagans. When Joshua led the Israelites into the Promised Land, they were commanded not to marry the people there. Those living in the area were pagans who did not follow God's way. God does not have a problem with interracial marriage, which is why in Ezra 10:16 the priest and judges sat down with each couple and examined the matter. God does have a problem with a professing Christian marrying a pagan. A pagan is anyone who does not believe that Jesus died for their sins.

Put your faith in God that He will provide a godly husband or wife for you in His sovereign timing. Also, some people must accept that singleness is the life God chose for them for His glory. If you are dating or single, rise up over your feelings and build relationships that center on Christ—for He blesses the obedient. Walk away from unhealthy and ungodly relationships. They can be extremely toxic. And if you are married to a pagan, you could be the one who brings them to Christ (1 Peter 3:1). *Are you asking God to bring godly relationships into your life, or are you settling for the company of people whom God does not intend for you to make your closest relationships?*

Day 78

Be Careful of the Heart's Desire

*"Solomon, my son, know the God of your father
and serve Him with a whole heart and with a willing mind,
for the LORD searches all hearts
and understands every plan and thought.
If you seek Him, He will be found by you,
but if you forsake Him, He will cast you off forever.
Be careful now, for the LORD has chosen you
to build a house for the sanctuary; be strong and do it."*
1 Chronicles 28:9-10 (ESV)

God has chosen you to be a child of God complete in Him. God gave you talents so you can serve Him with those talents. God does not just want a piece of your heart; He wants your whole heart. He wants you to surrender everything you love into His faithful and merciful hands.

But you can be sealed with the blood of Christ and still live in oppression. Satan does not want you to give your whole heart to Christ and leave no room for dark and deceitful things. God's light always penetrates the darkness, but Satan wants to keep you in the shadows. Yet, if you seek God, if you seek Jesus, the darkness becomes oppressive and far less comfortable for you.

So, be careful, and be strong in Christ. Solomon was not careful. As the wisest man in the Bible, Solomon allowed a woman to influence him to serve false gods, and he turned his heart away from serving God wholeheartedly. God has allowed you to be a living sanctuary, with the Holy Spirit dwelling in you. *Are you asking God to reveal to you what He is finding in your heart? Are you asking Him to fill your heart completely with His desires?* God only wants what is best for you, so seek Him today.

Day 79

Changes Through Love

*He who is prudent will keep silent in such a time,
for it is an evil time. Seek good and not evil, that you may live;
and so the Lord, the God of hosts, will be with you.
Amos 5:13-14 (ESV)*

This world is certainly evil. Turn on the news, look online, or watch a show on Netflix; discovering this truth is not hard. Sometimes following the culture, our friends, and sin proves easier. Sometimes following Jesus in these times proves extremely hard. Our minds get polluted with all kinds of images that are not of God.

Some people need to turn off the news. *Are you spending more time listening to God by reading the Bible than listening to the news on your phone or TV? If not, then why not make a change today?* As Christians, we should stand up for what is right, but in most cases, we should do so without yelling out our opinions. We need to make changes through love, not anger.

God has called you to a particular issue He wants you to address, but He is also sending out many chosen children. You are not expected to change everything wrong in the world, but He gifted you with a purpose. *Are you seeking the good that God wants you to do in this world?*

Day 80

Power in the Word

Whoever despises the Word brings destruction on himself,
but he who reveres the commandments will be rewarded.
Proverbs 13:13 (ESV)

Are you reading the Word, the Bible, every day? There is power in the Word of God. Jesus left you His Holy Spirit, your Helper (John 14:26). When you read the Word, His Spirit inside you ignites, guiding you and teaching you. Every day when you open your Bible, God wants to teach you something. Some days you will need to repent of areas that do not bring God glory. Other days He will answer your prayer in a way only obvious to you through His Spirit.

Oftentimes God is preparing you for what lies ahead. When times of comfort surround you, be thankful but watchful, and learn from God. *Be strengthened by Him*—so when the rug gets pulled out from under you, you will stand up, dust yourself off, and trust Him.

Day 81
The Whole Armor of God

*Be strong in the Lord and in the strength of His might.
Put on the whole armor of God, that you may be able to stand
against the schemes of the devil.
For we do not wrestle against flesh and blood, but against the rulers,
against the authorities, against the cosmic powers
over this present darkness, against the spiritual forces of evil
in the heavenly places. Therefore, take up the whole armor of God,
that you may be able to withstand in the evil day, and having done all,
to stand firm. Stand, therefore, having fastened on the belt of truth,
and having put on the breastplate of righteousness and,
as shoes for your feet, having put on the readiness
given by the gospel of peace. In all circumstances take up the shield of faith,
with which you can extinguish all the flaming darts of the evil one;
and take the helmet of salvation, and the sword of the Spirit,
which is the Word of God,
praying at all times in the Spirit, with all prayer and supplication.*
Ephesians 6:10-18 (ESV)

Each day you are in a spiritual battle, and Satan would love for you to keep thinking you're fighting an earthly problem, not a spiritual one. Your protection is the armor of God, so turn this passage into a daily morning prayer—which will prepare you for the day.

God gives us protection that covers us with His grace. Satan tries to condemn you, but God pardons you. So, stand firm on God's truth, where you can spot Satan's lies. Persevering with faith gives you salvation over every situation that Satan is trying to control. You do not have to know how or why; you simply need faith that God is working behind the scenes in ways you do not understand. *Do you feel defeated?* God says you can stand against the devil's schemes and have victory by the blood of Christ. You are Christ's warrior and He has suited you up. Jesus is your commander; He wants you to prayerfully seek His commands.

Day 82

The Lord Is Your Help

Be strong and courageous, do not be afraid or dismayed
before the king of Assyria and all the horde that is with him,
for there are more with us than with them.
With him is an army of flesh, but with us is the Lord our God,
to help us and to fight our battles.
2 Chronicles 32:7-8 (ESV)

God is helping you fight your battles. Life can pin you down, and everything can change in a moment, in a phone call, in an email, or a knock on your front door. But God has a mercy plan, an exit plan to get you out of battle. Tell yourself you have the courage to follow Jesus out of the line of fire. The shrapnel will still fly through the air until Jesus sees you completely through.

Do you have people in your life who do not want you to change? Are you with the wrong crowd? Hordes of people could be holding you back from change, from making decisions based on integrity, and from growing your desire for a life with Christ. But take heart.

God will draw healthy relationships to your side. So, today, prayerfully seek where God wants you to spend your time. Many of our battles exist in our own minds—such as depression, lack of self-control, anger, and bitterness—none of which comes from God. Instead, seek healthy, godly relationships. As we all wrestle in our own battles, we can learn so much through Christian fellowship.

Day 83

Break the Bondage of Words

Isaiah said to them, "Say to your master,
'Thus says the LORD: Do not be afraid
because of the words that you have heard,
with which the young men of the king of Assyria have reviled me.
Behold, I will put a spirit in him, so that he shall hear a rumor
and return to his own land,
and I will make him fall by the sword in his own land.'"
Isaiah 37:6-7 (ESV)

God says to not be afraid of the words you have heard. They have no power over you. *Yet, are you allowing words from the past to bring you down? What words were spoken to you that you will never forget?* Words can affect us drastically, which is why it remains so important to know who God says you are.

We all have experienced how words can cut us down, either as a child who grew up in a verbally abusive home, as a young woman or wife who has endured harsh words of strife, or as someone who has heard condemnation from a spouse, friends, family or co-workers. Therefore, God wants you to know what He says about you. He does not want you to give power to negative words ever spoken over you.

Do you realize that you can control whether or not you let people's harsh words have power over you? Do you know Whose you are? A child of God has his or her whole identity IN Christ. Your self-worth resides in the reality that you are a prince or princess. Your soul is eternally sealed in the blood of the Lamb. The King—King Jesus—wants you to remain confident in His power and in His words, which hold true power in your life. His words should be the only ones that cut you to the core. Be faithful to trust God's Words over those of the world. Right now, let this knowledge become a milestone in your walk of faith.

Day 84

Training from Heaven

*Be careful, be quiet, do not fear, and do not let your heart be faint
because of these two smoldering stumps of firebrands,
at the fierce anger of your enemy . . .
Your enemy has devised evil against you,
wanting to terrify and conquer.
But the Lord God says,
"It shall not stand, and it shall not come to pass."*
Isaiah 7:4-7 (ESV Paraphrased)

God is giving you instructions on how to handle your battles with other people. *Are you handling your battles the way God is instructing you?*

1. **Be careful**. Ephesians 4:1-3 says "to walk in a manner worthy of your calling with all humility, gentleness, patience, unity, love, and peace."

2. **Be quiet**. Proverbs 12:15-16 admonishes, "The way of a fool is right in his own eyes, but a wise man listens to advice. The vexation of a fool is known at once, but the prudent ignores an insult." You do not have to respond to everything people say to you. Be prudent and wise. Seek God in the moment of quiet. Take a deep breath of God, and let *Him* fill you up instead of negativity or put downs.

3. **Do not fear**. As provided in today's verse, God's sovereignty will rule your life if you surrender. Let it go, give it to God, and His perfect plan will succeed because He is completely on your side.

4. **Do not let your heart be faint**. Satan does not want your whole heart to surrender to Christ. Satan will try to wear you out, but God says, "Do not let your heart be faint"—period; end of discussion. Ask the Lord to let your heart be fixed on Christ, and you will see victory over the enemy.

Day 85

Sure-Footed on the Field

Do not be afraid or dismayed; be strong and courageous.
For thus the Lord will do to all your enemies against whom you fight.
Joshua 10:25 (ESV)

"He must reign until He has put all His enemies under His feet."
1 Corinthians 15:25 (ESV)

Our holy God has a plan that extends past our generation. Only He knows the beginning from the end. And He will defeat Satan. The victory is ours; yet the battle still rages. Most definitely, we will not see every battle won this side of heaven. And our complete healing will only come after we have ventured through life.

Always remember, victory can only be found in Christ alone. Joshua was God's diligent servant; he did exactly as God instructed him. As Joshua trusted God's sovereignty over all, he walked sure-footed on the battlefield. He was obedient all the days of his life. While he was a man of war, no war ever overtook him.

With all this in mind, now ask yourself some hard questions: *Are you letting the battles where God has placed you overtake you? Or are you diligently serving God throughout all your skirmishes and wars?*

Day 86

Surrounded by the Spiritual Realm

*"Do not be afraid, for those who are with us are more
than those who are with them." Then Elisha prayed and said,
"O LORD, please open his eyes that he may see."
So the LORD opened the eyes of the young man, and he saw,
and behold, the mountain was full of horses and chariots of fire
all around Elisha.
And when the Syrians came down against him,
Elisha prayed to the LORD and said,
"Please strike this people with blindness."
So, He struck them with blindness
in accordance with the prayer of Elisha.*
2 Kings 6:16-18 (ESV)

Our battle is not against flesh and blood (Ephesians 6). As Elisha knew the spiritual realm was surrounding them, he prayed for his servant's eyes to be opened to that hidden reality. So much is happening around you that you cannot see with your natural eyes. This passage gives us an awesome glimpse into the reality of that spiritual realm.

Are you prayerfully asking God to open your eyes to spiritual truths in the spiritual battles? God is in control of all the wars raging. He is aware of every obstacle you are fighting, and He can conquer the battles in your life. Don't walk around blind to the things God wants for you. Instead, pray your life into the one God chose for you to live—every day. Your mind has a hard time NOT thinking. So, start thinking things through with God, and He will give you sight.

Day 87

Jesus Prepares a Place for You

Do not let your hearts be troubled. You believe in God;
believe also in Me. My Father's house has many rooms;
if that were not so, would I have told you that I am going there
to prepare a place for you? And if I go and prepare a place for you,
I will come back and take you to be with Me that you also may be
where I am. You know the way to the place where I am going.
John 14:1-4 (NIV)

Believing God is always the first step in healing through His redemptive power. Belief was the first step when you accepted that Christ died for your sins. Belief is the first step in claiming you are being perfected in Christ, not on your own merit but by the grace of Jesus. His grace flows through a Christian's veins.

What promises from God have you not believed in? Do not let Satan lie to you; you have the most powerful force within your spirit. The Holy Spirit is a force to believe, and He will guide you in all truth. Jesus will guide you through His Spirit, not only here on earth but in Heaven. Just as He promised, Jesus has a place just for you—one that is perfect and more than you can imagine. Yet, we must wait, persevere, and believe He will come back for us. Believe His promises for they are true.

Day 88

Sealed by His Spirit

*For no matter how many promises God has made,
they are "Yes" in Christ. And so through Him the "Amen" is spoken
by us to the glory of God.
Now it is God who makes both us and you stand firm in Christ.
He anointed us, set His seal of ownership on us,
and put His Spirit in our hearts as a deposit,
guaranteeing what is to come.*
2 Corinthians 1:20-22 (NIV)

By estimation, over three thousand promises of God are found throughout the Bible, and the King James Version uses the word "promise" fifty times. Of course, promises on earth often get broken as people choose to not honor their spoken words. But God is not like man, and He cannot lie; therefore, His promises are true, and you can literally bet your life on the Word.

The promise of salvation over all your situations are founded in Christ. God's promises to help us stand firm. Just as the old-time hymn declares, *on Christ the solid rock I stand, all other ground is sinking sand.* We cannot stand long on our own, but if you stand with Christ, you will build a personal relationship with Him.

And like any relationship, communication is key. You are free to have constant chatter with Jesus. When you talk with Christ, He will let you know when it's time to move on past your circumstances or time to persevere. God promises He will make you stand firm. *Are you reaching for Him? Are you standing on the promises of God?*

Day 89

Not One Word Has Failed

*You know in your heart and soul that not one word has failed
of all the good things that the Lord your God promised concerning you.
All have come to pass for you; not one of them has failed.*
Joshua 23:14 (ESV)

Joshua spent the second half of his life in battle to conquer the Promised Land. God was judging the sin of the land and the sin of the people. *Why not go and seek God's wisdom in every battle you face, just as Joshua did, so that His mercy and blessing will give you victory?* Prayerfully, you can escape His judgment and win each struggle to reach the Promised Land—your eternal home of heaven. One day you will stand in front of Judge Jesus, and you can do so with joy and confidence when you have lived a life seeking and trusting Him.

God promises you freedom to live in His promises on earth. God has made you and knows you are sinful; He knows your heart is deceitful, but He also knows you are fearfully and wonderfully made. Life pulls you from one place to the next, but when you look up and stop allowing yourself to get bogged down by earthly problems, you will see His promises everywhere you look.

Sometimes He rescues us, but in the midst of the fray we often fail to see His promises of protection or healing till we move on. Later we can look back and see that He was moving in our battles and that He gave us needed strength when we had none. *Are you seeking His promises in the battles you face? Are you asking Him to show you His mercies of protection and trusting Him in the fray?*

Day 90

Never Alone

Behold I AM with you always, to the end of the ages.
Matthew 28:20b (ESV)

The great I AM is with you. Every moment of every day. Always and forever. God, the great I AM, is able to create anything out of nothing. He has control, He has the last word, and He wants to bless your life.

Are you asking God to bless your life? When we do not utilize our blessings, when we do not put them into action, it creates a stumbling block in our lives. We have not because we ask not.

Since I AM is with you always, why do you think your situation is too small, too inconsequential, to ask God about? Believe this truth: you are not bothering Him. He is not too busy—not too preoccupied to keep creating new life nor to honor His promises to you. He is capable of anything . . . all that is good, honest, pure, and true. In His love, He will fulfill every promise He has given to you.

If you are stuck in the middle of sin right now yet have Jesus Christ in your heart, stop telling yourself you cannot talk to God about the situation; you are not too sinful, and your situation is not beyond repair. Remember, He is already there waiting for you to be honest with Him. You cannot seek first the kingdom of God, in every situation, if you do not have the faith that God is right there, beside you and holding you in that moment.

Day 91

Accomplished in Christ

I can do all things through Christ who strengthens me.
Philippians 4:13 (ESV)

Stop saying "I cannot" and "never say never." Please remember you are redeemed. God knows how to redeem your whole life. Stop saying negative things about yourself. Stop being critical every time you look in the mirror. If you cannot say anything nice, do not say anything at all. This includes anything about yourself.

Start loving yourself the way you love others. You can do all things through Christ, and your whole identity is found in Christ. *Are you being too hard on yourself, too critical? Have you allowed yourself the mercy you need to accept past failures and do things differently in the future?* If God created you with a "flaw," it's only so His glory can be revealed through you. In your strength and in your flesh, you can easily believe the lies of your adversary. But when you stand with Christ, His strength will get you through. God called you to a purpose bigger than yourself; you need only Him to complete your calling. Self-help will not work. Only through God can your life be redeemed. *Do you know that you can learn to faithfully walk in courage on the path He has set before you?* Remember, God is not calling you to walk alone; He is calling you to walk with Him.

Day 92

Believe His Honest Wisdom

If any of you lacks wisdom, you should ask God,
who gives generously to all without finding fault,
and it will be given to you.
But when you ask, you must believe and not doubt,
because the one who doubts is like a wave of the sea,
blown and tossed by the wind.
That person should not expect to receive anything from the Lord.
Such a person is double-minded and unstable in all they do.
James 1:5-8 (NIV)

I prayerfully hope that everyone who reads this passage seeks to live it out. These verses offer you a promise for every situation in life that seems overly complicated and for those hidden blind spots in your heart. God wants a relationship with you in every area of your life.

How much faith do you have in God over the difficulties in life? Where do you doubt God? All Christians, those mature in the faith as well as those new to His promises, have doubts about Him. The disciples did, and they knew Jesus personally in His earthly flesh (Matthew 8:26).

These daily devotions are loaded with questions that I pray will lead you to seek God's wisdom. I constantly ask God questions, and God asks me many questions as well. Honestly seeking His wisdom will break chains that have tied you down too long. God does not look for faults in your words; He is looking for an open heart full of faith, trusting His power and wisdom, not your own.

Day 93

Unconditional Love

*There is no fear in love. But perfect love drives out fear,
because fear has to do with punishment.
The one who fears is not made perfect in love.*
1 John 4:18 (NIV)

Jesus is perfect love; He is the only answer. In Genesis 3, when sin entered the world, fear and shame did, too. Jesus is the answer to all our sin problems. Because He died for your sins and overcame death, your sins no longer hold any condemnation over you. Your identity in Christ says you are holy and pure, that your value is found in Christ. In Him, your boldness is peaceful and calm, justified by His actions and by His love.

Are you living like you are under the punishment of sin, a curse that keeps you down? If you have placed your faith in Christ, He has forgiven your sin, and His discipline should bring you to repentance, surrendering the outcome to God.

Sadly, some people have no idea how to love unconditionally. Perhaps their parents placed conditions on their love. Perhaps spouses, friends, and the world have told them that unconditional love does not exist; but God says it does. God intends for love and fear to not stand side by side. Perfect Love drives out all fear. When you are sanctified in the love of Christ, your relationships can flourish as you find your self-worth in Him. You will also leave unhealthy, toxic relationships behind.

When you choose daily to follow Jesus, His sovereignty and love are your identity. *Why not start today to hope in God alone? . . .* for only God is fully faithful, and He is perfect Love.

Day 94

Free from the Power of Sin

*For God has not given us a spirit of fear,
but of power and of love and of a sound mind (self-discipline).*
2 Timothy 1:7 (NKJV)

God gave you His Spirit when you accepted Christ. You can live with power, with love for God and others, and with a disciplined mind that seeks Him daily. But Satan wants you to remain oppressed, not fully relying on the Spirit of power and love. Satan wants you weak and full of fear, feeling condemned and in despair. But know this: you are completely free from condemnation.

Out of His love, God will convict you to the point of repentance, to form you into the image of Christ. He wants others to see Christ in you and encourages you to share your faith boldly. On the other hand, Satan wants to keep you repressed so he can ruin your testimony.

Hasn't Satan won enough ground in your life? Are you ready to take it back? You can have the self-discipline you need to be ready with a loving response. You have the ability to stay away from substances that ultimately harm or numb you.

Do you have the self-discipline not to lie and cheat yourself and the people around you? Are you willing to have the self-discipline to seek God daily, in prayer and in His Word? For He has told you He has already given you the power; *are you willing to claim it?* We do not have to accept everything "as is." We do not have to say, "I am depressed all the time; that's just how it is." That's not taking responsibility for the fears in our life. No, it does not have to be that way.

Instead, you can choose joy, and you can choose to live in the power of His love. You can have integrity through it all. This gift is promised to all who have found their identity in Christ.

Day 95

Immovable Love and Peace

"For the mountains may depart and the hills be removed,
but My steadfast love shall not depart from you,
and My covenant of peace shall not be removed,"
says the Lord who has compassion on you.
Isaiah 54:9-10 (ESV)

Sometimes, it's hard to see compassion in our society or concern for those suffering. The world simply says, "Toughen up," but not God. He wants us to be tender and meek, giving us gentleness as a fruit of the Spirit. If we would cultivate gentleness, some mountains in people's lives would melt away; many people simply need more compassionate and gentler responses.

In the heart of a believer, peace and anger cannot coexist. To allow His peace to fill you, know that your identity in Christ begins with God's steadfast love; His love covers all of you—who you were and who you will become. You are transformed into a new creation in Christ (2 Corinthians 5:17). Let your heart seek after how God wants you to show more compassion, and then you will find peace from God.

God is for you, He will never leave you, and His peace and gentleness can overflow from you; are you acknowledging these truths? No matter where you are, no matter how dark the circumstance, God's peace can rest on your soul.

Day 96

Open My Eyes to the Lies

If God is for us, who can be against us? Jesus is interceding for us.
Romans 8:31, 34 (ESV)

Do you feel that certain emotions, people, or challenges are standing against you? Do you feel at a loss over any area or any fear in your life? If so, pray this prayer today:

Heavenly Father, King Jesus, Holy Spirit, all the praise goes to You. I live in victory because You defeated Satan, who does not have the last say on anything. Thank You for choosing me for Your eternal plan. Unlike earthly fathers, You know how to protect, shield, and love Your chosen children, placing your authority over us in love. Jesus, thank You for leaving heaven, putting on flesh, and coming to earth. You understand our emotions as we know we are made for heaven while walking out faith here on earth. Lord, I have confidence to act boldly for You, knowing You are interceding for me. When my heart and mind are scattered, when my perception is blurred, You, King Jesus, intercede; You talk to Father God on my behalf. Nothing gives me greater confidence. Jesus, only You know my heart, mind, and soul. You know what I can and cannot handle. For I know the adversary will try to stop me, but I know, Jesus, that You can stop *him*. And You are praying for my strength and wisdom. God, open my eyes to the lies I have believed and replace those lies with Your truth. Jesus, I want you with my whole heart, confidently seeking you alone. Amen.

Day 97

Humbly Thrive Serving the Lord

Who is wise and understanding among you?
Let them show it by their good life,
by deeds done in the humility that comes from wisdom.
But if you harbor bitter envy and selfish ambition in your hearts,
do not boast about it or deny the truth.
Such "wisdom" does not come down from heaven
but is earthly, unspiritual, demonic.
For where you have envy and selfish ambition,
there you find disorder and every evil practice.
But the wisdom that comes from heaven is first of all pure;
then peace-loving, considerate, submissive, full of mercy
and good fruit, impartial and sincere.
Peacemakers who sow in peace reap a harvest of righteousness.
James 3:13-18 (NIV)

Do not let your heart fool you. Many people get stuck in situations due to a heart problem. They do not know what to believe as truth, only how to survive in the place they find themselves. Darkness, heaviness, and depression can all feel normal when they have defined you for so long; but herein lies a problem of the heart. The truth actually stings you, like a light that pierces your eyes. But after a time, your eyes adjust and the pain subsides. You can finally see beyond the heaviness . . . to see hope and joy surrounding you.

God does not want you living in survival mode; He wants you in thrive mode. *Unsure if a heart problem is besieging you?* Seek His wisdom. He wants you to live in His hope, to see your shortcomings through His eyes, and to press on. He wants you to be honest with Him and with yourself so you are no longer stuck in a certain situation.

Pride is strong, looking different for everyone. Anytime you rely on yourself, not seeking Him, your pride is offering false hope. God knows your heart—and your pride—better than you do. *Ask yourself, what am I taking credit for in my life?* All good things come from above . . . and from above, you can be completely healed.

Day 98

Imitate Good

Dear Friend, do not imitate what is evil but what is good.
Anyone who does what is good is from God.
Anyone who does what is evil has not seen God.
3 John 11 (NIV)

The word "evil" seems so dark and wrong. Often, people shy away from saying it. "Sin" is another word people avoid. Yet, the truth still stands: a little white lie is still a lie. A lie is a sin, not of God, so yes, a little white lie is evil. Consider the little bit of bitterness you have toward someone, the jealousy, the negative thoughts and attitudes—they are all evil; they are all sin; they are not of God.

Is your identity imitating God's way to handle life? Or, are you imitating the world with your bitter resentment and little white lies? As Jesus' blood covers every cell in your body, your identity in Christ is found in every cell as well. Sin can seem as small as a little cell: insignificant. But sin is like a cancer in the cells, multiplying rapidly. As God constructed your DNA, everything you do should honor Him. He made your every cell to glorify Him, and He wants you to imitate His love, faithfulness, mercy, goodness, and compassion. *How can you do so?* Spend time in the Word. Ask the Holy Spirit to fill your heart. Trust in God's grace, His forgiveness of your sins. And ask Him to help you imitate how Jesus loved others. You might be surprised at the motives and thoughts that begin taking shape and how others begin to notice that you have changed.

Day 99

Be a Blessing

All of you, be like-minded, be sympathetic, love one another,
be compassionate and humble.
Do not repay evil with evil or insult with insult.
On the contrary, repay evil with blessing, because to this you were called
so that you may inherit a blessing.
For, "Whoever would love life and see good days
must keep their tongue from evil and their lips from deceitful speech.
They must turn from evil and do good; they must seek peace and pursue it.
For the eyes of the Lord are on the righteous
and His ears are attentive to their prayer,
but the face of the Lord is against those who do evil."
Who is going to harm you if you are eager to do good?
But even if you should suffer for what is right, you are blessed.
"Do not fear their threats; do not be frightened."
But in your hearts revere Christ as Lord.
Always be prepared to give an answer to everyone who asks you
to give the reason for the hope that you have.
But do this with gentleness and respect.
1 Peter 3: 8-15 (NIV)

God knows exactly where you are. No one else may have a clue, but God knows. Your life might not have gone the way you wanted, the way you dreamed of years ago, but God is not surprised. You may think that life has been unfair or that people have mistreated you. But you are not called to settle the score or judge others. You *are* called to be humble, compassionate, sympathetic, and loving. You are called to be a blessing, even amidst the evil of the world.

People at work or in your family may not understand why you don't play their games to get ahead or seek revenge, but your confidence is found in Christ. Psalm 75:7 says, "For He brings one down and He exalts another." Your identity rests in how much you trust God, surrendering all to Him. If your mind is set on Christ, you have nothing to fear. If your mind is set on settling the score, on pride or judgment, His face is against you as today's verse states. *Are you humbly living the life God has called you to live?*

117

Day 100

Sealed in Christ

Set me as a seal upon your heart, as a seal upon your arm,
for love is strong as death, jealousy is fierce as the grave.
Its flashes are flashes of fire, the very flame of the Lord.
Many waters cannot quench love, neither can floods drown it.
Song of Solomon 8:6-7a (ESV)

We are the bride of Christ, covered in Christ's blood, and nothing can separate us from Him. The seal has been set, and your life should show evidence of Him. Christ's love for you brought Him to death on a cross: your S.O.S. moment. You needed a Savior and He died for you. Now, an extreme emergency is blazing—a dire need for people to know the saving grace of Jesus Christ.

His holy fire will burn away the things He does not want in your life. He is jealous for your love, and He wants you to put Him first, with nothing before Him. As He gave His best for you, created you, and loves you like no other, make Him the priority in every area of life.

Should you not give your best to Him? God knows you will fail Him, and He will extend mercy if you humbly repent. *How can you repent?* Acknowledge your sin and ask for forgiveness, turning away from the sin and back to Him. But even if you cannot see your sin, God will never take away your eternal home in heaven. Even if you find yourself floundering, God will not reject your eternal salvation. When you have sincerely asked Him to be the Lord of your life, your identity in Christ is hidden in the cross. Then, seeing you in the light of the cross, Father God covers all in His love for you.

Day 101

A Friend of Jesus

My friend, you whom I took from the ends of the earth,
and called from its farthest corners, saying to you,
"You are my servant, I have chosen you and not cast you off;"
fear not, for I AM with you; be not dismayed, for I AM your God;
I will strengthen you, I will help you,
I will uphold you with My righteous right hand.
Isaiah 41: 8b-10 (ESV)

Two is better than one, but a cord of three strands is not quickly broken (Ecclesiastes 4:9-12). God's Spirit dwells in you like a friend, but relationships with friends might take time to build trust. *Are you seeking friendships that glorify Christ?* God wants to bless you through friendships that build you up, not tear you down. Healthy relationships strengthen and encourage you in your journey through life. And friends who become prayer partners and prayer warriors on your behalf are special indeed; your relationships with them are built on faith and trust.

When you allow yourself to be fully honest with other Christians and pray for each other, you gain a godly insight that you otherwise might have missed. Plus, Christians hold each other accountable to the standards of Christ. When we enjoy blessed relationships the way God intended, we will love above all and seek Him in all we do together. Relationships centered on Christ protect and strengthen you to live and shine your light for Jesus.

Day 102

Completely Trust God

My God sent His angel, and He shut the mouths of the lions.
They have not hurt me, because I was found innocent in His sight.
Nor have I ever done any wrong before you, O' King.
The king was overjoyed and gave orders to lift Daniel out of the den.
And when Daniel was lifted from the den,
no wound was found on him because he trusted in his God.
Daniel 6:22-23 (NIV)

Daniel refused to bow down and pray to an earthly king, so he was thrown into the lion's den. In the first commandment, God says to "Have no other gods before Me" (Exodus 20:3). He is a jealous God (Exodus 34:14b). He wants your whole heart and expects you to put Him before everything else in your life.

Daniel had complete dedication to God, fearing God above man and lions. Of course, God created both man and lions, and He can control everything He created. Sometimes, He even protects you in ways that may seem illogical. Remember, Daniel had no idea what would happen to him in the lion's den, but he trusted God with his whole heart. Daniel had a personal relationship with God that gave him strength to follow God's law obediently, regardless of the possible outcome. God was making a good point; He was showing His sovereignty over all His creation, and He kept the lions' mouths closed, dispelling their appetite.

How can God close a lion's mouth in your own life? Well, perhaps ask yourself, *What is eating away at me? Is there something I need to trust God with so He can close the mouth of the lion roaring things that are false? Is God number one in my life, like Daniel? Metaphorically speaking, am I trusting God's protection in my own lion's den?*

Day 103

Hope in the Days to Come

The salvation of the righteous is from The Lord;
He is their stronghold in times of trouble.
The Lord helps them and delivers them;
He delivers them from the wicked and saves them,
because they take refuge in Him.
Psalm 37:39-40 (ESV)

False hope is any place you put your hope that is not of Christ. *What false hope are you clinging to?* A false hope is trying to nag your children or spouse into the person you wish them to be, and chances are your efforts will fail. But a marriage that places its hope in Christ becomes a powerful force, scaring Satan and his demons away.

Cling to Christ, pray together as a couple, and pray about your marriage. Marriage is a sacred vow (Matthew 19:4-6). As you will walk through many life difficulties together, let your love be strengthened and your words build each other up. Trust the sanctifying work God is doing in your loved one's life. Put your hope in God's hands, and surrender all your relationships to Him. Don't live in false hopes, but in the hope that He provides. Only He can truly protect your marriage or any relationship, and He will do so if you let Him.

Day 104

The Lord Is Faithful

*For not everyone has faith, but God the Lord is faithful,
and He will strengthen and protect you from the evil one.
We have confidence in the Lord that you are doing and will continue
to do the things we command. May the Lord direct your hearts
into God's love and Christ's perseverance.*
2 Thessalonians 3:2b-5 (NIV)

We live in a world full of nonbelievers, people without faith. They do not have the same mindset as Christians, nor the same morals and ethics. As Christians, our minds are to be set on things above, yet even some people attending church do not have a heavenly perspective; they are not setting their minds on the things of Christ. When the sin of this world creeps into our lives, we find that hurting people hurt people. Without a mature faith and trust in God, some people end up on the side of the evil one.

Redeemed souls should not put their trust in worldly solutions. A hammer in a carpenter's hands makes quick work, but Jesus is the best Carpenter. Only Jesus can fix certain broken areas in your life. A hammer in the wrong hands can destroy everything you worked so hard to build. When you faithfully work to build the life God designed for you, you can have comfort knowing God will protect His plan and His design. Father God is the architect.

Can you trust His design? Can you be content if He designed a shack for you instead of a mansion? Can you rely on the Carpenter to build you up the way God intended? People of the world can disassemble you or tear you down if you do not have confidence in the Lord.

Day 105
God Is Listening

God heard the boy crying, and the angel of God
called to Hagar from heaven and said to her,
"What is the matter, Hagar? Do not be afraid;
God has heard the boy crying as he lies there.
Lift the boy up and take him by the hand,
for I will make him into a great nation."
Then God opened her eyes and she saw a well of water.
So she went and filled the skin with water and gave the boy a drink.
Genesis 21:17-19 (NIV)

You have kept count of my tossings;
put my tears in your bottle.
Are they not in your book?
Psalm 56:8 (ESV)

Psalm 56:8, teaches us that God always hears the cries of His children. *Do you feel like God is not listening to you when you cry out to Him? Do you feel like you have been left alone in the desert to figure things out on your own?* This scenario does not describe the God we serve. *How can you forgo your stubborn ways and praise God in the storm?* Here is an example that you can pray right now:

Heavenly Father, thank You for always hearing Your children's voice when we get to the end of ourselves. Today I acknowledge that only You understand when I cry; only You have seen what lies in the past. Only You, God, have seen how I have been betrayed, and only You have the power to help me stand. Lord, please show me my stubborn heart. Please, quench my soul's thirst. I admit, I have not been seeking your protection for my healing. I confess that I have furthered my own suffering by not believing You are the Protector of my life, and I need to do things Your way from now on. Thank you, Jesus, for bridging the gap on the cross, bringing forth Your Holy Spirit, our true Living Water. Amen.

Day 106

The Apple of His Eye

In a desert land He found him, in a barren and howling waste.
He shielded him and cared for him;
He guarded him as the apple of His eye,
like an eagle that stirs up its nest and hovers over its young,
that spreads its wings to catch them and carries them on its pinions.
The Lord alone led him.
Deuteronomy 32:10-12 (NIV)

What area in your life is a dry desert? What areas are barren and full of waste? Are you misusing your time, your money, or your resources? You are the apple of His eye, but He cannot fully protect you unless you repent and take ownership of your desert wasteland. He is waiting to help you.

Sometimes it's hard to admit that someone else's sin toward you caused you to sin in return. And often, admitting that your mind is parched because you are filling it with the wrong things is not easy. The "wrong things" could be the movies you watch, the music you listen to, the places you find yourself, or the people you choose to get involved with. God did not intend for you to be influenced by negativity and foul speech. Often, we are what we listen to: garbage in, garbage out. It's time to take out the garbage, once and for all.

God does not want you there, stuck in the desert. *Are you the one keeping yourself there?* Have faith that He has a way out of the wasteland. God will shield you, but He is holy, and He has called you to be holy. He needs you to be honest with Him and with yourself. Redemption and protection come by escaping the desert. God will teach you to fly away, and when you fall, He will catch you. Let God lead you under the shadow of His wings—the safest place in all the world.

Protection

124

Day 107

Guarded by His Wisdom

For the foundations of the earth are the Lord's;
upon them He has set the world. He will guard the feet of His saints,
but the wicked will be silenced in darkness.
It is not by strength that one prevails.
1 Samuel 2:8-9 (NIV)

God has an eternal plan for you. He knows how many days you will live on earth. His will for you is good, and He knows the choices you will make against His will. He does not know you just a little; He knows your every thought, and He see your whole heart, mind, and soul. He understands you better than you understand yourself. He sees the wickedness in people.

Thankfully, God's protection covers us more times in our lives that we realize. The proof of His protection is often found in those times when things "almost happened" or in those "just shy an inch" moments; those times could have been disastrous. God has angels all around you, doing His work.

His protection is not always evident, but we do not know the "what ifs," and God does. If you are walking and talking with Jesus every day, you are in His will, so relax. God assigned many different platforms for people to stand on. *Can you be content where God has you today?* God has chosen you through the blood of Jesus; He never misses a soul. God may have needed you to walk your walk just so you could make an eternal difference in one person's life, maybe two. He also could have created you to be the loudmouth who shouts to thousands, "Jesus is King of kings and Lord of lords. He makes the eternal difference." In either case, God's eternal plan will succeed. He has given you the strength to prevail.

Day 108

Holy Anger

The Lord, the compassionate and gracious God,
slow to anger, abounding in love and faithfulness,
maintaining love to thousands, and forgiving
wickedness, rebellion, and sin.
Yet He does not leave the guilty unpunished.
Exodus 34:6 (NIV)

One of the blessings of our holy Father lies in His anger having no sin. His anger has patience and a pure motive. On the other hand, earthly anger is often wallowing in sin. Earthly anger can be bitter, unforgiving, and violent—physically and emotionally abusive. Not to mention prideful, not producing the righteousness that God desires (James 1:20).

Love is not absent from God's anger, and His anger is toward your sin. It's focused on your disobedience in listening to Him. The Bible is clear on how we are to live for Christ, and He is faithful to make us like Christ (Romans 8:29). God will sanctify your life so that you can respond and live as Christ.

Are you submitting to the way God wants you to heal? Are you submitting to His call on your life, to love others even when you are angry? Are you still angry with God for allowing pain and fear into your life? All of your sins—past, present, and future—have been nailed to the cross. Your anger does not have to control you any longer. Praise God for His blessing of freedom over the sin in your life, and praise God that His anger looks nothing like yours.

Day 109

Singing Over You

Sing aloud, O daughter of Zion; shout, O Israel!
Rejoice and exult with all your heart, O daughter of Jerusalem!
The LORD has taken away the judgments against you;
He has cleared away your enemies.
The King of Israel, the LORD, is in your midst;
you shall never again fear evil.
On that day it shall be said to Jerusalem:
"Fear not, O Zion; let not your hands grow weak.
The LORD your God is in your midst, a mighty one who will save;
He will rejoice over you with gladness; He will quiet you by His love;
He will exult over you with loud singing.
Zephaniah 3:14-17 (ESV)

What an awesome promise. God is in your midst; you shall never again fear evil, so let not your hands grow weak. Do not be shaken, be steady, be firm; you are strong in Christ. Rejoice, God wants you to sing praises with your whole heart, unreserved for Him. God is rejoicing over your victory. He is singing over you.

Jesus is perfect, so He must have perfect pitch all the time. *Can you imagine how beautiful that sounds? Do you sing to God yourself? Do you worship Him in Spirit and truth? Have you learned to give your whole self to Him during worship?* Nothing will ignite your Spirit like worshipful music. If your soul needs an uplift, then lift up your voice to God almighty; He can change the atmosphere. He can open your mind in newfound ways when you learn to keep your eyes fixed on His goodness with a thankful heart. If you have a pattern of negative thoughts, praising Him will break the cycle of negative thinking. His blessings surround you. Sing a song of praise back to your Savior.

Day 110
Daily Bread Needs

Just as you received Christ Jesus as Lord,
continue to live your lives in Him, rooted and built up in Him,
strengthened in the faith as you were taught,
and overflowing with thankfulness.
For in Christ all the fullness of the Deity lives in bodily form,
and in Christ you have been brought to fullness.
He is the head over every power and authority.
And having disarmed the powers and authorities,
He made a public spectacle of them, triumphing over them by the cross.
Colossians 2:6-7, 9-10, 15 (NIV)

Your salvation in Christ is a daily salvation. You do not come to Christ and pray to receive Him and then that's it, thinking you are done serving the Lord. Your eternal salvation is the beginning; you must die to yourself daily. You should ask Jesus to ignite your Spirit every day.

His is your Daily Bread. His mercy is new every morning, and so is your need for daily salvation. God can save you from many troubles when you turn to Him and seek His wisdom. We are doomed without Christ walking with us every day. Satan hates to see us thankful for the fullness of Christ; he wants to distract us. But Jesus' glory shines Satan right out of your territory.

Have you asked God to reveal His sovereign hand over things that happened to you in the past? Can you see that the road behind you held blessings, even in the pain? Nothing you do is in vain (1 Corinthians 15:58). God shapes and molds us to His freedom, one step at a time. Through the pain and the sorrow, there resides a faithful Love. A good loving God has disarmed the powers of sin and death. The more faith you have in Christ, the more thankful you will become, and you will seek your salvation daily.

Day 111

Hope in the Day of Trouble

*Offer to God a sacrifice of thanksgiving and perform your vows
to the Most High, and call upon Me in the day of trouble;
I will deliver you and you shall glorify Me.*
Psalm 50:14-15 (ESV)

When you are drowning in a sea of pain where nothing feels right, when you are not even sure if you should take the next step, life may appear dark, confusing, and often overwhelming. In this moment, you can be a sacrifice of praise. Yes, it may seem to go against the grain, but it's true. When you turn your face to heaven and praise Him, you are winning the battle as He pours His supernatural mercy back into you. And you are glorifying Him, letting others know that He is real, which brings the deepest of all blessings into your heart.

Are you praising God in the storm? When everything on earth is etched with pain, God is still enthroned in heaven. Jesus Christ is still your eternal salvation, and that is the only hope you need. So, when nothing makes sense, hope in the day the pain on earth will cease and you will be in eternal glory with Jesus. You will see again all those you loved on earth, all who knew Christ. And while you wait, praise God with a thankful heart that your pain and suffering will end one day. If not on this side of heaven, then when you step into heaven in the blink of an eye. Praise God that He cares when you are hurting. He wants you to call on Him when life is good and when life is harsh. He wants you to talk out your fears and worries with Him, and then what a great blessing and comfort you will receive . . . and even be for others.

Day 112

Lift Up Your Voice

Go on up to a high mountain, O Zion, herald of good news;
lift up your voice with strength, O Jerusalem, herald of good news;
lift it up, fear not; say to the cities of Judah, "Behold your God!"
Behold, the Lord GOD comes with might, and His arm rules for Him;
behold, His reward is with Him, and His recompense before Him.
He will tend His flock like a shepherd;
He will gather the lambs in His arms; He will carry them in His bosom,
and gently lead those that are with young.
Isaiah 40:9-11 (ESV)

The Messiah has come; this prophecy has been fulfilled. Your testimony in Christ is to be known. We are to herald the Good News of Christ—lifting our voices so people can see the work of Christ in us. Fear not to tell of His glory! You are to shine in every place and situation you face. God's light is to be illuminated in every dim room or dark circumstance. Temptations and difficulties may besiege you the whole way, but our Helper tends to our needs and our heart's desires.

Have you learned to share your testimony of faith in Christ? Are you comfortable talking about the work of Jesus in your life? Do not let your harsh ways wall off His gentle leading. Praise His mighty works today as He leads you to share His great Name.

Praise

Day 113

A Steady Walk

Though the fig tree does not bud and there are no grapes on the vines,
though the olive crop fails and the fields produce no food,
though there are no sheep in the pen and no cattle in the stalls,
yet I will rejoice in the LORD, I will be joyful in God my Savior.
The Sovereign LORD is my strength;
He makes my feet like the feet of a deer,
He enables me to tread on the heights.
Habakkuk 3:17-19 (NIV)

Even though they oftentimes live in harsh environments, deer are sure-footed and confident. In season, their food is plentiful while other times scarce. Deer live in many eco-systems, yet each is perfectly created for the place God has ordained for them. As God loves the deer, He loves you, created in His image, even more. He has left His Spirit with you.

He created you to be born on earth in His perfect timing, for a reason during this season. He does not make mistakes, and He never creates an accident. So, ask yourself, *are you confident and sure-footed?* If not, then *why not?* Satan wants you to doubt yourself, but he is a liar. Do not fear the path where God has set you. You need to keep moving with sure steps, walking with Christ.

As you seek Christ, your faith in Him will build your confidence in His plan for you. Seasons come and seasons go, yet only God is unchangeable, with the power to change any situation or storm. He can bring a calm to give you peace. Praise Him for the confidence you have in Christ. Praise Him as you travel through the seasons of life, sure-footed, assured of His love, and guided each step by Christ Himself.

Day 114

Grace Transforms Suffering

I AM now going to allure her;
I will lead her into the wilderness and speak tenderly to her.
There I will give her back her vineyards,
and will make the Valley of Trouble a door of hope.
There she will respond as in the days of her youth,
as in the day she came up out of Egypt.
"In that day," declares the LORD, "you will call Me 'My husband';
you will no longer call Me 'My master'. . ."
Hosea 2:14-16 (NIV)

God will always deal with our sin; He loves us too much to let our sin continue to destroy areas of our lives. One reason God takes our sin so seriously. Sin separates us from our communion with Him. Nothing and no one can take away our eternal salvation, but our sin makes our relationship with Jesus distant and unsatisfying.

God is holy, and He wants you to put all your trust and hope in His power to cleanse your heart and soul. Have you done so? Have you given yourself the same mercy He has given you? God allows consequences and situations in your life to lead you into the valley of trouble . . . but He is carrying you still. Sometimes this path is borne from your sin, and sometimes we must walk through "the valley of the shadow of death" as the way to become more like Jesus.

But you know that your ultimate hope lies not in the desert, but in Him, the Living Water. Only the Holy Spirit can quench your thirst. Only through trusting God's way can you hope for a better tomorrow. Only through relying on Jesus, every step of the way, can you find the desire for the things of God. God has a joyous song for you to sing. Let His grace transform your suffering. Prayerfully seek God's perspective, ask Him to reveal the areas in your life you need Him to cleanse. *What is holding you hostage, and why not choose today to break free?*

Day 115

Peace with God

Since we have been justified by faith,
we have peace with God through our Lord Jesus Christ.
Through Him we have also obtained access by faith
into this grace in which we stand,
and we rejoice in hope of the glory of God.
Not only that, but we rejoice in our sufferings,
knowing that suffering produces endurance,
and endurance produces character, and character produces hope,
and hope does not put us to shame,
because God's love has been poured into our hearts
through the Holy Spirit who has been given to us.
Romans 5:1-5 (ESV)

On the day of your salvation, every sin you have or ever will make was covered in the blood of Christ. If you have faith in Jesus, you have made peace with God with nothing to fear. Jesus paid the price of sin, giving you the free gift of grace. Plain and simple, Satan cannot have you. Even though he will try to take away your confidence in grace, all he says and does are lies.

God wants you to be like Jesus—to have his same traits and characteristics. All of Jesus' hope was built on His firm belief in every word of the Father. His hope was built on knowing with certainty that God will do what He says He will do. And you, too, can have that same solid trust.

Do you place all your hope in the Word of God? On the cross, the power of sin and hell was broken. Jesus risked it all that day because He knew God would resurrect Him. Nothing on a cross is pleasant; the horror and excruciating pain are real. Yet, Jesus could not save the world unless He suffered.

Are you suffering now for Christ or for the sin you're holding onto? Turn your back on sin and put your hope in the love of Christ. Your suffering will produce endurance, character, and a sure hope, and through the power of the Holy Spirit, you will look more like Jesus every day.

Day 116

Dependable Holiness

*So, when God desired to show more convincingly
to the heirs of the promise the unchangeable character of His purpose,
He guaranteed it with an oath, so that by two unchangeable things,
in which it is impossible for God to lie,
we who have fled for refuge might have strong encouragement
to hold fast to the hope set before us.
We have this as a sure and steadfast anchor of the soul,
a hope that enters into the inner place behind the curtain.*
Hebrews 6:17-19 (ESV)

God's character does not change; His purpose does not change; His promises do not change. He swears by oath, and He cannot lie. He is perfect, He is holy, He is pure. He is not corrupted by sin. Our minds cannot fully comprehend this truth on this side of heaven, but try. You are the heir of the promise, and you have the Holy Spirit living inside you.

Do you know you are perfectly loved just the way you are? God promises He will protect you through all of life: the good, the bad and the ugly. In Him you find your strength and hope, not in the world. It can seem like such a long journey on earth, but God promises we have an anchor in our soul, linked to a hope that reaches the big and small places in our hearts. We are told to hold fast to this hope, so do not let it slip through your fingers. God is your refuge; when you cling to Him with hope, He will encourage you and keep you steady.

Day 117

A Glorious Storm

They cried out in fear. But immediately Jesus spoke to them saying,
"Take courage! It is I. Fear not."
Matthew 14: 26b-27 (BLB)

Jesus sent the disciples into the storm. Why? To show the glory of God. To prove He has dominion over everything. Only God can change the environment. Only God has sovereign control. If you put your hope or fears in your situation, your hope is false and your fear unwarranted. Jesus tells us to take heart, to be courageous. Sometimes Jesus needs you to enter a storm as the only way to bring God's glory to a situation. Not every bad thing that happens in your life results from your sin (John 9:3). The Great I AM, the only One with your best interest at heart, is telling you to not fear, even when the bad weather, the tumultuous circumstances, are tossing you around.

Are you looking to Him to find your purpose in the storm? Nothing is wasted when you look to Jesus when the hurricanes blow. The most courageous Christians are those who place all their hope in Christ alone. *What are you hoping for?* Never give up hope in Christ because of the storms in your life. In an instant, He can help you navigate the storm or even calm it completely. So, my friend, take courage.

Day 118

The Lord Preserves the Faithful

Dear Lord, it's in You I have taken refuge;
let me never be put to shame . . .
Into Your hands I commit my spirit; deliver me, LORD,
my faithful God. I hate those who cling to worthless idols;
as for me, I trust in the LORD. I will be glad and rejoice in Your love,
for You saw my affliction and knew the anguish of my soul.
You have not given me into the hands of the enemy
but have set my feet in a spacious place. Be merciful to me, LORD,
for I am in distress; my eyes grow weak with sorrow,
my soul and body with grief. My life is consumed by anguish
and my years by groaning; my strength fails because of my affliction,
and my bones grow weak. Because of all my enemies,
I am the utter contempt of my neighbors and an object of dread
to my closest friends—those who see me on the street flee from me.
I am forgotten as though I were dead;
I have become like broken pottery. For I hear many whisperings,
"Terror on every side!" They conspire against me
and plot to take my life. But I trust in You, LORD;
I say, "You are my God." My times are in Your hands;
deliver me from the hands of my enemies, from those who pursue me.
Let Your face shine on Your servant; save me in Your unfailing love.
Psalm 31:1, 5-16 (NIV)

Do you recognize the value of your eternal hope? You have eternal salvation in Christ. While Jesus does not heal everyone this side of heaven, and sometimes situations do not improve, in heaven there is no sickness, pain, or mourning (Revelation 21:4). Our eternal hope is Christ, and our earthly pain and suffering will not follow us to our eternal home. Heaven is the hope, and Jesus is the gatekeeper (John 10:3-13). He will keep heaven safe, allowing no evil to enter. Dear one, in all your grief and all your affliction, believe this truth today: He will shine His face on you and save you in His unfailing love.

Day 119
Trust the Process

*May the God of hope fill you with all joy and peace as you trust in Him,
so that you may overflow with hope by the power of the Holy Spirit.*
Romans 15:13 (NIV)

This verse spills over with action. Meaning, to live out this verse, you have to do your part. This verse begins, "May the God of hope fill you . . ." *Are you letting God fill you?* He will not force you; His blessings are a gift. God wants to fill you with the good gifts of joy and peace.

This verse also says, ". . . as you trust in Him," so the filling of your soul is a process, not a one-hit wonder, but wonderful all the same. Seeking God daily, you will witness your perspective change in ways that align with God's thinking. When you think things through with God, you will see His hand all over your life.

Can you allow yourself to submit and put all your hope in trusting His process? You cannot have peace when you are trying to force situations in life that go against His will. God will stop at nothing to get your undivided attention. We all have to reach the end of ourselves in order to see our need to completely depend on trusting His every word. Putting all your hope in God's process will result in finding joy and peace. When your Spirit connects to Jesus through the Holy Spirit, His work will become obvious, and then you cannot help but overflow with the hope of Christ. *Why not bow your head right now in submission to Him and ask Him to help you place your trust in His perfect process?* He will answer you, and He delights in you.

Day 120

Restored Comfort

God says, "I have seen your ways, But I will heal you;
I will guide you and restore comfort to you,
creating praise on the lips of the mourners.
Peace, peace to those far and near," says the Lord,
"and I will heal them."
Isaiah 57:18-19 (NIV)

God sees all your ways, not just the ones you admit to Him. He sees all of your heart and understands how you operate and think. You cannot hide anything from God, yet still He loves you unconditionally and will heal you. *Are you allowing Him to heal your heart, mind, and soul by doing the work on yourself He is requiring of you?* He can restore and comfort you when you learn to put Him in His holy, righteous place in your life.

What priorities are you putting above God? Do you have integrity in all your dealings? Only God is sovereign, and He always listens to a repentant heart. You can turn to God and rely on His Law, His direction, His Word; turning to Him will never disappoint. Jesus is our Peace, our mediator to God. He knows the challenges of the flesh. He knows the wars in your mind.

Can you trust His sovereignty over your life? Over your marriage? Your job? Your children? Your negativity? Your self-worth? Your abuse? Are you carrying things God did not intend for you to carry? Lay everything down before Him. Know that His sovereignty can bring you peace, "peace to those far and near." As you become obedient to His Word and see His fingerprints in every life area, you will begin praising Him with your whole heart; you are a miracle of His making.

Day 121

A Promise You Can Stand On

*God causes all things to work together for good to those who love God,
to those who are called according to His purpose.*
Romans 8:28 (NASB)

God has a sovereign purpose for everything in your life. If you are seeking God and putting Jesus in the middle of everything, then through God's providence you are right where God wants you to be. When the rug has been pulled out from underneath your feet and nothing makes sense anymore, meditate on this verse. This is a promise you can stand on. Only a loving, sovereign Lord can cause all things to work for good. *What area in your life do you still feel the need to control? What are you holding back from God? What do you fear in letting go of your control?* The heartbreak and disappointments in your life can work together in God's mercy to bring about new forgiveness, compassion, empathy, and love. Most of the time God does not do what we expect; His ways are higher. He knows the beginning and the end. He knows the "what ifs." He knows what is best for everyone involved.

Are you frustrated with trying to do things your way? Surrender your expectations and everything you are trying to fix; God is telling you that meaning can come from the mess and purpose from the pain. He makes all things work for good for those who love Him.

Day 122

Punishment Belongs to God

God is just. He will pay back trouble to those who trouble you.
And give relief to you who are troubled.
2 Thessalonians 1:6-7a (NIV)

God does not condone abuse. God does not want you in any type of abusive relationship. God does not desire for you to be with people who tear you down. If you are still in an abusive relationship, please seek help. There are many organizations that help people get free from abuse and into a healthy environment. God will judge the people that abused you, but He does not expect you to sit idle and let it happen. Part of being courageous for Christ is being strong enough to get out of toxic relationships.

The sovereignty of God in your life should produce an assurance of trust and faith. God is just; His justice and rule are perfect. In addition, God cannot be put in a box; He does a lot of out-of-the-box thinking—setting us on paths that we could never conjure up in our minds—and He sees those who are troubling you. Trust His faithfulness . . . that He is who He says He is, and that He will do what He says He will do.

Are you listening to the still, small voice speaking to your heart? Are you holding onto things He is asking you to release? Are you seeking His relief? Sometimes we are called to persevere while other times we should remove ourselves from the trouble in our lives. *Have you surrendered control of your worries and woes to God?*

Day 123

Leave Room for God's Wrath

Do not repay anyone evil for evil.
Be careful to do what is right in the eyes of everyone.
If it is possible, as far as it depends on you,
live at peace with everyone. Do not take revenge, my dear friends,
but leave room for God's wrath, for it is written:
"It is Mine to avenge; I will repay," says the Lord. On the contrary:
"If your enemy is hungry, feed him; if he is thirsty,
give him something to drink.
In doing this, you will heap burning coals on his head."
Do not be overcome by evil, but overcome evil with good.
Romans 12:17-21 (NIV)

Are you trying to settle the score with someone? Have you ever thought, "Why be nice to someone? They sure are not nice to me." In our sinful flesh, anger and bitterness can destroy. We are to love and forgive. Move on; let it go. *Do you not know how to stop replaying that broken record in your mind?* Replace negative thoughts with Christian music, meditating on God's Word, and pray in honesty with the One who completely understands. Not only does God understand you, but He also understands the ones who dishonor, disrespect, and treat you poorly. Living peaceably with everyone means that you depend on the strength of Christ, knowing His sovereignty redeems the evil in our hearts and others.

Do you honestly believe the power of the cross cancelled the debt of everyone's sin? When you choose to settle the score and act in revenge, you are telling God you will judge that person, that you do not trust His judgment over sin. Living courageously for Christ will expand your heart to love the sinner but not the sin. Revenge is a heart problem. Take the heart of the problem and leave it at the cross.

Day 124

Good Intentions

Joseph said to them, "Don't be afraid. Am I in the place of God?
You intended to harm me, but God intended it for good
to accomplish what is now being done, the saving of many lives.
So then, do not be afraid. I will provide for you and your children."
And he reassured them and spoke kindly to them.
Genesis 50: 19-21 (NIV)

Joseph offers us such a great example of living out our faith and trusting God. Because of his brothers' evil actions, Joseph was sold into slavery, yet he did not seek revenge. He knew God's plans would prevail, even when he had no idea what they entailed. As it turned out, God's plans for Joseph included years in prison for a crime he did not commit, yet he did not complain. Joseph endured hardship throughout his life, yet he did not question God or ask, "Why me?"

In Genesis 45:7, Joseph makes it clear that God is in control of everything; God can even use sin for His purpose. For example, the sin of Joseph's brothers directed him down a path that led straight to his earthly calling. Years before when he was young and arrogant, before he was sold into slavery and sent to prison, Joseph had a God-given dream that was eventually fulfilled.

Has God given you a dream or vision that is meant to keep you moving forward in His direction? God often gives His people dreams—beautiful, personal promises that inspire you to keep looking heavenward with tenacity and faith. Then, when you cultivate your dreams and they start to materialize, don't be too disappointed if they bring you to a surprising place. God can use your dreams to send you in the direction He wants you to go, but you cannot fathom all His ways; He wants to do things you cannot even imagine. *Can you be content in who you are in Christ when people blame you for things you did not do? Are you still asking God, "Why me?" Can you be loyal to God, knowing God is shaping you each step of the way?*

142

Day 125

Teach the Children

He brought His people out like a flock;
He led them like sheep through the desert.
He guided them in safety, so that they were unafraid,
but the sea engulfed their enemies.
Psalm 78:52-53 (NIV)

This psalm named "Teach the Children the Deeds of the Lord" contains both a warning and a promise. We are expected to teach our children of all the Lord's works. God entrusted you with children in your life, and by the words of your testimony, they should know they are redeemed in Christ. Tell them of God's protection over your life, and watch them find courage by trusting God's leading in their own life. Teach them the way they are to go (Proverbs 22:6). Be an example. Childlike faith can move mountains. *Growing up in today's harsh world can prove challenging, so why not help your kids see God's sovereignty when they are young?* Then they can build their identity on who God says they are instead of who the world says they should be.

Are you sharing God's sovereignty over your life with your children, young or old? God sovereignly gave you children; now your duty lies in raising them in the knowledge of God or continuing to instill your older children with His truth. They will make their own decisions and you cannot guarantee their salvation, but you can fulfill your calling as a parent who loves the Lord and seeks to influence your children with a strong faith.

How can you do so effectively? Children often want to know why they are being instructed, and "because I said so" is not the best way. God wants you to inform your children about how He has changed you, how He has instructed you, and why He has done so. God always has a reason, and He does nothing by coincidence. Explain that truth to your children, and they will learn better through you. God has a perfect design for all His children as He leads each one in the way to go.

Day 126

Speak the Truth

*I purposed in these days to bring good to Jerusalem
and to the house of Judah; fear not.
These are the things that you shall do:
Speak the truth to one another; render in your gates judgments
that are true and make for peace;
do not devise evil in your hearts against one another, and love no false oath,
for all these things I hate, declares the LORD."*
Zechariah 8:15-17 (ESV)

How honest are you with yourself? How honest are you in all your dealings? God hates lies, and little white lies are still lies. By God's standard, there is never a good reason to lie. God is truth, and you are to speak the truth as well. God wants you to have honest gains and honest answers, with integrity of the heart and mind. You have been called to speak the truth in peace and love. This is what pleases God.

God protects right living and righteous lips. In James 3, God's Word points out the difficulty of taming the tongue. He knows you are flawed and will give you mercy, but that is no excuse to do things your way. *Are you depending on God's sovereignty instead of lying your way through life?* Know that He blesses obedience. He blesses the repentant heart. He blesses the humble. In that light, stop buying into Satan's lies, and believe the truth that God created you perfectly to accomplish His will and purpose. He has already given you everything you need today to live out life honestly. *Why not ask Him today to revile the lies you have been telling yourself?* You have the power of God to stand on His truth—so start today to put that power into action.

Day 127

Covered by the Blood

The Passover: The blood shall be a sign for you,
on the houses where you are. And when I see the blood,
I will pass over you, and no plague will befall you to destroy you,
when I strike the land of Egypt.
Exodus 12:13 (ESV)

In our humanness, does this description of smearing blood on doorways sounds a bit repelling? How can it be pleasing to God? Using blood as a sign to wash you clean . . . how can that be? In God's Word, blood is actually a sign of His saving grace. *"Why?"* Let's first take a look at Genesis 3.

After Eve ate the forbidden fruit, she felt naked and ashamed, and while Adam and Eve decided to cover themselves with fig leaves, God gave them garments of animal skins to cover their shame. This signified the first animal sacrifice—and God had done it. For centuries, humans tried to cover their sins with the blood of animal sacrifices, but Jesus was the only sacrifice that would take care of the world's sin problem. Just like God covered Adam and Eve's sin with an animal sacrifice, Jesus covers your sin with His own sacrifice, and the blood of Jesus should still be a sign for you of that reality.

Father God now sees you through the work of the cross, and He wants you daily to accept and proclaim this same forgiveness. He wants you to mark your own home with the "blood of Jesus," meaning He wants you exemplify for your neighbors how to live for Christ. Jesus wants to Pass-over you in judgment as you are found in Him. Anyone not recognizing that Jesus is the God-sent sacrifice will not be passed over but have a judgment of sin over their eternal life. *What area in life are you trying to hide?* God wants to expose your sin so He can give you saving grace. Some days you need to face your sin's ugly reality so it can stay at the foot of the cross.

Gospel

Day 128

Oaks of Righteousness

The Spirit of the Sovereign LORD is on Me,
because the Lord has anointed Me to preach good news to the poor.
He has sent Me to bind up the brokenhearted,
to proclaim freedom for the captives and
release from the darkness for the prisoners,
to proclaim the year of the LORD's favor
and the day of vengeance of our God, to comfort all who mourn,
and provide for those who grieve in Zion—
to bestow on them a crown of beauty instead of ashes,
the oil of gladness instead of mourning,
and a garment of praise instead of a spirit of despair.
They will be called oaks of righteousness,
a planting of the LORD for the day of His splendor.
Isaiah 61:1-3 (NIV)

How is the state of your soul? Does it need release from the darkness? Perhaps your spirit is in despair . . . feeling grieved and full of mourning. He wants to give you a garment of praise. All God promises in Isaiah 61 resides in His hands—not in your own. *Do you feel responsible for your own healing?* Only He can help you. Yes, you need to cooperate with God, trusting Him and doing what He tells you. But you cannot make your brain heal completely from trauma; only Jesus can do that. You can't accomplish the work of Jesus on the cross; only Jesus can do that. Only Jesus could put Satan in his place, and only He can release you from the self-proclaimed prison that shackles your mind. Jesus comforts and brings you peace. Your duty is to have faith that God will do what He promises you. Without faith, it is impossible to please God (Hebrews 11:6). You may never understand how God can turn your ashes into gladness, but He can. He alone is the miracle worker; your job is to show up and have faith. The Gospel, accepting that Jesus died for your sins, is only the beginning. God wants to resurrect all that has died in you. The Gospel in your life is a daily ritual; daily you need to die to self and live the life of Christ. Because He lives in you and sustains you, you are His precious child, holy and pleasing to Him.

Day 129

Jesus Is the Beginning

He is the image of the invisible God, the firstborn of all creation.
For by Him all things were created, in heaven and on earth,
visible and invisible, whether thrones or dominions or rulers
or authorities—all things were created through Him and for Him.
And He is before all things, and in Him all things hold together.
And He is the head of the body, the church.
He is the beginning, the firstborn from the dead,
that in everything He might be preeminent.
For in Him all the fullness of God was pleased to dwell,
and through Him to reconcile to Himself all things,
whether on earth or in heaven, making peace by the blood of His cross.
Colossians 1:15-20 (ESV)

These verses help explain how we have one God but three dimensions of Him: the Holy Trinity. Father God is Spirit, and He created Jesus. Jesus is the firstborn of all creation, and Father God placed the fullness of God into Jesus—all His glory, power, and wisdom.

Before Jesus went to the cross, He promised His disciples He would leave them a Helper, a part of His Spirit: the Holy Spirit (John 14:26-27). After you accept the Gospel of Christ, the Holy Spirit enters you. With the Spirit's power, you can do miraculous work— and do all things through Christ—knowing what direction to take. When your spirit connects with the Lord through the Word of God, you can ignite the Spirit within. God wants to shape you into His "Gospel saving plan," but He won't do it alone. He is asking you to yield to the power residing within you. If you continue to ignore the Spirit's prompting, you grieve the Holy Spirit within you and forgo a blessing God intends for you. If you fan the fire of the Spirit, God will burn away the things in your life not of Him. *Are you fanning the flames of the Holy Spirit or dousing them with water?* Ignite your flame to burn for the things God values and see God's plans for your life light up as well.

Day 130

Tell of His Healing

The angel told the woman
"Do not be afraid, because I know you are looking for Jesus
who was crucified; He is not here!
For He has been resurrected, just as He said.
Come and see the place where He lay.
Then go quickly and tell His disciples."
Matthew 28:5 (CSB)

As you have tried to navigate through all the harsh realities of this world, have you been left feeling marginalized and unimportant? If so, know this deep in your heart: God does not marginalize women or men. It was a woman who carried baby Jesus in her womb, a woman who washed His feet with her tears, and a woman who first learned that Jesus was resurrected, just like He said. Everything Jesus said will come to pass. Every promise He has made, He will keep. And for every commandment He has put in place, He is watching you to bless your faithfulness.

The last commandment Jesus left in Matthew 28:19 was to "Go and make disciples of all nations and baptize them." Your home, work, and peers may make you feel marginalized, but Jesus will not. Jesus has an important place for you in *HIS*tory. Jesus needs you here and now, to do the will of God. Your place in society is not by chance; it is by divine placement. God needs you to go and tell people about His saving grace. People need to know about Jesus' healing work. People need to hear your story of how you came to a place of great loss, to a tomb-like place resounding in death and sorrow, but now Jesus is resurrecting your whole life. You have no idea how many days you will be with the people around you, how many chances you will get to tell your story; no one can know what God has done for you unless you seize the opportunity to put words and actions to your redemption. The Gospel story in your life is a story God wants you to tell repeatedly—as one marked by a testimony of healing and grace. *Have you begun to understand the work of Jesus in your life so you can share it with people who need to hear your story of a resurrected heart?*

Day 131

Deep Roots

When anyone hears the message about the Kingdom
and does not understand it,
the evil one comes and snatches away what was sown in his heart.
This is the seed sown along the path.
The one who received the seed that fell on rocky places
is the man who hears the Word and at once receives it with joy.
But since he has no root, he lasts only a short time.
When trouble or persecution comes because of the Word,
he quickly falls away.
The one who received the seed that fell among the thorns
is the man who hears the Word,
but the worries of this life and the deceitfulness of wealth choke it,
making it unfruitful.
But the one who received the seed that fell on the good soil
is the man who hears the Word and understands it.
He produces a crop,
yielding a hundred, sixty or thirty times what was sown.
Matthew 13:19-23 (NIV)

This Gospel message should resound in the deepest part of your heart. *Is your soil well-worn, rocky, thorny, or richly fertile?* You cannot bear heavenly fruit if you are hindering the great Gardener from cultivating, pruning, and weeding out the things that don't look like Christ.

Is your sole purpose to bring God glory in all that you do? Do you let the Son water your soul? Have you submitted all your land to the Lord? Are you fighting what the Gardner wants to take out of your life? Even one weed left can be bad as it blossoms and spreads, affecting the good in your life. Satan wants to snatch away the work of God, but if your roots are deep and your soil yielding, God will work through the situation, building your confidence in His power. Your healing is possible only by the work on the cross—as you depend on the Gospel message over every situation. The cross brought humanity forgiveness and purity. If you are in Christ, you can ask Him to lead you to forgive those who betrayed you . . . and He will. If you choose to stay bitter and unforgiving, your soil will dry out. Don't allow it! God wants you to be fertile ground.

Day 132

The Living One

When I saw Him, I fell at His feet as though dead.
Then He placed His right hand on me and said:
"Do not be afraid. I AM the first and the last. I AM the Living One;
I was dead, and behold I AM alive forever and ever!
And I hold the key to Hades [Hell]"
Revelation 1:17 (NIV)

God is before all things, and God is behind all things; He is omnipresent. Only God can be everywhere at once. Jesus was the first of all creation, and Jesus was the first to be resurrected from the dead. Jesus will be the last to close the gates of heaven; no one will enter without His approval. With Jesus, no end exists; He will reign forevermore with eternal saving grace. Because of an empty tomb, the Gospel of Christ was poured out on all humanity.

With all this in mind, ask yourself some key questions: Are there dead areas in your life that God is asking you to wake up and walk out away from? Do you know the tomb of despair, of bitterness, or of pride? God wants you to first think of Him and consider the dead areas of your life that He wants to resurrect. Jesus left the tomb, so you could find His courage to leave behind the sin in your life—which always brings death. The Living One wants to make your whole life fruitful, but you have to recognize that He is the only saving grace. God wants to be First and Last in everything you do. He wants you to pause and include Him in the equation before you make a decision. He wants you to run to Him first when life gets difficult. He wants you to seek Him when you are trying to change your behavior. Self-help books won't heal; only Jesus brings true healing to a person's soul. God also wants to be your rear guard and watch how you walk on His path. *God wants to protect you from behind, but are you trusting His protection or looking behind you constantly? Do you have a hard time letting things go and moving on? Why not talk to Him today, this moment, about all that makes you afraid, and allow His Spirit inside you to give you courage?*

Day 133

A Holy Escape Plan

In Mount Zion there shall be those who escape, and it shall be holy.
Obadiah 1:17 (ESV)

Jacob, a founder of our faith, had a brother Esau, who rebelled against The Lord; Esau's people become the Edomites, who worked against Israel for about 1,000 years. Edom's sin of pride brought upon them great judgment, but our always-merciful God has a redemption plan, an escape plan, for those who choose to be a part of His plan; no one is outside the grace of God.

While the book of Obadiah is only twenty-one verses long, these verses show the judgments of the Lord toward those who put their trust in themselves instead of God. Pride is a sin, and everyone has to deal with this sin at some point in life. Verse 3 says, ". . . the pride of your heart deceived you." *Do you exude pride in some areas, like in the things you are "good" at doing?* God will bring you down, as mentioned in the next verse: "Though you soar like the eagle and make your nest among the stars, from there I will bring you down." The original sinner was Satan because his pride got the best of him. Satan's fall occurred long before Adam and Eve were created, and he still wants the Lord's glory by manipulating your desires, making you think you are the star, the pretty one who gets her way, or the strong one whom no one can defeat.

All your talents are tests for God to see where your allegiance stands. You can stand with God and give Him thanks, or you can stand alone where Satan loves to see you isolated. Esau wasted his God-given birthright; do not end up like him. When you are born of Christ, you are given birth rights through the Holy Spirit; learn them and depend on them. Take five minutes today to read the verses in Obadiah, and keep in mind you are the prideful one needing redemption. God's judgment is just, and when you turn from your pride, His blood covers your fleshly ways and allows you to escape the sinful desires of today's world.

Day 134

Shine the Glory

Let no one say when he is tempted, I am being tempted by God,
for God cannot be tempted with evil, and He Himself tempts no one.
But each person is tempted when he is lured and enticed
by his own desire. Then desire when it has conceived gives birth to sin,
and sin when it is fully grown brings forth death.
Do not be deceived, my beloved sisters and brothers.
Every good gift and every perfect gift is from above,
coming down from the Father of lights
with whom there is no variation or shadow due to change.
Of His own will He brought us forth by the Word of truth,
that we should be a kind of firstfruits of His creatures.
James 1:13-18 (ESV)

Satan brought the darkness of sin into our world, deceiving Eve and thus bringing forth the knowledge of good and evil. Before they ate the forbidden fruit, Adam and Eve were pure and complete, with safe, God-given boundaries to keep them in His glory and presence. Now, sad but true, Satan deceives you every chance he can. He does not want you to shine the glory of the Lord around your world.

At the same time, God will test your faithfulness (James 1:2-4) to make you strong in Him. The only way to completely shine the light of the Lord is through complete faith in Jesus, especially when everything around you seems dark and difficult. Every time you call to Jesus, He is there; He never leaves you. When life is shaking you, you can hold onto His truth. Nothing can stop His truth from shining forth, His glory is eternal, and His light never ceases. He is always good, and His intentions for you are good. Jesus already went to the darkest place and defeated sin, hell, and Satan; therefore, do not let Satan deceive you any longer. Hold onto the truth of who God says you are, and bring Jesus into your every thought. *In what area of your life is Satan deceiving you? Are you letting your temptations get out of hand?* God wants to shine His glory on your darkness.

Day 135

Expose Your Dark Places

For you were once darkness, but you now are light in the Lord.
Live as children of light for the fruit of light consists in all goodness,
righteousness and truth, and find out what pleases the Lord.
Have nothing to do with fruitless deeds of darkness,
but rather expose them.
For it is shameful even to mention what the disobedient do in secret.
But everything exposed by the light becomes visible
for it is light that makes everything visible.
Ephesians 5:8-14 (NIV)

Our society can ravage people who are kind and pure, but in God's light we are to live with tenderness and compassion, with "goodness, righteousness, and truth," as Paul says in Ephesians. Some circumstances can prove more challenging to remain tender and pure, rather than rude and harsh. In addition, our social environment is set up more for helping someone to "forget" their troubles instead of deal with them. Yet here's the truth: if you do not deal with your past, your past will deal with you. God expects you to consider your life; you are not to walk around as a fool.

One reason to openly share your God-given life with others is so they can express how they have gone through something similar—and thus you can learn from them, just as you can also share how God is working in your own life; unless you openly talk about the things of God in your daily activities, you are missing out on showing compassion to others and giving God glory.

Ask yourself now: How do I handle my burdens? Whom do I look to for help and guidance? Do they have a healthy relationship with Jesus? Do they help to strengthen my faith or tear it down? And do I share how God is working in me to bring Him glory? Always talk more with God about your problems than you do with people, but God wants you to fellowship with other Christians so you cannot only learn from them but, in your honest sharing, expose what is shameful in your own life. Others' stories can give you hope in ways you might otherwise never know.

Day 136

Nothing Is Hidden

God is light; in Him there is no darkness at all.
If we claim to have fellowship with Him yet walk in darkness,
we lie and do not live by truth. But if we walk in the light,
as He is in the light, we have fellowship with one another,
and the blood of Jesus, His Son, purifies us from all sin.
1 John 1:5 7 (NIV)

You are pure! Regardless of what your past looks like before you met Jesus, you are now found in the light, in Jesus. When you accepted Jesus as Lord over your life, He turned on the light in your soul. Yet perhaps part of your soul wants to stay in the dark; part of you does not want to be found out. Ask yourself why you are hiding, keeping secrets in your soul. *Nothing is hidden from God, so why are you lying to God or lying to yourself? What are you not wanting to expose, and what are you afraid of that keeps you in the shadows?* God's light has already exposed all the darkness of your heart; your duty now is to stop trying to cover it up.

It's time to get honest with yourself. As God sees all your ugliness, you are hurting yourself by not accepting your God-given gifts. Resisting the light does not hide anything; in fact, your resistance is from Satan. When Satan see that God is shining His light on the dark spots of your soul, he wants you to resist the work of Jesus. Know that God will sanctify you, and God will teach you key lessons, but the more you fight His light, the more you hurt yourself. The complete healing God wants to bring you is thwarted when you try to hide yourself. *Who are your fellow peers who love the Lord?* God wants you to connect with other believers who have walked a similar road as you; He wants to encourage you through the battles of the shadows to bring you wholeness and peace.

Day 137

No Longer Stranded

For God, who said, "Let light shine out of darkness,"
made His light shine in our hearts to give us
the light of the knowledge of the glory of God in the face of Christ.
2 Corinthians 4:6 (NIV)

In Mark 10:18 Jesus said, "No one is good, except God." Apart from Christ, you are completely in the dark; you cannot conjure up light from within. It's only by the saving grace of Jesus that you have the eternal light of Jesus Christ within you; it's a miracle you are no longer stranded in the dark. You are a child of light, and you now have a path lit up by the light of Jesus. God's Word is a lamp unto your feet. And if you depend on His light to lead you, you will not stumble.

The Word of God is your knowledge on how to live in the light, and through knowledge you gain wisdom when you act in faith. Figuratively speaking, many souls walk around in the dark; they have no idea that the light of Christ offers a better way. And not just the people who claim there is no God are doing so. Some Christians walk around in the shadows in assumed comfort. But God does not want anyone to live there; He wants Christians to claim their victory over depression, over self-belittling and shame, and over the negativity keeping them shackled. God wants you to have the fullness of Christ residing in you, and that can happen only if you are willing to call the light into the darkness. Satan hates the glory of God shining into your darkness because he knows that you will see his tactics, which in turn gives you authority over him. Freedom from the darkness is found in the light of Christ. *What area in your heart still remains in the dark? Where do you need to ask God to shine His holy light so the darkness can flee?*

Day 138

I Will Rise

As for me, I watch in hope for The Lord. I wait for God my Savior;
my God will hear me. Do not gloat over me, my enemy!
Though I have fallen, I will rise,
though I sit in darkness, The Lord will be my light.
Micah 7:7-8 (NIV)

How embarrassed are you when you trip and fall in front of people, both literally and figuratively? People can be so harsh, laughing at your pain, acting as if they have it together, but the reality is, only God is holding everything together. Only God can bring His light into the darkness. As a Christ-image bearer, you have been gifted with His eternal light.

Are you hoping someone will see you fall and run over to rescue you? Are you hoping for them to lend a hand so you can get back on your feet again? Do not rely on man with what only God can provide. Regardless of what the people around you are waiting and hoping for, ask yourself this: *Where are you placing your hope? Are you waiting patiently for God to come in and be your Savior? When you stumble and fall, is your hope set on God so He can be the One to gently shine His light on the areas of your life that need a new direction? Do you have confidence that God hears every prayer?*

He is waiting for you to ask Him to look into your soul and shine His holy light, where freedom and redemption are found. People can have words that cut you deep in the dark, but God is gentle with you there. *When your self-esteem is low and depression is all your feel, where is your hope? Is your hope in the light of Jesus or in your coping skills?* Jesus knows when you fall. He is right there when you hit rock bottom and can pull you out of the pit of despair. Ask Him to do so, extend your hand, and He will rescue you, flooding your soul with love and grace.

Day 139

When the Dawn Breaks

The people walking in darkness have seen a great light;
on those living in the land of deep darkness a light has dawned.
You have enlarged the nation and increased their joy;
they rejoice before You as people rejoice at the harvest,
as warriors rejoice when dividing the plunder.
For to us a Child is born, to us a Son is given,
and the government will be on His shoulders.
And He will be called Wonderful Counselor, Mighty God,
Everlasting Father, Prince of Peace.
Of the greatness of His government and peace there will be no end.
He will reign on David's throne and over His kingdom,
establishing and upholding it with justice and righteousness
from that time on and forever.
The zeal of the LORD Almighty will accomplish this.
Isaiah 9:2-3, 6-7 (NIV)

A Light has dawned, and Jesus is His Name. *Do you need Him daily to change your life? Do you need the Son to come up over your past mistakes?* When the dawn breaks, you will feel the pressure of those around you who don't want you to change. You can feel so out-of-sorts doing things differently, perhaps feeling you cannot keep up with God's standards. So, what can you do?

Oh, precious child of God, relax in His arms. *Why not ask Him to hold you and help you rejoice?* God has beauty planned in the sunrise over your changing ways. He did not call you to a comfortable place right now, but is calling you out of the darkness and into His light. And while this change may feel strange, and you may begin to wonder if anything will ever come naturally, God is growing you, pulling you away from the things of your past because you are His. God increases your joy when you focus on His work in you, and He will do so in a way you can endure. Only Jesus can counsel your heart in a personal and directional way, and you must follow His leading to truly rejoice. *Are you leaving the dark and fearful places behind and trusting Him as your Wonderful Counselor, Mighty God, Everlasting Father, and Prince of Peace?*

Day 140

The Bridge Over His Grace

*Do not fear them (people), for there is nothing covered
that will not be revealed and hidden that will not be known.
What I tell you in the dark, say in the light,
and what you hear whispered, proclaim on the housetops.*
  ˈ Matthew 10:26-27 (NASB)

God sees everything; nothing is out of His sight. Therefore, He knows all the evil thoughts and plans that people conspired against you, and they will be exposed in the light of Jesus on Judgment Day. You may not see the justice of God here on earth, but you can have confidence, peace, and comfort knowing that Jesus will question them on that Day and do what seems right.

You, too, will stand with Jesus, and "you will give an account for every single, careless thing you said against someone" (Matthew 12:36). God delights in honesty, and He expects you to do the same. Lying, critical words, and negativity are not the ways of God. In addition, God does everything for a reason. When He created the universe, He created light first. Jesus is also a first. Jesus, the Light of the world, overcame death and hell on the cross, and thus Jesus brought His light into the realm of the dead, for the first time creating an eternal way into His light and glory forever. Jesus, our Light, is a bridge between you and the cross and into the presence of God, where peace and healing are found. When you choose to follow the bridge of His grace, you escape the darkness. God wants to uncover the wrongs in this world and include you in the process, but first you must look to your own heart. Our compassionate Father wants to shed His light in your darkness to reveal the things you try to keep hidden—not to harm you, but to make you whole. *Can you allow yourself to become softened by God, exposing the things you find too uncomfortable to deal with?* When you do, you will want to run and tell those you love what God has done for you.

Day 141

The Bread of Life

Jesus declared, "I AM the bread of life.
Whoever comes to Me will never go hungry,
and whoever believes in Me will never be thirsty.
But as I told you, you have seen Me and still you do not believe.
All those the Father gives Me will come to Me,
and whoever comes to Me I will never drive away.
For I have come down from heaven not to do My will
but to do the will of Him who sent Me.
And this is the will of Him who sent Me,
that I shall lose none of all those He has given Me
but raise them up at the last day.
For My Father's will is that everyone who looks to the Son
and believes in Him shall have eternal life,
and I will raise them up at the last day."
John 6:35-40 (NIV)

Jesus wants to nourish your soul. As much as you need to eat, that's how much Jesus wants you to need Him. So, don't starve yourself from His nutrition. Just as you take in nutrition by eating a variety of foods, so you also absorb the nutrition of Jesus into your soul by taking Him in through different avenues. Feast on the Word of God as a starting point for receiving nourishment in Christ, but singing to the Lord and worshipping Him also prove key to your spiritual health. Spending time with God in prayer, fasting, being still in the Lord, and finding your peace in Christ all nourish your Spirit. Your body and mind should ache when you have not fed on spiritual food.

Are you drinking in the Spirit so much so that you overflow with the goodness of God? If you starve yourself from the spiritual nourishment you need, how can you be an example for Christ? You cannot give to others what you do not take in. *God often talks about our harvest; you will know them by their fruit (Matthew 7:10), but how do you plan on being fruitful if you are not tilling up the soil of your brokenness?* You can fully heal through God, and He wants to nourish your fields, but you must seek His food and water or your field will dry up and become unfruitful.

Day 142

The Light of the World

I AM the light of the world.
Whoever follows Me will not walk in darkness,
but will have the light of life.
John 8:12 (ESV)

God commands us not to fear, and He will give us all we need to replace our fears with His courage, but in faith we also must turn our eyes to Him and do our part. God is so omnipresent that you must make room for Him each and every breath you breathe. This side of heaven, obedience can seem so harsh and brokenness so lonely, but these are also the places where God wants to teach you how to rely on Him. God will take you to the end of yourself so you can learn this lesson.

The great I AM brought light and life into this world, each in infinite capacities, so they exist both way out in space as well as in the deepest places within your being. Everything you have suffered and endured can be swallowed up in His bright light of complete joy and healing if and only if you surrender each and every breath.

By the breath of God's mouth, the world was created (Psalm 33:6). Each and every breath you breathe can bring about shadows, words, reactions, and thoughts that do not glorify Jesus, separating you, in that moment, from God, which ultimately brings spiritual death. In contrast, you can invite Jesus' light into any situation, bringing forth truth, compassion, light, and life. In John 12:36, Jesus said, "While you have the light, believe in the light, that you may become sons of Light." Today you have the choice to make room for God and allow the great I AM to bring complete healing into your soul. But you must remain open to receiving Him, making room in your heart and life for God. *Have you asked God to expose the reason for your fear and doubt, asking Him to empower you with His holy courage to do His will?* The old saying is true: if He brought you to it, He will bring you through it.

Day 143

The Good Shepherd

I AM the gate; whoever enters through will be saved.
He will come in and go out, and find pasture.
The thief comes only to steal, kill and destroy;
I have come that they may have life and have it to the full.
I AM the Good Shepherd.
The Good Shepherd lays down His life for the sheep.
John 10:9-11 (NIV)

Do you find comfort knowing that Jesus is the Good Shepherd who leads you to the gates of heaven? Jesus did the work on the cross to save you and now leads you in love and grace, but it's your responsibility to follow. Yet many people make following Jesus more challenging than needed; sheep do not question the shepherd every turn they make. They just follow; it's that simple.

Notice that this verse highlights what Satan is about: he is the thief wanting to rob you of your security in Jesus. Satan wants to destroy your trust in the faithful great I AM, and he wants to kill your reflection of God's glory. Don't let him. Remember, by the power of the great I AM, you can live a life full of the fruits of the Spirit—love, joy, peace, patience, kindness, goodness, faithfulness, gentleness, and self-control (Galatians 5:22-23). Satan wants to rob you of your God-given fruit because he fears what you will do in the power of the Holy Spirit.

The Bible says that Satan was the craftiest of all those God made (Genesis 3:1), so he isn't stupid but monstrously evil. Know that, by the power of the great I AM, you can resist the Devil and live in the fullness of life that Jesus intends for you. Satan is scared by you believing in God's promises, so when you believe with all your heart that Jesus laid down His life for you, you can overcome the evil one. If you believe in the work of the Holy Spirit who lives inside you, Satan has nothing on you. He is lying, so stop believing the lies. The Good Shephard wants to lead you to a life free from fear. *Are you living in the courage of Christ so that you can do God's work?*

Day 144

The Resurrection

Jesus said to her, "I AM the resurrection and the life.
Whoever believes in Me, though he die, yet shall he live,
and everyone who lives and believes in Me shall never die.
Do you believe this?"
John 11:25-26 (ESV)

The great I AM is asking you today's question. *Do you believe that Jesus is the Resurrection and the Life? Do you believe that He can resurrect every dead area of your life?* All you have suffered may still bring you pain, and you may feel that the joy, peace, and security of your life are dead. Numb to your feelings, perhaps you still have moments where breathing itself feels strenuous and heavy. Certainly, God wants you to have life—abundant life on earth as well as eternal life in heaven—but sometimes some things need to die so, through their death, you can experience the joy and peace of life in Christ.

Perhaps you can think of this truth whenever you see a flower. A flower produces seeds and then dies, and the seeds lie still until they germinate and grow. If you have negative thinking, if you talk down to yourself in any way, God is asking you to put to death the negative thinking and believe He can be the life of your mind. God wants to heal your mind so that it rests in His peace, and when your thinking is clear, you will notice how God has transformed your mind.

Stop complicating the simple ways of God. Stop making certain things bigger than they need to be. *Do you believe the drama and confusion brought on by Satan? Or do you believe with every cell of your body that the great I AM can restore you?* Your body on earth is set to fail; but though your heart will stop beating, you will instantly be filled with joy as you meet Jesus face-to-face. *What is so fabulous on earth that it seems better than spending eternity with the great I AM?* Heaven will be greater than you can ever imagine, so set your eyes and hope on things above!

Day 145

The Way, Truth, and Life

Let not your hearts be troubled. Believe in God; believe also in Me.
In My Father's house are many rooms.
If it were not so, would I have told you that I go
to prepare a place for you? And if I go and prepare a place for you,
I will come again and will take you to Myself,
that where I am you may be also.
And you know the way to where I am going.
Thomas said to Him, "Lord, we do not know where you are going.
How can we know the way?"
Jesus said to him, "I AM the way, and the truth, and the life.
No one comes to the Father except through Me.
John 14:1-6 (ESV)

The great I AM does not want your heart troubled, so first ask yourself, *"What is troubling me?"* In response, Jesus calls us to believe in God as well as in Him. In the NIV, the above verse replaces the word "trust" with "believe"; many times, different versions of the Bible trade out the two words. You cannot trust something unless you believe it first, but on the other hand, you cannot believe in something unless you know it is trustworthy. Biblically speaking, "trust" and "believe" are interchangeable. If you believe the great I AM, you will trust Him.

How can you believe that Jesus is in heaven, preparing heaven for you, when you do not trust that He is also the Truth and the Life here and now? How is it possible that you can trust that Jesus has your eternal home set, but you do not believe that He is sovereign over your daily life? God's truth will set you free, but you do not get to pick and choose what His truth is. Choosing to ignore any part of the Bible does not discredit His truth. There is only one way into heaven: through Jesus. There is only one way to courageously live in freedom from the lies and the death of sin: His name is Jesus. The great I AM is all you need. *What do you need God to do in your life?*

Day 146

The True Vine

"I AM the true vine, and my Father is the Gardener.
He cuts off every branch in Me that bears no fruit,
while every branch that does bear fruit He prunes
so that it will be even more fruitful.
You are already clean because of the Word I have spoken to you.
Remain in Me, as I also remain in you.
No branch can bear fruit by itself; it must remain in the vine.
Neither can you bear fruit unless you remain in Me.
I AM the vine; you are the branches.
If you remain in Me and I in you, you will bear much fruit;
apart from Me you can do nothing. If you do not remain in Me,
you are like a branch that is thrown away and withers;
such branches are picked up, thrown into the fire and burned.
If you remain in Me and My Words remain in you,
ask whatever you wish, and it will be done for you.
This is to my Father's glory, that you bear much fruit,
showing yourselves to be My disciples.
As the Father has loved Me, so have I loved you.
Now remain in My love. If you keep My commands,
you will remain in My love,
just as I have kept My Father's commands and remain in His love.
I have told you this so that My joy may be in you and
that your joy may be complete."
John 15:1-11 (NIV)

Jesus wants you to know that if you have heard and believed His Word, you are already clean, free from sin's condemnation. Whatever has happened to you does not define who you are. Yes, the past fiery storms have shaped you, but they are just a part of you. Your future will not define you either, even as hard things lie ahead. The moment you accepted the Lord into your heart, you were grafted into the family of God; your salvation day is your defining moment. Accept the reality that you will have trials ahead, that you will be tested and tempted, as these are the storms of life. How you respond will show the world your faith in the Gardner. Your faith flourishes if you remain in the love of Christ. When you spend time with Him, His Word becomes nourishment—and the more evident your faith and stronger your branches. But if you choose to neglect the duties of the garden, your growth withers. Just like the garden in your yard, the weeds will sprout and choke out God's radiance if you don't pull the weeds. If you don't spend time pruning, some areas of your life will take over and become wild. When God prunes, you may feel the pinch or the squeeze, but have faith in knowing all branches must be pruned to flourish. Roses display their beauty most splendidly after being cut back for a new growing season. *Are you allowing the Gardner to tend to your branches? Are you afraid of being cut off from your peers or from God?* Trust that God has a new growing season for you, allowing you to shine for His glory.

Day 147

Loving You Regardless

In Your unfailing love You will lead the people You have redeemed.
In Your strength You will guild them to Your holy dwellings.
Exodus 15:13 (NIV)

In that short little verse, God is mentioned six times and those He has redeemed are mentioned twice. God is the One that redeems, God is the One that leads, and God will not stop loving you regardless of how you feel or what you have done. No one is too dirty for God because your sin was redeemed through the work of Jesus on the cross.

Jesus has already dealt with the sin you are committing. No matter where you are physically and mentally right now, no matter the substance that may saturate your mind, God has dealt with it. This moment right here has been redeemed, and you can follow the leading of God right where you are.

Are you willing to say "no" to God because you do not feel this moment is redeemed? God has asked you to follow His guidance, even in the middle of everything you find your hands doing. God is asking you to follow Him to a holy dwelling. *He can clean you up, but are you following Him?* Jesus put death in its place so that you can live a redeemed life in the freedom of Christ. Your freedom is not freedom to do as you choose, but freedom from the power of sin and over the work of Satan. Your freedom is found in loving others the way God intended you to. You are not free to live out your fleshly or sinful desires.

Redeemed people are being guided to His holy dwelling—a place of refuge and peace. Father God wants you to live like Jesus did. More than anything or anyone, Jesus knew God. *How well do you know God?* You get to know Him best by reading His Word with an open heart. Invite His redeeming love to guide your steps, and they will be aligned with His.

Day 148

Cry Out to the Lord

Give thanks to the LORD, for He is good; His love endures forever.
Let the redeemed of the LORD tell their story—
those He redeemed from the hand of the foe,
those He gathered from the lands, from east and west,
from north and south. Some wandered in desert wastelands,
finding no way to a city where they could settle.
They were hungry and thirsty, and their lives ebbed away.
Then they cried out to the LORD in their trouble,
and He delivered them from their distress.
He led them by a straight way to a city where they could settle.
Let them give thanks to the LORD for His unfailing love
and His wonderful deeds for mankind,
for He satisfies the thirsty and fills the hungry with good things.
Psalm 107:1-9 (NIV)

Here you read how the people cried out to the Lord and He redeemed them . . . and He delights in doing so. But if you read the entire psalm, you will see how they actually cried out to Him four different times, and each time He redeemed His chosen ones and they praised Him. But each time, they slowly became rebellious once more or their courage melted away. Fear often has to do with punishment, with sin. A rebellious heart will have a difficult time finding courage for the things of God. But God always listens to an honest, repentant heart.

Is there something in your life that repeatedly creeps in slowly, and over time, it has become something that makes you willing to sin? God wants you to trust His redemption over this difficult situation that you cannot seem to reign in. God knows what mistakes you will make down the road, yet He chooses to redeem you repeatedly. God knows the places in your heart and mind that are still not redeemed. He will bless you with redemption over these areas if you invite Jesus to help you with your troubles. *Why not do so today?*

Day 149

Royal Family

Do not fear; you have committed all this evil,
yet do not turn aside from following the LORD,
but serve the LORD with all your heart.
And you must not turn aside for then you would go after futile things
which cannot profit or deliver, for they are futile.
For the LORD will not abandon His people
on account of His great name,
because the Lord has been pleased to make you a people for Himself.
1 Samuel 12:20-22 (NASB)

Sometimes, other people's sin committed against you caused you to sin in ways you still do not even realize; it has become such a part of you that it feels natural. Certainly, brokenness can feel comfortable when that is all you know. Numbness can be an escape so that you stop feeling anything. Perhaps, you have no idea what it would look like to be whole, to fully honor and respect yourself the way God does. As God is the Creator of life, only He can breathe life into all your dead places. Without a doubt, He is pleased with you being a part of His royal family, and His unconditional love for you can redeem the little white lies you tell yourself; He can redeem the gushing hole in your heart.

Can you put your faith in God and be confident that He will not abandon you, regardless of the sin you have committed? God will not abandon you, regardless of the shame you feel because of all the muck and despair someone else has brought you through. Ask yourself, *what areas in my life do I need redeemed by the power of Jesus? What bad intentions do I need redeemed? What relationship do I need redeemed?* God is with you, He will not leave you, and He will fight for you.

Day 150

In Perfect Company

"Fear not, for I AM with you; I will bring your offspring from the east,
and from the west I will gather you.
I will say to the north, 'Give up,' and to the south, 'Do not withhold';
Bring My songs from afar and My daughters from the ends of the earth,
everyone who is called by My name, whom I created for My glory,
whom I formed and made."
Bring out the people that are blind, yet have eyes,
who are deaf, yet have ears!
All the nations gather together, and the peoples assemble.
Who among them can declare this, and show us the former things!
Let them bring their witnesses to prove them right,
and let them hear and say, it is true.
"You are My witnesses," declares the LORD,
"and My servant whom I have chosen,
that you may know and believe Me and understand that I AM He.
Before Me no god was formed, nor shall there be any after Me.
I, I AM the LORD, and besides Me there is no savior."
Isaiah 43:5-11 (ESV)

You were created for His glory. *In your daily life, do you pause and ask yourself, "Am I bringing God glory right now by doing what I am doing?" Did you know not bringing God glory is a sin?* If you know what is right yet choose not to do it, you are sinning in God's eyes. Jesus is your only hope to learn and live for His glory, and Jesus is all you need. Jesus is with God, and He is praying for you. Jesus can give you sight in the areas of life you have been blinded from seeing, and Jesus knows how to whisper in your deaf ears so you can awake to His calling.

Are you living your daily life like Jesus is right there with you? Does He feel close or distant? Are you seeking His presence? Are you seeking His wisdom? Jesus gathers His community to Himself, but He then asks you to be His witness to the glory in your life. Obey Him by doing so and see His heavenly blessings unfold—peace in the trials, a new joy in your heart, and all the fruit of His Holy Spirit poured out in and through you.

Redeemed

Day 151

Serve Him Without Fear

"Blessed be the Lord God of Israel,
for He has visited and redeemed His people
and has raised up a horn of salvation for us
in the house of His servant David,
as He spoke by the mouth of His holy prophets from of old,
that we should be saved from our enemies
and from the hand of all who hate us;
to show the mercy promised to our fathers
and to remember His holy covenant,
the oath that He swore to our father Abraham,
to grant us that we, being delivered from the hand of our enemies,
might serve Him without fear,
in holiness and righteousness before Him all our days.
And you, child, will be called the prophet of the Most High;
for you will go before the Lord to prepare His ways,
to give knowledge of salvation to His people
in the forgiveness of their sins, because of the tender mercy of our God,
whereby the sunrise shall visit us from on high
to give light to those who sit in darkness and in the shadow of death,
to guide our feet into the way of peace."
Luke 1:68-79 (ESV)

God knows how sin has shaped our world, and He knew we needed Jesus, our Redeemer. God always has a plan and is not worried; He is in complete control. You must trust that God placed you in your world for a purpose and has assigned jobs for you. These jobs might put you in harm's way, in hostile places, and with unpleasant and challenging people—things that will be too much for you to bear without Him. Thus, you must rely on His strength, not your own. *Are your flesh and desires getting in the way of surrendering every part of yourself to God?* Surrendering your enemies to God will allow Him to have the final say on how things should go.

Are you trying to get even with the people who have harmed you? God blesses those who rely on His grace and mercy. Holiness and righteousness cannot stand with fear because redeemed children of God have been washed in His holiness and righteousness and by the blood of the Lamb; you have been set free from the oppression of sin and fear. Your days with Him are secure.

Day 152

Grow Strong

*Abraham did not waiver in unbelief at God's promise
but was strengthened in his faith and gave glory to God,
because he was fully convinced that what He had promised
He was also able to perform.*
Romans 4:20-21 (HCSB)

I encourage you to pick up your Bible and read Genesis chapters 12 to 22 sometime, but for now here's a quick overview. Abraham offers a prime example of faith in God, but that faith had to grow strong. In the same way, your strong faith doesn't develop overnight; it's a lifelong journey. God called 75-year-old Abram and said He would make him into a great nation and that all the people on earth would be blessed through him. Abram had no children and did not know how God will fulfill His promise, but he had enough faith to obey God. He left his home and built an altar, showing his loyalty to God. Once he arrived in Egypt, however, Abram's faith faltered. He lied about his beautiful wife, calling her "my sister" as he feared the people. Even in our humanness, we cannot quench God's will; His plans will move forward. God inflicted diseases on the Egyptians, which got Abram back on God's intended path. In Genesis 12:17, God told Abram His promise again; however, because he was human, Abram and his wife doubted God's timing and Abram impregnated the maidservant. God reminded Abram of His promise a third time, and his wife laughed. In the end, God did exactly what He said He would do through Abraham.

Is God doing something in your life that does not look the way you think it should? Are you leaving room for the miracles of God? Close to the end of Abraham's life, he believed the Lord completely, and God credited it to him as righteousness (Genesis 15:6). God knows that your faith grows when you see His hand in your life over time. Your faith walk may not progress perfectly, but He will lead you to be fully convinced that God can do what He says He will do.

Day 153

Perfection Found in Christ

Without faith it is impossible to please God,
for whoever would draw near to God must believe that He exists
and that He rewards those who seek Him.
For whatever does not proceed from faith is sin.
Hebrews 11:6 & Romans 14:23b (ESV)

Faith is believing and loving God with your whole heart, mind, and soul. It is trusting Him and His every word. Faith is not doubting that God can do what He says He will do. Faith is knowing His power is strong enough to deal with everything without exception. No one in this world is completely trustworthy; only God is fully trustworthy. No one really loves unconditionally except Jesus. No one can control the universe but God. God has characteristics that you can depend on. *Do you know God's character?*

God knows the heart of every person, and He remains faithful to all He has created. Because He is holy and He is Truth, only God is fully trustworthy. Without a doubt, His standards should be the plumb line in your faith walk. While everyone on earth lies, God cannot lie. In the flesh, we can find it hard to have faith in God's purity because we live in a sin-filled world. We have never seen anyone "perfect," but faith is believing perfection is found in Christ. Our faith should run deep, and if you place your faith in the One above all, you can reach deep into your soul and find freedom from anything that keeps you from receiving the reward He has planned for you. If you want Jesus to redeem your whole soul, you must learn to live in faith. God wants to redeem your wounds, your abuse, and your wrong thinking, but you must seek Him for healing. You must trust Him that He will see you through. You do not have to understand how God will redeem your past, but just have faith that He will. *Can your faith that God will redeem your past begin today?*

Day 154

Divine Inspiration

Should a person like me run away?
Or should one like me go into the temple to save his life? I will not go!
I realized that God had not sent him,
but that he had prophesies against me because someone hired him.
He had been hired to intimidate me
so that I would commit a sin by doing this,
and then they would give me a bad name to discredit me.
Nehemiah 6:11-13 (NIV)

God calls missionaries into all parts of the world—because both the scariest and most comforting places all need the love of Christ. God is calling every Christian to a life of ministry, and He will equip you for your mission field, sovereignly putting you in the right place at the right time. *What is the catalysis for how much mission work you do for God?* Answer: *your faith.*

All Christians are prophets of the Lord. A prophet is a person who speaks by divine inspiration or as the interpreter through whom the will of God is expressed. Anyone who spends time in prayer will have God's will expressed to them. This explains why it is so important to pray for the ones you love; you could hear a word from God that you need to speak into their life. God does the real work, but through faith you can relay God's message.

The Bible highlights the prophets with the biggest faith, those who asked God to send fire down from heaven, like Elijah, or close the mouth of a lion, like Daniel. Like He spoke to these prophets, God wants to talk to all His children. He wants us all to prophesy, not just the elite few. Your faith will take you as far as you will faithfully go. No matter if Satan tries to thwart you, God will get His mission accomplished and get the glory. He could do it all Himself, but He chooses for you to be a part of His miraculous work as a blessing and privilege. *Are you willing to stand in faith against those intimidating you?* Through faith, you can do what God has called you to. Fear of God's calling is the opposite of faith in His sovereign plan.

Day 155

Distinguish the Truth

But you, beloved, building yourselves up
in your most holy faith and praying in the Holy Spirit.
Keep yourselves in the love of God,
waiting for the mercy of our Lord Jesus Christ that leads to eternal life.
Jude 20-21 (ESV)

Jude wrote to defend the truth of God against false teachers. He said, "Men who spoke abusively were like unreasoning animals, and some had secretly slipped in among them." These people tried to distort the will of God, but God's message says to build yourself up and steer clear of distorted people who will try to tear you down. *How can you be built up in faith? Is it by knowing the Word of God, praying continually throughout your day, and putting all your faith in the Faithful One?* Those who walk closely with God can distinguish between God's truth and the lies of false teachers. An important way to defend the Truth is to faithfully pray in the Holy Spirit that you will respond in mercy toward those who doubt God's faithfulness. You must educate yourself on the One who holds your eternal destiny, not only for yourself but for the people around you.

Are you building up those in your life or using critical words? Have you let some unreasonable animals secretly slip into your circle of friends? God is alright with you ministering to these types of people, but not alright with them influencing your decisions and leading you where He does not intend for you to go. *Do you have faith that God will give you the tools you need to build yourself up, beginning in His Word?* God gives generously to those who ask Him and those who seek Him will be found in Him. God will not look away from you when you come to Him with an honest heart. He wants your heart's cry to be spilled upon His altar in prayer, and He wants to show you something new. He can only do so if you have faith that God will build you up for His calling on your life.

Day 156

Fight the Good Fight

*. . . pursue righteousness, godliness, faith, love,
endurance, and gentleness. Fight the good fight of the faith.
Take hold of the eternal life to which you were called,
when you made your good confession [in Christ] . . .*
1 Timothy 6:11b-12 (NIV)

What things or desires do you pursue? What do you do in your spare time? Do you have a godly vision, or do you pursue your own goals? All you do in faith as a service to Christ is blessed. To attain righteousness, one needs to know with certainty that Jesus is faithful and holds our eternal life in His hands. Flowing from Jesus' faithfulness is a love that helps us endure the difficulties.

How much gentleness did you show the last time you lost your temper? Gentleness comes from our own sense of peace overflowing, knowing Jesus is faithful and the One in control of our days. Your identity in Christ must be built upon the fact that God is faithful—even when the world is crumbling around you. God's original design was created without confusion, abuse, lying, hate, or death.

God "puts your tears in a bottle" (Psalm 56:8). He knows what causes you to cry. If you want to feel God's comfort, you must yield to the fact that God is faithful. Period. Any doubt you have about God's faithfulness is a lie straight from Satan. This is how you fight the good fight of faith: you depend upon His faithfulness, and you faithfully follow Jesus, living in the manner and character of Christ. Endure the lies of Satan by allowing your faith to swallow up his lies; your faith is grounded in God's holy Truth found in His Word. If your identity is anchored in the faithfulness of Christ, your actions will swallow up the fiery darts that Satan throws your way. Sometimes things must get harder before they get better. In this testing of your faith, God is right there beside you in His Holy Spirit. You can depend on His strength to pull you through.

Day 157

Heartfelt Devotion

If then you have been raised with Christ, seek the things that are above,
where Christ is, seated at the right hand of God.
Set your minds on things that are above, not on things that are on earth.
For you have died, and your life is hidden with Christ in God.
When Christ who is your life appears,
then you also will appear with Him in glory.
Put to death therefore what is earthly in you: sexual immorality, impurity,
passion, evil desire, and covetousness, which is idolatry.
Colossians 3:1-5 (ESV)

This Scripture passage does not imply that all are saved in Christ. Step one of following Jesus is to accept His salvation through the work of the cross. If you have truly accepted Him, repenting of your sins, and trusting that He has taken away all condemnation, then He has deposited His Holy Spirit into your soul, making you a new creation alive in Him. This is a supernatural change that will take place if you have accepted His saving grace.

But His saving grace spills over into every area of life, and you must accept that also. Often in the Christian culture, you hear it called "surrendering to God"—simply accepting that God is in control of your finances, job, household, mental state . . . God is in control of it all. People who choose not to accept God's sovereignty ultimately forsake the ability to remove themselves from many out-of-control situations. Your desire for control can put you in a tailspin that leads to a downward spiral; God wants to teach you, but you refuse His guidance. You refuse to surrender.

What are you seeking in life? Is it what God wants you to seek? Is your mind set on the things of God? We are to work and provide for our families, *but are you taking Jesus to work or school with you? Do the people in your life know you live because Christ lives in you?* Your real identity can only be found in Christ and His calling on your life.

Day 158

Be Filled by the Holy Spirit

"When the unclean spirit has gone out of a person,
it passes through waterless places seeking rest, but finds none.
Then it says, 'I will return to my house from which I came.'
And when it comes, it finds the house empty, swept, and put in order.
Then it goes and brings with it seven other spirits more evil than itself,
and they enter and dwell there,
and the last state of that person is worse than the first.
So also, will it be with this evil generation."
Matthew 12:43-45 (ESV)

This passage offers a warning to anyone who does not yield to God's way in any area of their heart. The demonic realm torments the people of earth, and you are protected only by the power of the Holy Spirit. Always remember, Jesus gave you a Helper, the Holy Spirit— the power and force behind everything you can do in Christ. Satan has control over people that choose to reject Jesus. *Are you willing to ask God to reveal what negative state of mind is suppressing your Holy Fire?*

Do not forgo your healthy mind by rejecting the way God wants you to live. When evil thoughts come to mind, the best cure is meditating on the Word of God. God is the One who can replace your suicidal and negative thoughts with His truth of who you are in Christ. Satan and his demonic spirits hate the Word of God, which is the power of Jesus. If you learn to put your whole identity in who God says you are and fill your heart with the things of God, then the Word can cast out all demonic depression.

When your heart is fragmented spiritually, torn between living for Christ and living for the world, your desire to pursue Christ wholeheartedly is blindsided by your will and pride—further depressing your unhealthy heart and giving Satan victory. Christians can prayerfully ask God to free a person from demonic influences. But, if that person chooses not to accept Jesus as their Savior, they will be worse off than before. God's Word waters our soul, keeping us from the desert places, and bringing our spirit to a place of refreshment where the fruits of the Spirit can thrive.

Day 159

Positive Thinking

Finally, brothers, whatever is true, whatever is noble, whatever is right,
whatever is pure, whatever is lovely, whatever is admirable,
if anything is excellent or praiseworthy, think about such things.
Philippians 4:8 (NIV)

God has a lot to say about what we should think about and how we should talk to one another. *Do you know people who always find a reason to complain? How much fun are they to be around? What about you? Do you normally see the good in a situation? Do you look for the excellence in the moment with a thankful heart, or do you sometimes see the glass as half empty?*

Life is hard, trauma is traumatizing, but God breathes life into traumatic situations. Even in your hardest times, He wants you to see that He is true, noble, righteous, pure, lovely, admirable, excellent, and praiseworthy, and that He fills your life with these traits as well. He wants you to focus on these attributes, thinking of how they relate to everything in your world.

In other words, God wants you to think about the good in life and not focus on the bad. However, the bad stuff in life can teach you a lot about your relationship with God. We all go through hard challenges, but a Christian's hope remains in Christ. Our faith is centered in the truth that He is in control, and His plan for you is not to get stuck on everything wrong with a situation. God wants your attention focused on a situation's blessings, the provision right in the moment when you needed it most.

Satan brings evil, disharmony, confusion, and lack of love into the world. Satan wants to take your eyes off Jesus so that you focus on the problem, but God wants you to trust Him so that you see His hand in everything. *Would you ask Him now to help you think about things that are true, noble, right, pure, excellent, admirable, and praiseworthy?*

Day 160

Exalt the Will of God

We destroy arguments and every lofty opinion
raised against the knowledge of God,
and take every thought captive to obey Christ.
2 Corinthians 10:5 (ESV)

Look up the definition of lofty, and you might see some differences in meaning. On one hand, the Lord Jesus Christ is "lofty," meaning noble and exalted. But "lofty opinions" describe just the opposite, meaning proud and self-important views. Knowledge of the Word gives you wisdom so you can not only do what the Word says but also distinguish between "lofty opinions" and God's noble and exalted will for you.

You can exalt the will of God in your life, or you can serve your flesh, trying to control your time, your situation, your raw emotions, your future. You can "take every thought captive to obey Christ," or you can let your mind wander to the dark, the ugly, and the lewd, to the shame you feel, the guilt and the anger. *Have you asked Him to help you direct your mind so that your thoughts "are captive" and in His will?*

Do you know your tipping point when your patience is wearing thin? Can you be rational when people become heated with you? Jesus knows your heart; He knows when you are numb from the pain; He knows when you are uncomfortable with new ways of responding, trying to change. Perhaps you are used to the feelings of being misused and used to things not of Christ. But Christ wants you to break free from living like this. Change is not easy, and truly being honest with yourself takes time and practice. You must find the ways God wants you to live and how He wants you to think. God wants your thoughts to align with the Word of God, which will lead you to a better understanding of who God says you are.

Day 161

Ponder Before You React

Whoever is slow to anger has great understanding,
but he who has a hasty temper exalts folly.
A tranquil heart gives life to the flesh, but envy makes the bones rot.
Proverbs 14:29-30 (ESV)

The Lord is slow to anger, and we should be likewise. As Christians striving to be like Jesus, our slowness to anger reflects the Lord's heart and tells the world where our identity lies. *Do you have a problem with anger, or are you slow to anger?* You do not have to prove yourself to other people; you must be faithful and confident in who God created you to be and the direction He is leading you. Lovingly looking to God for guidance in a difficult conversation can sway the conversation to a positive outcome. You can pray in your mind while you speak with another person. God can extinguish the flames of the fiery tongue, and He can give you a peace from above that will make your heart tranquil.

A tranquil heart is not fearful but confident in God. God is the life-giving Source, and when people respond or react in anger, they are usually choosing to sin against God—separating themselves from Him as all sin does. Learn from this scenario. In your moment of anger, look to God for understanding so that you avoid the folly of creating a gulf between yourself and God in that moment. When someone accepts God's will and turns to Him, allowing the Holy Spirit to free them from anger's clutches, God in that moment protects those who are faithful. Anger is an emotion, and you are to exert self-control over your emotions. *How well are you keeping your emotions in line with your identity in Christ?*

Day 162

Speak with Kindness

Let no unwholesome word proceed from your mouth,
but only such a word as is good for edification
according to the need of the moment,
so that it will give grace to those who hear.
Do not grieve the Holy Spirit of God,
by whom you were sealed for the day of redemption.
Let all bitterness and wrath and anger and clamor and slander
be put away from you, along with all malice.
Be kind to one another, tender-hearted, forgiving each other,
just as God in Christ also has forgiven you.
Ephesians 4:29-32 (NASB)

To live a life completely free in Christ, a person must know how God wants him or her to live. This is the portal to live a life free from fear. Your identity is found in knowing who God says you are. You are His child, He loves you more than you can ever imagine, and He does not have favorites (Romans 2:11). God gives you the same power as He gives other Christians. The difference is that some people choose to believe God above everything else; they let Him rule over all their situations. When you have the right understanding of who you are in Christ and how much God has sacrificed for you, you begin to realize that God did that for all the people in your life. Therefore, we are to speak life into conversations, not death. We are to extend grace to others, for we all fall short of the glory of God. Not one of us is good.

If the people closest to you were to describe your identity, would they claim that you are someone who speaks well of everyone? Do you gossip? Do you use words out of spite, or are your words pleasant to all who hear? Are your words filled with bitterness, or forgiving and tender? God puts great importance on words. He spoke the world into existence; we have the Word of God in our Bibles. Words are no small matter, but in our culture, words get thrown around like they are weightless. Above all, God wants you to love people through words and deeds.

Day 163

Change Is Possible

By the mercies of God, present your bodies as a living sacrifice,
holy and acceptable to God, which is your spiritual worship.
Do not be conformed to this world,
but be transformed by the renewal of your mind
that by testing you may discern what is the will of God,
what is good and acceptable and perfect.
Romans 12:1-2 (ESV)

Jesus was the last blood sacrifice. In the Old Testament, animal sacrifices were an act of worship. Then Jesus changed all that. Now, people who are in Christ are to sacrifice their fleshly desires. Christians are now to present their own bodies as a sacrifice to God in service to the Lord. Jesus made you holy, and you are to sacrifice your ungodly thoughts and actions, the things you are tempted to do that are not holy.

God has given you the power and the resources to overcome your temptations. For example, Christ has sealed you with His Holy Spirit (Ephesians 1:13-14). Your citizenship is in heaven (Philippians 3:20). You are not of this world (John 15:19). Reading God's Word has power as God speaks to you through its promises and truths. In addition, you are to stay focused on the Word of God so that your mind and soul know who God says you are.

While God's Word transforms your mind, it also tells you His will for your life. Both your body and soul belong to God. So, be completely focused on God's will for your life. His perfect will is perfect for you. *Have you learned how to rely on His mercy to change your errant ways?* Transforming your mind is a process. Throughout the process you will fail to do things in all the right ways, but that is alright. This marks the place where you need to give yourself mercy. Many wrongs can make it right when you choose to seek God. Seek Him about the ways that your thinking is misaligned with His ways, and let Him change your perception.

Day 164

Keep Your Composure

*Patience is better than pride. Do not be quickly provoked in your spirit,
for anger resides in the lap of fools.*
Ecclesiastes 7:8b-9 (NIV)

What has recently been thrown in your lap? You do not want to
deal with it, but there it is. Perhaps you are stuck with dealing with
the alcoholic in your life or with another person's anger. *How on
earth are you not to get angry with this mess thrown your way?* The
moments you never thought would happen to you are now real: your
child ended up in jail, your boss forced himself on you, your closest
friend betrayed you. You did not see it coming, you are beyond
stressed, you can hardly breathe, but it has been thrown at you, and
now you must deal with it.

You have a choice. A fool will choose to get angry, which hardly
brings about a healthy resolve, or you can be patient, looking to God
for solutions. This does not mean you deny the pain. Allow yourself
grieving time, but when you trust that He brought this problem to
light, freedom can be found. Work together with Christ and those
around you. Sometimes you are the answer to the problem, but in
your anger, you can leave it with God so negativity does not bog
down your spirit. Solutions are found when your mind is patiently
waiting for God to reveal His answer.

*When your spouse or a close friend hurts you deeply, do you
patiently listen to their side, even when they are yelling at you in
anger? How do you respond?* Pride makes a person want to be right
and want to be heard, but God says to love your enemies, especially
those who are your brothers and sisters in Christ. A fool does not
know Christ, but God gives wisdom and joy to those who please Him
(Ecclesiastes 2:26). The only way to please God is to accept His Son
Jesus as your personal Savior and accept the challenge of whatever
He has allowed to fall in your lap. The joy of the Lord can extinguish
the fiery darts that Satan tries to throw your way.

Day 165

The Truth Sets You Free

*Jesus said " If you hold to My teaching, you really are My disciples.
Then you will know the truth and the truth will set you free."*
John 8:31-32 (NIV)

The Word of God is alive and active. That means that when a person chooses to be in the Word every day, God can direct his or her steps more closely toward His purpose. He created you so He could love you and work through you. He has work for you to do for Him, but it remains your responsibility to learn His will through His Word and prayer.

Memorizing Bible verses allows the Word to penetrate your heart—so you can recognize Satan's lies, even when they seem to mirror God's words. Just like with Eve in the Garden, when the serpent said, "Did God really say?" you will be able to say, "No, He did not." And Jesus shows us how we are to respond. In Matthew 4:1-11, Jesus was tempted in the desert, but He used the Bible as His defense against the adversary. Satan tried to twist the Bible and distort God's Word, but as Jesus is the "Word which became flesh." He knows the Bible perfectly and how Satan was distorting its context. In His humanness, Jesus passed His test of faith and proved His spiritual allegiance to God the Father.

Jesus wants you to know and love your Bible because freedom is found when you live out its words. You can discern between God's truth—the Christian's standard for living—and the world's truth. You already have victory over Satan and can live a life of freedom in Christ, but you must do your part: know the Word of God and follow in His footsteps without complaining about everything not going your way. *Do you rely on the fact that Jesus overcame death and nothing, not anything, can separate you from the love of God? Do you have areas in your life where you are questioning God and not trusting His victory?*

Day 166
Overcome the World

This is love for God: to obey His commands.
And His commands are not burdensome,
for everyone born of God overcomes the world.
This is the victory that has overcome the world, even our faith.
Who is it that overcomes the world?
Only he who believes that Jesus is the Son of God.
1 John 5:3-5 (NIV)

Only Christ overcame the world; no one can do it on his or her own merit. Jesus was the only answer for the world's sin problem. His victory over death allowed us to be born again, grafted into the family of God. Jesus does exactly what He says He will do. Only Jesus can make a promise and not break it. In our humanness, we will fall short every time. But Jesus says we overcome the world, and through the Holy Spirit, we have the power of Jesus to overcome this world.

Difficult times will come, harsh words will break your heart, but you do not have to stay bitter or consumed by the world's problems; the Spirit comforts and teaches us when we believe and place our hope in the only One who can save us. God is still in control. He has not closed His eyes to what is going on in the world, nor to your situation. He knows where you place your faith; honestly, it should always be with Jesus. *But does your faith reside in something other than Jesus, perhaps merely in a crutch that helps you limp along without really healing you, not really helping you to become whole again?* Victory is found in laying your crutches down and placing all your faith in the victory of Christ.

Victory

Day 167

Acknowledge His Blessings

Through You we push back our enemies;
through Your name we trample our foes.
I do not trust in my bow, my sword does not bring me victory;
But You give us victory over our enemies,
You put our adversaries to shame.
In God we make our boast all day long,
and we will praise Your name forever.
Psalm 44:5-8 (NIV)

How is your gratitude toward your victories through God? Did you praise His name for the promotion at work, a process that required supernatural patience on your part? Did you praise His name when you escaped from that violent marriage? Did you praise His name when you barely survived a car accident? God is not just watching over the human race and blessing those who are "good." God is watching over everyone, and He knows the intent of everyone's heart. Some people devise evil in their minds against you but are thwarted in their plans, yet you have no idea how that intervention happened this side of heaven.

God allows some terrible things to occur, and while we sometimes cannot fathom His purposes, He knows what is happening; for those who love God, He is working all of it for good. He will step in and give you victory amidst the storm just when you need it most. God's timing is always perfect, regardless of how you feel. God may be growing your faith, and sometimes He tests our faith to make it stronger. *How faithful are you in the battle? Do you praise Him in the struggles besieging you?* There is victory found when you praise the Lord with a grateful heart, regardless of where you are standing on the battlefield.

Day 168

Proven Faith

Do not fear what you are about to suffer.
Behold, the Devil is about to throw some of you into prison,
that you may be tested . . . you will have tribulation.
Be faithful unto death, and I will give you the crown of life.
He who has an ear, let him hear what the Spirit says to the churches.
The one who conquers will not be hurt by the second death.
Revelations 2:10-11 (ESV)

Many Christians around the world are sadly imprisoned or martyred for their faith in Christ. And due to their love for Christ, many others are being tested through tribulations. Persecution is not new; it has been around since Jesus left us the Great Commission to go and tell the world of His Good News. Jesus was martyred on the cross; His time on earth was difficult.

In this light, why are you surprised that some people do not want to hear how God is helping you heal? Why are you surprised when you suffer? If you know your Bible well, you are aware that God does not promise you a blissful life here on earth. God promises He will be with you in the fire; He will fight your battles when you are on the battlefield.

Jesus was faithful every moment on the cross. Jesus brought glory to God when God raised Him from the dead. Jesus also conquered death so you could have the victory over death. If you conquer your life on earth by being faithful to God, He will give you the most splendid crown there is: the crown of eternal life. Nothing on earth compares to the plans God has for you in heaven, a place where there will be no more sin to make you fearful. You have an eternal victory that will never be taken away.

Day 169

The Righteous Judge

With righteousness He will judge the needy,
with justice He will give decisions for the poor of the earth.
He will strike the earth with the rod of His mouth;
with the breath of His lips He will slay the wicked.
Righteousness will be His belt
and faithfulness the sash around His waist.
The wolf will live with the lamb, the leopard will lie down with the goat,
the calf and the lion and the yearling together;
and a little child will lead them.
The cow will feed with the bear, their young will lie down together,
and the lion will eat straw like the ox.
The infant will play near the cobra's den,
and the young child will put its hand into the viper's nest.
They will neither harm nor destroy on all My holy mountain,
for the earth will be filled with the knowledge of the LORD
as the waters cover the sea.
Isaiah 11:4b-9 (NIV)

If Jesus is King over your life, you will have justice for the injustice that has been done to you. God's Word is a sword, a reliable tool as you put your trust in His judgments. For no one on earth has ever been a righteous judge; only God can judge the whole world with faithfulness to us all.

There is victory when you accept that you have been justified through belief in Jesus' sacrificial life. Only through the blood of Jesus do you get to step into heaven, and one day in heaven you will stand before Jesus and give an account for everything you ever said (Matthew 12:36).

God spoke the world into existence and gave you His holy Word to depend on and find victory. Words have power. *Are you choosing the victory of building people up, or bragging about how you destroyed someone?* Be careful what you say; God is listening.

Day 170

God Wants to Be Invited

Rejoice in the Lord always; again I say rejoice.
Let your reasonableness be known to everyone.
The Lord is at hand. Do not be anxious about anything,
but in everything by prayer and supplication with thanksgiving
let your request be made known to God
and the peace of God, which surpasses all understanding,
will guard your hearts and you minds in Christ Jesus.
Philippians 4:4-7 (ESV)

This verse says to let your reasonableness be known to everyone. *When you don't see eye to eye with someone and face friction, how reasonable do you become? How reasonable are you when confused about the difficult situations you encounter?* God wants to be the center of your entire life, but you must invite Him in. He wants you to rejoice in the things He has done. He wants you to be aware of His presence. God not only cares about the huge issues of your life but wants you to be anxious for nothing. He does not want you to worry about all the little details. He does not want you to be stressed out or anxious. He wants you to be at peace and rest in His plan.

God is asking you to trust Him with all your life's concerns. He cares that you give Him respect, honor, and glory in everything you do. Whether you are at the grocery store, at work, with your friends, out to dinner—anywhere you find yourself and with anything you find your hands doing—God wants to be invited in. Then because you will sense God with you, you will act reasonably in all situations. But He will not force His way into your life; He gave you free will.

Prayerfully invite Jesus into your mental conversations. Trusting His leading, you will find the peace that only He can offer, and your heart and mind will be steadfast on His ways. Inviting Jesus into your mental conversations also guides your mind to be reasonable, and people will take notice of how you have changed. Slowly, day by day, He guides you through the changes.

Day 171
Faith in God's Plan

*After I looked things over, I stood up and said to the nobles,
the officials and the rest of the people, do not be afraid of them.
Remember The LORD, who is great and awesome,
will fight for your brothers, your sons, and your daughters,
your wives and your homes.*
Nehemiah 4:14 (NIV)

The people of Jerusalem were rebuilding the walls of Jerusalem, and the officials in the land near Jerusalem were furious about it. They taunted the Jews and wanted to start a war with them, but God frustrated their evil plans. Nehemiah knew the Jews' situation was not good, but they prayed and brought God into the mess. When Nehemiah remembered the Lord and had faith that He could fight for them, God directed them on how to protect themselves from invaders. The whole Jewish community had to have faith in God's plan for it to work, and their faithfulness was blessed, even through all the intimidations. In Nehemiah 6:16, the enemies learn the wall was completed and become intimidated, losing their confidence and realizing the monumental task was accomplished by our God.

Are you letting the world intimidate you on your God-given assignment? Are you praying with a faithful heart for God to give you protection in a dangerous situation? God listens to the prayers of His saints, and when you pray for your family, your home, or your spouse, God will fight for them. God wants you to talk to Him not only about yourself but about all the people you love; all your concerns are His concerns. The prayer you send to God may be the prayer that sparks a courageous heart in the person who concerns you. Never stop praying for lost people in your life; God knows how they are intimidated by the glory of the Lord, and you could be the one person standing up for them in Christ.

Day 172

Attentive to Your Voice

The Lord is my rock and my fortress and my Deliverer, my God,
my Rock in whom I take refuge, my Savior.
You saved me from violence.
I call upon the Lord, who is worthy to be praised,
and I am saved by my enemies.
2 Samuel 22:2-4 (ESV)

Call upon the Lord when your fear is crippling and the confusion in your mind leads you nowhere. When your heart is sad, call upon the Lord. Your God has His ear attentive to your voice; He listens and cares.

What violence do you know? What hatred have you experienced? God does not want you to live in a state of trauma, regardless of the depth of trauma you have experienced. When life's waves crash in, let them crash onto the bedrock of Jesus; if He is your cornerstone, He can mend you and deliver you into a peaceful mindset.

Are you your own worst enemy? God can replace your negativity when you focus on praising Him. When you learn to pray with assurance that Jesus is the only Savior, then moment by moment Jesus can save your day. There is no wrong way to pray to God unless you are not wholehearted. God will do what He thinks necessary to get you to a place of learning, where you will realize that only through prayer can some chains be broken. Only through prayer will you see your Deliverer's power to achieve what is the desire of your heart.

God knows what is best for you, and He will do what is right in His eyes. God wants to have a relationship with you. He wants to be included in your planning process and in your battle plan; He wants your vision to include Him at its center. If you learn to include God when your enemies attack, He will fight your battles with you. You are not alone, but you must remember God's faithfulness to you.

Day 173

Do Not Give Up

When Zechariah saw him, he was startled and was gripped with fear.
But the angel said, "Do not be afraid Zechariah;
your prayers have been heard.
Your wife Elizabeth will bear you a son,
and you are to give him the name John."
Luke 1:12-13 (NIV)

Is there something in your life you keep praying for, but you are left wondering if you are wasting your time because God has not answered in a "timely" way? Are you beginning to wonder if you will ever find freedom from your memories? Are you wondering if your broken home and relationships can ever be mended? Do not give up on the prayers that are in line with the promises of God. God's timing is not always the same as what you think it should be.

Look to the example of Elizabeth and Zechariah. Elizabeth was barren. She and her husband, Zechariah, had prayed long and hard, and because of their age, they had probably given up on the idea of having children. But God wanted Elizabeth to be the mother of the one that Jesus said "was the greatest prophet to ever live" (Matthew 11:11). John's birth was a miracle. Plus, he was the earthly cousin of Jesus. Elizabeth and Zechariah were searching for God's fingerprint on their lives and must have openly talked about God day to day. After John was born and grew to manhood, we know that he was a great communicator, dressed in simple clothes, and ate interesting food. Baptism started with him, and he even baptized Jesus. Elizabeth probably never dreamt of being the mother of such a blessed man, but God can work in ways that we do not consider. No matter how far off in the future you think the desires of your heart will ever come to pass, do not give up; keep praying for God's miracle to happen.

Day 174

Face The Task

Elijah was afraid and ran for his life . . . He prayed that he might die.
"I have had enough, Lord."
Then he lay down under the bush and fell asleep.
All at once an angel touched him and said, "Get up and eat . . ."
He ate and drank and then lay down again.
The angel of the Lord came back a second time
and touched him and said, "Get up and eat,
for the journey is too much for you."
So he got up and ate and drank.
Strengthened by that food, he traveled forty days and forty nights
until he reached Horeb, the mountain of God.
There he went into a cave and spent the night.
And the word of the Lord came to him:
"What are you doing here, Elijah?"
He replied [lamenting], "I have been very zealous
for the Lord God Almighty.
The Israelites have rejected Your covenant,
torn down Your altars, and put Your prophets to death with the sword.
I am the only one left, and now they are trying to kill me too."
The Lord said, "Go out and stand on the mountain
in the presence of the Lord, for the Lord is about to pass by."
Then a great and powerful wind tore the mountains apart
and shattered the rocks before the Lord,
but the Lord was not in the wind.
After the wind there was an earthquake,
but the Lord was not in the earthquake.
After the earthquake came a fire,
but the Lord was not in the fire . . .
And after the fire came a gentle whisper.
A voice said to him, "What are you doing here, Elijah?"
[Elijah repeated his lament to the Lord.]
The Lord said to him,
"Go back the way you came, and go to the Desert of Damascus.
When you get there, anoint Hazael king over Aram.
Also, anoint Jehu king over Israel,
and anoint Elisha to succeed you as prophet . . .
I reserve seven thousand in Israel—
all whose knees have not bowed down to Baal
and whose mouths have not kissed him."
1 King 19:3-13, 15-16, 18 (NIV)

God is asking you, *"What are you doing here?" Why are you running from His purpose? Have you reached your wits' end, is your fear crippling, and does death look like a better option than life?* Elijah was done. He saw no way out. He would rather have his trusted God take his life instead of the enemy killing him, but God is faithful. God sent an angel twice in one evening to feed Elijah and strengthen him so he could do all God had planned for him.

Once he got to where God told him to go, Elijah was blessed by God speaking to him in a gentle whisper. While Elijah felt completely alone, like he was the only one that still followed the Lord, there were actually a host of people whom God could use and trust to accomplish His plan. Elijah was not alone. Always remember, God gives us hope when life seems completely hopeless.

Day 175

Give attention to Your servant's prayer and his plea for mercy,
O Lord my God. Hear the cry and the prayer
that your servant is praying in Your presence . . .
The Lord responds: "When I shut up the heavens so that there is no rain,
or command locusts to devour the land
or send a plague among My people,
if My people, who are called by My name,
will humble themselves and pray and seek My face
and turn from their wicked ways, then I will hear from heaven,
and I will forgive their sin and will heal their land."
2 Chronicles 6:19 and 7:13-15 (NIV)

God wants you to confess your sins to Him and forgives you when you repent. Just like when people talk things out with friends, when you talk with God, you can better hear what you are saying; it helps you more closely understand why and how you sinned against God. When you share your heart out loud and not just keep your concerns in your head, you will see the difference it can make. Satan lies to you in your mind, but God wants you to verbalize to Him the areas you need repentance. God is active and knows your thoughts, but does not take up residence in your mind. He is omnipresent and fills the whole earth at all times. He expects you to think about how you live, and as a jealous God, He wants you involved in your own forgiveness process.

Living a life full of Christ is your calling as a Christian. You cannot overflow with His love if you are not being filled with the things of God. Ask God to empty yourself and fill you with the Holy Spirit. You cannot lose your salvation in Christ; therefore, Christians always have the Holy Spirit with them, but are not always filled by the Spirit. Only when you deny your fleshly desires and turn to the righteous One for guidance can the Holy Spirit fill you. God knows how you need mercy. *Are you responding to His perfect prompting? Are you living a life of repentance?*

Day 176
Fasting for a Cause

Is such the fast that (God) chose, a day for a person to humble himself?
Is it to bow down his head like a reed,
and to spread sackcloth and ashes under him?
Will you call this a fast, a day acceptable to the Lord?
Is not this the fast that I choose, to lose the bonds of the wickedness,
to undo the straps of the yoke,
to let the oppressed go free and to break every yoke?
Then you shall call, and the Lord will answer,
you shall cry and He will say "Here I am"
if you take away the yoke from your midst,
the pointing of the finger and speaking wickedness.
Isaiah 58:5-6, 9 (ESV)

When fasting for the Lord, you are to do so in a personal way, not obvious by how you look on the outside. Fasting is a time set aside for you to seek His will and direction, not a time for selfish requests or personal gain. You can fast for someone to be healed, when you feel unhappy or depressed, or when you are in mourning. You can fast when waiting for an answer from God. When done for the right reasons, fasting brings your relationship closer to Him. The righteousness of God happens through you when you humble yourself daily, not just during a fast. God wants your loyalty to His ways, including helping the oppressed and not letting wickedness prevail. He is a God of peace and wants you to work hard at bringing His peace to this world. Satan lets you believe you have power when you show hostility toward others who have wronged you. But, fasting can be a way to break the bondage of your anger.

God cares how you treat everyone in every position. *When you are on the phone with a customer service rep and are upset about something, do you stop and ask God to come into the situation? Have you ever noticed how He can direct those moments when you stop and pray so He can work through you?* There is a time and place to fast, but God cares more about the attitude of your heart; He wants you to pray and seek His love, whether things are going your way or not.

Day 177

Unwavering Faith

If you do not stand firm in your faith, you will not stand at all.
Isaiah 7:9b (NIV)

Satan does not want you to stand firm. He wants the waves to crash over you with every emotional blow, and as you hear his lies in your mind, unable to discern them from your own thoughts, he wants to take you down. Satan wants to tear you apart so your loyalty to God is unsteady. Your testimony can be tarnished if your faith in the Word of God is not strong or resilient.

Don't let your faith grow soft or lukewarm, but keep your eyes focused on Jesus and stay planted firmly in God's Word. When you stand on the Word, you stand on the Cornerstone. Jesus is holding out His hand to help you stand, giving you strength when Satan is trying to knock you down. Have faith that God is a good God all the time.

Have you asked God to unveil your eyes so you can see the lies from Satan? God is your only hope to stand firm. Nothing in this world can satisfy your soul like the love of God. You must drink the Lord in deeply, and then He can wash away the root of despair, the root of bitterness, the root of every rotten and weedy thing that needs to be removed. When He does this, when you accept Him as your Lord and Savior, you can live a courageous life for Christ. Be certain of this: Jesus is your foundation, and He will help you to stand firm.

Day 178

Hold to the Traditions

God chose you . . . to be saved,
through sanctification by the Spirt and belief in the truth.
To this He called you through our gospel,
so that you may obtain the glory of our Lord Jesus Christ.
So then, brothers and sisters,
stand firm and hold to the traditions that you were taught by us,
whether by spoken word or by letter.
Now may our Lord Jesus Christ Himself, and God our Father,
who loves us and gave us eternal comfort and good hope through grace,
comfort your hearts and establish them in every good work and word.
2 Thessalonians 2:13b-17 (ESV)

"God chose you . . . to be saved, through sanctification by the Spirit and belief in truth." God had a distinct time and place for you to be born, and only God can create life; only He can create a soul. Only Jesus could overcome death and resurrect all the rot in this world.

One day Jesus will put Satan in his place but until He does, will you stand firm in the "traditions," the Word of God? God did not just choose you; He loves you. *Can you fully accept His love? Do you stand firm on His love, knowing that He gave you a hope when He died on a cross for you? Do you allow Him to comfort your heart?* Jesus Himself establishes you, sanctifies you, and teaches you the good work He has planned for you. *Are you standing firm on your God- given dreams?* God chose you because He has good work for you to do. Stand firm in confidence as a child of God.

Day 179

Taking Sides

You will not need to fight this battle.
Stand firm, hold your position,
and see the salvation of the Lord on your behalf.
Do not be afraid and do not be dismayed.
Tomorrow go out against them, and the Lord will be with you.
2 Chronicles 20:17 (ESV)

As a Christian you are to hold your position and not waiver. Many brave military heroes know the fear of standing at enemy lines, knowing a battle is about to erupt; yet, they hold their positions and face the fear head on. They are trained to stand firm and hold their position so no enemy may pass. Regardless of the fear they feel, they know they must be obedient to all the authority over them.

How often do you question God about His authority and His direction for your life? Life is a battle, and you will get through it. *The question is, are you too afraid to do what God has ordained for your life, even when knowing the Lord will be with you?* Fear is a feeling, and feelings are not wrong, but being controlled by them is. Satan loves to see us controlled by our emotions, but Jesus can and will win the battle for you if you stand firm on the salvation of the Lord.

Are you training yourself so you can hold your position? Do you know what your position is? In how many situations in your life have you been unsure what position you should take? God expects you to pick a side. He does not want you to stay in the grey area. God called you out of darkness and brought you into the light, which shines a holy knowledge on the side you should take or position where you should stand. God is light, and His Word is clear as to how you should live in the light. Hold your position regardless of the fear you feel. The more you face your fears, the more courage you have to stand firm in the freedom of Christ.

Day 180

See Salvation

Moses said to the people, "Fear not, stand firm,
and see the salvation of the Lord, which He will work for you today.
For the Egyptians whom you see today, you will never see again.
The Lord will fight for you, and you have only to be silent.
Exodus 14:13 (ESV)

The parting of the Red Sea was just about to take place. Already, the Jewish people had seen ten plagues brought onto the Egyptians by the Lord. They had seen miracles and were learning to trust God through the journey to a better place, but the hardened hearts of the Egyptians did not want them to find freedom. The Egyptians were much like the Devil in your own life—relentlessly in pursuit, chasing you down—but God wants to fight for you. God wants to part the Red Sea for you so you can walk on dry ground and not be swept away. God will destroy the enemies.

Are you worried about when it will happen? How are you at staying silent and not spouting off all your anger and fear when adversity is closing in on you? God knows that waiting and being quiet are not easy for His children. In your mind, you might want to trust the things that actually keep you defeated, the things of this world, but they will only keep you from the will of God. The victory of God can only be seen when you stand firm and trust in His Name. Stand firm on the promises of God; He will fight this battle, and then, when you fully have faith, you can see the victory in Christ.

Day 181

On the Lookout

Be on your guard; stand firm in the faith; be courageous;
be strong. Do everything in love.
1 Corinthians 16:13-14 (NIV)

What keeps you on your guard? Have you guarded your opinion
because your words seem to fuel someone else's fire? Do you keep
your heart guarded because you are tired of being hurt and let down?
Christians are not supposed to compromise their beliefs when the
world around them forsakes following Christ, but standing firm in the
faith can be a huge task. Sometimes the enemy tries to sneak his way
into your life while, at other times, he blatantly bombs you with
attacks, over and over again. Some things seem obvious, and standing
your ground in certain areas are clear, like abortion, lying, taking
money for unjust gain, gossip, wearing immodest clothes, sex outside
of marriage, being a drunkard . . . yet all these sins are common in the
world we live in.

God wants you to pick a side on issues, not to be lukewarm in
your faith but bold and courageous, which means not waffling or
being persuaded to agree with wrongdoing. These sins may be
common in today's world, but they still hold the holy weight of God's
judgment. The world is comfortable committing these sins, but they
should make you sad and uncomfortable. When the culture around
you makes light of the Ten Commandments, you must be on your
guard. It proves easier to slip into sin when the world around you is
casually sinning. It takes perseverance to keep your eyes focused on
Jesus and to stand firm, knowing His way leads to an everlasting joy.
Sin will separate you from a holy God, and Satan loves it when the
culture makes sin look so appealing because he knows this separates
you from God. God is with the humble, and when you stand firm on
His truth, you can have a holy confidence that His love, His joy, His
peace will empower you to be courageous to fight the good fight of
faith.

Day 182

Sin Has No Grip on You

For freedom Christ has set us free; stand firm therefore,
and do not submit again to the yoke of slavery.
Galatians 5:1 (ESV)

The verdict is clear: humans, in their own power, cannot fulfill the whole law that God gave us. His standards are perfection, and we are not perfect—only broken, sinful, and shameful people. We have no hope in eternity if left to our own devices. Therefore, we needed a Savior from sin; we needed to be justified, and only Jesus could make atonement for our sins. If all you have is the faith that Jesus sacrificially died for your sins, then eternally you have all you need. Your faith should squarely rest upon the work and obedience of Jesus through the love of God the Father.

You are to stand firm on the fact that Jesus has set you free from sin, so why do you keep sinning? Why do you keep buying into the lies of Satan that what you did, or what was done to you, keeps you from being holy in Christ? Your sin is as far from you as the east is from the west. Your sins cannot touch you anymore unless you give them power and authority in your life. It was Jesus that made you white as snow; so, claim what is yours. Believe with whole heart that the love of Christ wants to keep you free today from sin's bondage. And know that as you stand firm on your freedom in Christ, you are a slave to sin no more. Jesus did not leave you alone to figure it out; He left His Spirit to dwell in you. Stand firm on the power of the Holy Spirit to resist the sin that keeps calling you back and tempting you. Through the Holy Spirit, you can overcome your slavery to sin because Jesus overcame the cross. Live in freedom from shame and regrets, from any guilt of the past or fear of the future. God loves you more than you will ever know, and He wants you to take off the yoke of sin holding you back and, now, live free.

Day 183

Recognize His Attributes

The Lord is a refuge for the oppressed,
a stronghold in times of trouble.
Those who knew Your name will trust in You.
For You, Lord, have never forsaken those who seek You.
Psalm 9:9-10 (NIV)

Do you grasp the holiness of God? Do you understand that His wisdom is so vast that He can see the entire situation and act in love? When you have a hard time understanding yourself, it can be extremely hard to trust yourself and how you will respond. *Years of abuse dwindles a person's trust, so how are you to trust a God when you do not grasp His holiness, His power, or His sovereignty?* Ask God to increase your understanding of who He really is and that you can rely on what He says. If you need motivation to find the answers of your heart, stop looking within; stop doing what you are "used to" doing and start recognizing that God is with you. He has given you instructions on how to live the way that He intends. Then when you are obedient to His Word, you will find the freedom to live without fear and in the courage of the Holy Spirit.

When you are relying on the Holy Spirit to make your daily decisions, when you are talking to God throughout your day and reading His Word, then your thoughts and actions put God in His right place in your life, and you will fall into the place God wants you to be. The Lord never forsakes those who seek Him; what a blessed promise! When your heart is broken, God alone is trustworthy, and you can hold onto Him. Humans have good intentions, but even those closest to you will often let you down or break a promise. But God's promises are true. When you do not feel loved, know God loves you. When you feel too weak or afraid, trust in a God who goes through the fire with you. Only God is truly trustworthy because only God is in control.

Trust

Day 184
When the Waves Crash

They woke Him and said to Him,
"Teacher, do you not care that we are perishing?
And He awoke and rebuked the wind and said to the sea,
"Peace! Be still!"
And the wind ceased, and there was a great calm.
He said to them, "Why are you so afraid? Have you still no faith?"
And they were filled with great fear and said to one another,
"Who then is this, that even the wind and the sea obey Him?"
Mark 4:38-41 (ESV)

Have you ever been in a place where you feel you are about to perish? The waves are crashing, and you feel certain you will drown in the pain and sorrow overtaking you. *Do you feel life is so out of control that you have no idea if God really cares about the storm you are battling? In your anguish, have you cried out to God?* He can rebuke the storms in the water, and He can rebuke the storms in your life. God's miracles always show you His glory. Just maybe God has taken you to this place so you can understand the glory of God. Just maybe you need a miracle shown to you so you can put your complete trust in Him.

Jesus knows how to get your attention; do you have the faith to weather the storm with Him? God created everything through Jesus (Colossians1:16), and God has complete control over everything. Our human brains cannot completely wrap our minds around why God chooses to do what He does, but you must trust that He is always good and always acts in love for you. Humans have no idea what living in a world without sin would be like; therefore, we are partially blinded to His holiness and His goodness. In Mark 10:18, Jesus said to him, "Why do you call Me good? No one is good except God alone." If you believe with your whole heart that the Bible is true, and that Mark 10:18 is speaking His truth to you, then ask Him to turn your fear into trusting the only One who is good.

204

Day 185

A Way Out

Be strong and courageous,
do not be afraid or tremble at them
for the LORD your God is the one who goes with you.
He will not fail you or forsake you.
Deuteronomy 31:6 (NASB)

What in life has you feeling defeated? What has knocked you down repeatedly? Where do you feel shame? What part of your life do you want to keep secret? Who is abusing their power over you? Do you feel safe? Know that God's design is not abusive.

Can you trust there is a way out? Getting out of an abusive place can seem extremely frightening. All the unknowns can seem daunting, but God wants you out of any dangerous places; on the other side, you will find freedom from fear—a path that will lead you toward people who will build you up and not tear you down.

Have you kept quiet so long that you feel you have lost your voice? God wants you to speak boldly, relying on Him. God can give you the wisdom to act and speak obediently to God's will for your life, but you must trust Him through the process. The people of Israel were just about to go over the Jorden River into the Promised Land, but they had to obey God's directions. God needed them to fight a war to overtake the evil communities that were a breeding ground for Satan's workers of lawlessness. In the same way, God wants to remove you from the abusive places holding you back from His will for you.

Are you willing to trust that the war you are fighting is not in vain? There is a purpose for it all, and God wants you to be a faithful servant. Do not show your fear toward those who are abusing you; pray for God's courage, move forward in faith, and through His leading, take back the power you have over your life.

Trust

Day 186

Use What You Have

*Be strong and let us use our strength for our people
and for the cities of our God,
and may the Lord do what seems good to Him.*
1 Chronicles 19:13 (ESV)

King David wanted to deal kindly with the Ammonites, but they greatly shamed David's men by shaving off their beards and cutting off their garments in the middle at their hips (1 Chronicles 19:4). This in turn started a war that could have defeated David's army. David's commander Joab saw that the battle was set against them, so they devised a plan and spoke the words in 1 Chronicles 19:13. Joab had both faith in God and a willingness to use all his personal strength to fight the battle all around them.

Are you surrounded by people who put you to shame? Has something in your past caused you to feel the burden of dishonor or humiliation? Can you trust that God will do what is good, even when it looks like everything is set to fail? His intentions are not to shame you but to set you free from the wars encircling you. His good intentions work out for your benefit in the end if you trust what "seems good to Him"—His good and sovereign plan that will mold you more closely to look like Jesus, that will help strengthen your faith, that will bring Him glory and benefit you eternally. You have not lost your battles if you continue to trust that God can see you through.

God wants you to fight with Him; He wants you join Him in the struggle, to let His courage bring you courage so you can do things differently. God wants you to bring your faith, your hopes, your strengths—all He has created you to be—to the table, and then He can multiply what you have with His miracles. God expects you to join Him wholeheartedly in your healing. God wants to change you from the inside out, but you need to first let go of some obstacles in your life that God wants you to release . . . and then "be strong" in His strength.

206

Day 187

Know the Danger

For even when we came into Macedonia, our bodies had no rest,
but we were afflicted at every turn—fighting without and fear within.
But God, who comforts the downcast,
comforted us by the coming of Titus.
2 Corinthians 7:5-7 (ESV)

A faithful servant of the Lord, Paul trusted God's huge plans for him. Nevertheless, he faced relentless difficulties. He was paving the way for Christian living, but it brought him peril after peril: beatings, being stranded on an island, and imprisonment, just to name a few. In Acts 16:16-40, we learn that while Paul and Silas are imprisoned, the God of the universe causes an earthquake, opening the jail doors. Instead of fleeing, Paul stays and saves the jailhouse guard's life, both physically and spiritually. Paul trusts Jesus with every cell in his body and goes where God instructs him, knowing the danger but trusting God regardless.

Paul was one of the most courageous Christians in *HIS*tory, but he still had to face his fears and trust that God had a purpose, regardless of the mission's danger. When a person is saved from hell, Satan is unhappy and thus tries to provoke Christians so fear overtakes the task that God is calling them to do. The only way to live courageously for Christ is to prayerfully face your fears head on, trusting God as your Comfort. The more you learn to operate under the uncomfortable places of fear, the more He will teach you how to break free from fear's power.

You will learn that opposition is not always God closing doors but Satan trying to keep you in fear so you forsake the work of Christ. As iron sharpens iron, so fellowship with other believers proves important to our encouragement and strength—and why it was such a blessing for Paul to see Titus. *Can you recognize the difference between Satan opposing God's work in your life versus God telling you to move on? Why not ask God to confirm His plans for your life?*

Day 188

Gained Confidence

"An angel of God said, 'Do not be afraid, Paul;
you must stand before Caesar; and look!
God has graciously given you all those who are sailing with you.'
Therefore, keep your courage, men,
because I believe God that it will be just the way it was told to me."
Acts 27:24-25 (NASB)

Trust

As the storm was about to overtake them, the ship's men were losing all hope. But then the angel of God appeared. Some theologians believe this angel was answering Paul's prayer, and in return, Paul trusted the message that he was to go proclaim the Gospel in Rome before Caesar. Paul's confidence remained firm that the Creator of the storm was in control of what that storm would do: leave them shipwrecked. By human standards, the scenario was terrifying; however, Paul was able to show the entire ship's crew as well as the native islanders that God provided powerful healing through miracles. Not one of the men on the ship was lost—a miracle in itself—and God gave Paul favor as he was able to minister to the islanders for three months. Had Paul not been shipwrecked, these people may have never known about the saving grace of Jesus.

Paul gained confidence when he prayed to God when all hope seemed lost. He faced His fears with unwavering faith and a willingness to follow God wherever He wanted him to go. *Are you looking for a miracle but not willing to go into the dark places that God is calling you to face?* God does not want you to stay stranded on an island of hopelessness. He wants to show you His glory through the miracles that will follow when you allow your healing to happen to the glory of God. Although you may sometimes feel God has abandoned you, feelings are not trustworthy and often wrong. You must trust that God wants you to find the end of yourself and cry out to Him. He will wash away your hopelessness, giving you a new beginning, with restored hope and trust in Christ. Your miracle is waiting.

Day 189

Without Question

*"Get yourself ready! Stand up and say to them
whatever I command you, do not be terrified by them,
or I will terrify you before them . . .
They will fight against you but will not overcome you,
for I AM with you and will rescue you," declares the Lord.*
Jeremiah 1:17, 19 (NIV)

How ready are you to do whatever God commands you? Are you prepared to handle the hardships of the world in a godly way? Can you control your lips, your anger, your pride? These hard questions often prove insightful as God works to mold your character and refine your faith and confidence in Him.

Are you ready to fight the good fight for the things that God says to stand up for and do? Are you comfortable with the status quo, or are you getting yourself ready for the places God wants you to shine His light? When He asks you to go into the dark places of this world, you are ready to bring His light to those there without succumbing to their evil and skewed ways? As soldiers prepare for battle, they train themselves in faithfulness and discipline. They must know the rules and regulations that their commanders set before them. They do not question why they are assigned a task but follow their leader with loyalty and devotion. In the same way, you must know the Word of God so you can know God's standards, trusting God's authority over you and accepting the work He lays before you. One battle at a time wins the war.

In Revelation, we learn that Jesus wins the war—a victory that lasts for eternity. As a soldier in God's army of those who trust in Him, it is your duty to follow through with His orders without questioning why He has called you to battle. You must be close to God to hear His whisper, and then you will learn to hear His voice. He will speak to you personally as He helps you fight against all the hardships and trauma you have faced. You do not need to fear.

Day 190

Stand Up for Yourself

*Listen to Me, you who know righteousness,
the people in whose heart is My law;
fear not the reproach of men nor be dismayed at their reviling.*
Isaiah 51:7 (ESV)

The God of the universe wants you to listen to Him and obey Him, even when people attack, criticize, and insult you. God knows people will verbally abuse you but does not want you to stand idle while people cut you down with their words; no, the opposite is true. God wants you to respect yourself and see yourself through His eyes so their words cannot tear you apart. People who verbally abuse you are doing the work of Satan, not of Christ. You cannot control how people treat you, but you can pray that God will punish them as He sees fit. You can ask God for guidance on how you are to talk to the person who seems to think treating you harshly is alright. You can speak up for yourself in a respectful way. You can ask someone, "Why do you talk to me that way? What makes you think it is alright to treat me the way you do?" There is nothing wrong with letting them know that they are talking to you with disrespect and you do not have to tolerate it. You can seek resolution with that, or maybe you need to be removed from the person's life.

God comforts those whose hearts are turned toward His righteousness. Peace can overcome violence, but often it takes time. God knows that abusive people bring about all kinds of fears in the abused. Importantly, God does not minimize your abuse. He wants you to listen to His voice so you can have courage to act righteously. Only by listening for His voice can you be certain if God wants you to persevere and see a miracle happen in someone's life, or if He is directing you to take steps to get yourself into a safe place. Who is constantly speaking to you in a rude, negative way? *Are you prayerfully listening for God's voice on how to deal with this person?* With God, you can have an action plan for dealing with verbally abusive people in your life.

Day 191

Acting in Favor

But Daniel resolved not to defile himself with the royal food and wine,
and he asked the chief officials for permission
not to defile himself in this way.
Now God had caused the officials to show favor and sympathy
to Daniel, but the officials told Daniel,
"I am afraid of my lord the king, who has assigned your food and drink.
Why should he see you looking worse than the other young men
your age? The king would then have my head because of you."
Daniel then said to the guard whom the chief official
had appointed over Daniel, Hananiah, Mishael, and Azariah,
"Please test your servant ten days;
Give us nothing but vegetables to eat and water to drink"
... At the end of the ten days they looked healthier and better nourished
than any of the young men who ate the royal food.
Daniel 1:8-12, 15 (NIV)

As a loyal Jew who wanted to serve the Lord wholeheartedly, the prophet Daniel strove to adhere to the ways of the Jewish people. Yet he and his fellow Jews had been taken captive and now lived in a pagan world. Jewish law stated that specific food was forbidden and drunkenness was a sin, but both were celebrated in the pagan king's court. Daniel gives us biblical proof that when you set your heart on being faithful to God, then our sovereign God will act in our favor.

The officials were afraid of the pagan king, but Daniel wanted to honor God over man, so He gave Daniel a plan—a way to eat as God instructed while showing the people that God's way was the best way. Just as He did with these officials, God can move anyone's heart. The Holy Spirit also dwells within you; your body is God's holy temple, so He wants you to be faithful with what you put inside it. *Are you paying attention to what you are putting into your body? Do you have self-control?* Be obedient, do not pollute your body, follow God's plan for you ... and be blessed, just as Daniel was as he gave glory to God.

Day 192

Respect Authority

. . . like Sarah, who obeyed Abraham and called him her master.
You are her daughters if you do what is right
and do not give way to fear.
1 Peter 3:6 (NIV)

Abraham is the father of our faith, making Sarah, his wife, the mother of our faith. In faith, she obeyed the leading and authority of her husband. God has a holy plan for authority; He designed authority to bring wisdom into life situations. But in many cultures over the centuries, and particularly in today's culture, authority can be twisted because of sin. Also, you do not give a child authority; authority is given to people who have earned it by learning how to handle their particular job or task. Any colonel of the U.S. Air Force has been enlisted for a certain number of years, going through many tests and passing them. This officer has trained and performed better than others around him or her; God gave the ability to earn a position of authority.

Respecting authority is being obedient to the ways of God. Our culture has taught us to be strong, independent men and women; in turn, this can cause us, in the flesh, to become too controlling of our own lives when, in fact, only God has complete control. Some people's lives have caused them to fear authority due to the abuse of authority in their environment. Yet, God did not create authority as a means of punishment; many times, it is Satan that twists it toward sin. God desires both husband and wife to love Him with all their heart, soul, and mind—to seek the Lord first, then come together to work together. God speaks in and through both parties.

Are you respecting your spouse by truly listening, or are you too afraid you are wrong? Are you too afraid to lose an argument? Are you too afraid to back down? So instead, you demand and argue in ways that do not bring God glory. *Can you come under the authority that God has designed for you?*

Day 193

Abide in the Teaching

Watch yourselves, so that you may not lose what we have worked for, but may win a full reward. Everyone who goes on ahead and does not abide in the teaching of Christ does not have God. Whoever abides in the teaching has both the Father and the Son.
2 John 8-9 (ESV)

Watch yourself; it is your responsibility to make certain you abide in the teachings of the Lord. Do not act as some people do, who hear the calling of the Holy Spirit and ask Jesus to be the Redeemer of their soul, but attend church and read the Bible only for a while. One Saturday they stay out too late and have too much fun. Skipping church the next morning, they lounge around the house and find it relaxing. Before long, sleeping in on Sunday mornings becomes a habit, and they no longer go to church nor open their Bible. Their prayer life shrivels from lack of nourishment. And they have no Christians in their life, no one encouraging their faithfulness to live for God instead of the world.

God wants you to love Him more than anyone else on earth. He wants your full attention. *What has your focus? How are you spending your time? Are you obediently seeking the wisdom from above, or are you more often seeking just the counsel of friends?* This verse offers a warning from God; distractions that you can touch can easily become an idol, and idols will destroy your relationship with a jealous God who wants your full affection. Abiding in Christ means you never lose sight of Jesus. Those who seek Him first abide in the teachings of Christ.

Day 194

Tending the Sheep

I will place over them One Shepherd, My Servant,
and He will tend them; He will tend them and be their Shepherd.
The Lord will be their God, and My servant will be Prince among them.
I the Lord have spoken. I will make a covenant of peace with them . . .
They will live in safety and no one will make them afraid.
Ezekiel 34:23-25a, 28b (NIV)

Sheep need protection from an able shepherd; they do not know how to find the best pasture, how to fight off wild animals, nor how to get out of tight places by themselves; they also follow the crowd and easily get lost. Perhaps that's why our all-knowing God sometimes calls His children sheep. Compared to God, we are not smart. We cannot see every angle of a situation and cannot read people's minds, but God can. Many times, people get stuck in a crowd just because they find themselves there, and they would rather not be the black sheep of the family. Unfortunately, this sheep-like behavior can easily lead someone off the path of Christ, and their soul becomes lost.

Jesus is our good Shepherd who tends to us, and He chases after you. *Can you stop running long enough to see where He wants to lead you?* Jesus is your Covenant of Peace. You can have confidence in Christ that He keeps you safe; God says no one will make you afraid. *Do you claim that promise? Do you live in that peace? Are you allowing Him to tend to you, or are you running to other things, other people? Do you know how to leave your concerns and worries at the foot of the cross?* Jesus knows exactly what you need. Jesus knows you better than you know yourself. Jesus knows your tomorrow, and He knows your every moment. Find peace in Jesus because He is the only true refuge for your sheep-like soul.

Day 195

Shalom Is Permanent

"Peace I leave with you; My peace I give you.
I do not give to you as the world gives.
Do not let your hearts be troubled and do not be afraid."
John 14:27 (NIV)

You are created in the image of God, and you have a godly purpose in this life. You are called to look more like Jesus every day as you follow after Him. What does Jesus look like? He is not worried about anything. He remains calm in anxious situations. He is dependable. And as you live for Him, reading His Word, spending time with other believers, and praising Him daily, you are becoming more like Him, too. But sadly, the world around you is not.

Some of the people you have loved are not dependable, causing you anxiety. When you become anxious, you are not standing in peace. You cannot be anxious and peaceful at the same time. You are to overflow with the peace of Christ, bringing Shalom into the chaotic world. God's peace, Shalom, is much deeper than earthly peace. Shalom mirrors the character of God. It is not about the circumstances you live in but about being whole and complete in Christ, living for your eternal prosperity, eternal safety, and eternal spiritual health.

The world cannot give you these things; only Jesus can. Shalom is permanent while the world's peace, as we often know it, is fleeting. Jesus came into a chaotic world to bring a permanent peace to the souls of all who follow Him. As image-bearers of Christ, we accept the call to bring permanent, peaceful solutions to the chaos of the world. Every time you feel anxiety swell in your belly, ask yourself and God these questions, *"Why am I allowing Satan to cast doubt and fear in my mind? Why am I allowing Satan to steal my peace?"* You have two options: to trust God and stand in the peace of God, or to hide in fear and accomplish nothing spiritually. Peace in Christ comes when you learn to work through your fear. He is calling you deeper.

Day 196

A Grateful Heart

Let the peace of Christ rule your hearts,
to which indeed you were called in one body.
And be thankful. Let the Word of Christ dwell in you richly,
teaching and admonishing one another in all wisdom,
singing psalms and hymns and spiritual songs,
with thankfulness in your hearts to God.
Colossians 3:15-16 (ESV)

God does not desire your heart to war with itself. With God's complete love ruling sovereignly over your life, you should be confident in God's faithful character, which remains steadfast and never changes. God's good plans for you will mold you into the person He desires you to be. Sometimes shaping hurts deeply, especially when you lose a best friend to cancer or an overdose of pills. Or when you find out your spouse was dishonest and hurts the whole family. But God still has His eyes on you. His permanent safety and peace for you do not change.

God wants the Word to dwell in you so you can cling to His promises and you will know how to defend against Satan's attacks. *Are you asking God where you can bring Him glory in this mess? Are you so stunned that "this" happened to you? You might be exactly in God's will, but is your perception of the situation the same as Christ's?* Serving the Lord in a world full of unrest can drain you, but the almighty God empowers you. You will never, ever be separated from Christ; you are eternally His. That alone is reason enough to praise Him within your heart, but you have even more to be thankful for. *Can you recognize it?* You will never have peace if you are unwilling to face your fears honestly with God and trust that He has you in this place and time for a reason. You can bring God glory when you accept that He gives you peace in every moment you face, but you must trust Him. The world's peace is superficial, but God's peace can saturate your heart when you trust His sovereign plan.

Day 197

Working on Your Behalf

O man greatly loved, fear not, peace be with you;
be strong and of good courage.
Daniel 10:19a (ESV)

Even though Daniel enjoyed a rich relationship with God, the plans of God for him proved challenging. When Daniel refused to bow down to man, maintaining faith in God alone, he wound up in a lion's den (Daniel 6:1-23). Still, Daniel's heart was so aligned with God's that he prayed earnestly to God about everything, especially all his trials in the pagan land. God heard Daniel's prayer and wanted to send a mighty angel in response, but Satan intervened and fought this mighty angel for twenty-one days (Daniel 10:13). Then the mighty angel brought Daniel the encouraging words of today's verse. Just like this scenario, Satan wants to intervene in God's work in your life, but you can trust that God and His mighty angels are fighting on your behalf.

You have no idea what is really happening around you, all the war being waged in the spiritual realm. Thus, you can accomplish the work of God in faith and stop living in fear. God will send in His holy angels to answer your prayers when you pray for His will to prevail. God wants peace to rule your heart, regardless of the pit you "feel" stuck in. All of Daniel's confidence could rest on the promise that this angel brought him because he trusted God's words.

Angels, God's messengers, get to see Jesus in all His glory. The angel's news in this passage encouraged Daniel enough to keep him moving on his predestined path. Daniel had to face his fears repeatedly by trusting God completely. God laid the groundwork and provided safety; it was up to Daniel to listen and obey God's instruction. With God, all things are possible, even when your God-given task looks too daunting and dangerous. *Can you find God's peace by trusting His will for you, even in your conflicts?*

Protection

Day 198

Keep the Peace

For there shall be a sowing of peace.
The vine shall give its fruit, and the ground shall give its produce,
and the heavens shall give their dew.
And I will cause the remnant of this people to possess all these things.
And as you have been a byword of cursing among the nations,
O house of Judah and house of Israel, so will I save you,
and you shall be a blessing. Fear not, but let your hands be strong.
Zechariah 8:12-13 (ESV)

Just like the people in Zechariah's time, Christians have a coming peace and prosperity that will not be seen this side of heaven. God will accomplish everything He said He would, but it might not be when you expect it. God's timing is perfect, but it does not always feel perfect. God's protection can take you through a winding path of treacherous ground underfoot. *Will you allow God to sow peace in your life where people have cursed you? Do you look to be a blessing all around you, or just to the people you like?*

God knows the difficulty of bringing peace into a chaotic world. *Can you find your strength in Christ to not fear the conversations you are avoiding?* God's protection is often found when you keep the peace. Sin is often present when anger flares. Peace is not hostile but loving. *What fears inside are keeping you from bringing peace and blessings to those who have cursed you?* Weaker people often rely on the fist of iron to get the job done and their point across. But God says to let your hands be strong and not fear. Bringing peace to a hostile scene is possible when you trust God's protection and truth.

218

Day 199

Stand in the Presence of God

The Lord is good, a stronghold in the day of trouble;
and He knows those who take refuge in Him.
Nahum 1:7 (ESV)

Take in those words for a moment: the Lord is good. In Him, there is nothing false or weak, negative or bad. God has no evil intent, no desire to trick you. He is holy and just. God alone is pure, and in Jesus He puts all His glory. Jesus went to the cross to protect you from eternal separation from God. Jesus' work on the cross built a bridge between you and your heavenly Father. You now can stand in God's presence, asking Him for His protection over every area of your life. You have found liberty.

When difficulties come your way, whom or what do you run to? Do you allow yourself to seek God's protection? Can you trust His goodness, even when life's troubles weigh you down? God knows the hearts of those who run to Him when life hurts. He watches over them so that evil and eternal death do not overtake them. God's perfect protection might allow something negative in your life so you are driven to be the man or woman of God He intends for you to be, molded into His image and character. And then to carry that wisdom, compassion, and love for others into the next difficult situation. A child often has to learn from the consequences of choices made. Just like a parent, God allows us to endure seasons of suffering to train us not to find our joy in anything or anyone other than Him. He protects us as our refuge, our stronghold in the day of trouble.

Day 200

Walk in Integrity

For the Lord gives wisdom;
from His mouth comes knowledge and understanding.
He stores up sound wisdom for the upright;
He is a shield to those who walk in integrity,
guarding the path of justice and watching over the way of His saints.
Proverbs 2:6-8 (ESV)

One of the most beautiful parts about walking with Christ is how He slowly changes your perception so it lines up with His trustworthy ways. Knowledge, understanding, and wisdom are blessings from God, poured out upon those who walk in integrity. Integrity is a heart issue because people who have their heart set on the ways of God will have their heart in everything God allows them to do. When you put your whole heart into the work of God, you do it to the best of your ability; you don't cut corners.

God is watching you closely and shields you according to His plan for you. Thus, He sometimes sends you in a different direction from the way you've been walking, surprising you with where you end up. Sometimes God uses your dreams and desires to send you to one place, only then to steer you down a completely different path. You went to school with one thing in mind but got a degree in another. You set out to live in one place, only to find yourself across the country in a different locale. Sometimes He steers you clear of a fight or altercation, a clear case of divine intervention. Sometimes the doctor orders blood work done at the perfect time, catching the cancer before it gets worse. God knows you need red lights at intersections to get you from point A to B; you need them in your life, also. He knows how to orchestrate your day so you are protected in ways you might not even realize. *Are you willing to be more patient with your time, knowing God is patiently protecting you?*

Day 201

God's Direction Leads to Safety

At my first defense no one came to stand by me, but all deserted me.
May it not be charged against them!
But the Lord stood by me and strengthened me;
so that through me the message might be fully proclaimed,
and all the Gentiles might hear it.
So I was rescued from the lion's mouth.
The Lord will rescue me from every evil deed
and bring me safely into His heavenly kingdom.
To Him be the glory forever and ever.
2 Timothy 4:16-18 (ESV)

Have you ever felt so alone, thinking no one can understand what you are going through? Do you feel like no one is there to defend you? Well, God is there. *Have you asked Him to show Himself?* Only God knows exactly what you are suffering. Only God understands why you made your choices. Broken people have a tendency to break others, but you do not have to continue that pattern of living. You can do things differently than your family has done. You do not have to make the same mistakes others have made. If God has allowed you to be present during other people's suffering, then perhaps you can objectively look at their attitudes and actions so you can learn from them. You can grow in wisdom by seeing things through the lens of forgiveness and protect yourself from making the same mistakes.

Have you asked Him to strengthen you? The Lord never leaves or forsakes His children. When others have deserted you, be confident that God is with you. Pour your heart out to Him; He knows exactly where you are. Your faith will grow when you spend daily time with Him in prayer, a quiet time when you can listen to His answers in His Word, as well as in that still, small Voice that resounds in your heart. Rely on God's direction and He will lead you to safety and help you understand His protection. God will make the evil around you clear, showing you what and whom to avoid and whom to turn to for help and hope.

Day 202

Loyal Fellowship

*Do not fear, for I will show you kindness
for the sake of your father Jonathan,
and I will restore to you all the land of Saul, your father,
and you shall eat at my table always.*
2 Samuel 9:7 (ESV)

God puts people in your life whom you need to protect. You need to make good on your words and remain loyal to the people around you. *Where does your loyalty stand toward the people in your life whom God has entrusted to you?* David loved his friend Jonathan, and they made a covenant of friendship together (1 Samuel 18:3). They had a godly bond, completely loyal to one another. After Jonathan's death, David wanted to show kindness to Jonathan's family. So, as a follower of God, David followed the law of God and protected Jonathan's son, who could not walk; he was lame (Deuteronomy 10:18, 15:7, 23:23, 27:19).

This story exemplifies how God has a way of protecting the "least of these," as Jonathan's son certainly was. You could also look to David himself, the smallest brother in his family, to illustrate this truth. God gave David victory on the battlefield, which led to him becoming the second king of Israel. In the same way, God's kindness toward you is never-ending, and you are to extend this kindness to others, especially when you have spoken words that promise your loyalty. Every covenant you make needs loyalty backing it up. God is completely, totally, 100 percent kind, faithful, and loyal; He does not go back on His Word. As a follower of Christ who is being transformed into His image each day, "Let your yes be yes and your no be no" (Matthew 5:37). Be completely true to your word. Making a pledge or covenant you cannot fulfill will not give you or another person protection; however, when your heart is loyal to others, you are showing His kindness with integrity and faithfulness, making you look more like Jesus and giving Him glory.

Day 203

Longing for a Safe Place

Help, Lord, for no faithful one remains;
the loyal have disappeared from the human race.
They lie to one another;
they speak with flattering lips and deceptive hearts.
May the Lord cut off all flattering lips
and the tongue that speaks boastfully.
They say, "Through our tongues we have power; our lips are our own—
who can be our masters?"
"Because of the oppression of the afflicted and the groaning of the poor,
I will now rise up," says the Lord.
"I will put the one who longs for it in a safe place."
The words of the Lord are pure words,
like silver refined in an earthen furnace, purified seven times.
You, Lord, will guard us;
You will protect us from this generation forever.
The wicked wander everywhere,
and what is worthless is exalted by the human race. Amen.
Psalm 12 (HCSB)

The world we live in today sounds a lot like the times when this psalm was written. Words have power, and sometimes it takes wisdom not to let them oppress you. Hurtful words can lose power when you hear them filtered through the knowledge of God. For example, when someone speaks down to you or resorts to name-calling, you can call on God to give you wisdom from above (James 3:17); then, the insulting words become dulled, unable to cut so sharply.

When you feel oppressed by others' negative words, reach for your Bible so you can learn who God says you are. When you discover that you are His beloved, redeemed, perfect in His sight, wonderfully made, His child, and much more, other people's words lose power, and God's Word gains traction in your life. *If you believe every Word of God, have you submitted to the whole Word of God?* God wants you to cry out to Him about your oppression. He wants you to cling to Him faithfully. When no one else is faithful, God is. When all you hear are lies, God's truth remains. When you are forced to something not of God, He is still there. *Can you rest in that? Will you trust Him for your eternal destiny?*

Day 204

Bold with Christ

You shall not fear them, for it is the Lord your God who fights for you.
Deuteronomy 3:22 (ESV)

Sometimes you need to take hold of your courage and do what needs to be done. Stand up where you need to stand, not only for yourself but for your nation, your family, and your God. Sometimes the feeling of fear will not depart while you do what God has placed on your heart. But take courage, face your fear, and keep moving forward, even if the fear does not diminish. Doing what is right and standing up for the things of God can give you a fearful feeling, but you are not controlled by your emotions. At some point in life, God will let you know the places where you will want to take a stand; these times will exemplify your God-given purpose, and He has protection for you there.

You are anointed to do a godly task, so as you take a stand, keep talking about what is right. Keep talking about the work of Jesus in your life, even if you fear the rejection of people. If God has called you to speak in front of an audience, even if you are afraid, *do it*. God called you to do a mighty work; He called you to proclaim the Good News of Jesus. When you are bold for Christ, He will protect you. He will fight for you when Satan tries to throw too much fear your way.

Satan wants to cripple the plans of Christ, and many people play his pawn. For every holy battle God wants you to face, Satan has an evil plan to destroy your work. So, what can you do? Call on Jesus and God's angel armies, who will fight for you. Call on your faith and your favorite Scripture that you have memorized for such a time as this. Call on the Holy Spirit to fill you with faithfulness and self-control. *When you can't shake your fear, will you call on your Risen Savior?*

Day 205

Focus on the Problem-Solver

The fear of the Lord leads to life; then one rests content,
untouched by trouble.
Proverb 19:23 (NIV)

Because God alone holds the keys to your eternal home, you may have reason to fear Him if you have not placed your faith and trust in Jesus, who died on the cross to redeem you from your sins. Jesus is perfect Love, and He alone is the Gatekeeper in heaven. He will not let sin inside heaven's gate, while sin will be bound in hell eternally. Separation from Christ is a fearful thing for those who have denied His call to follow Him. And if He is Your Lord and Savior, the fear of the Lord—a deep respect and incredible awe for Him—is the only fear that should reside in you.

On earth, here and now, Satan can throw all kinds of trouble your way, and if you fixate on the problems of life instead of focusing on the best Problem-Solver there is, you will rob yourself of resting "content, untouched by trouble." Jesus fixed all the world's problems when He died on the cross. Jesus, and Jesus alone, is strong enough to overpower Satan. Satan's eternal home is set; his time is coming to an end, but you have an eternal promise that Satan cannot touch.

Can you accept that God wants you content, knowing you are safely His forever? The "fear of the Lord" can give your faith a positive push as you respect and "fear" the Lord too much to deny Him or grieve the Holy Spirit. God wants you content every day of your life on earth, for you will live forever in Christ Jesus. God has a mission on earth for you to complete, but He also has an eternal purpose for your soul. His plan for you includes a perfect, sinless, shameless, completely honest, loving eternal home. No trouble will ever overtake you there as you rest in His arms.

Day 206

Follow His Law Faithfully

Moses said to the people
"Do not fear, for God has come to test you,
that the fear of Him may be before you, that you may not sin."
The people stood far off,
while Moses drew near to the thick darkness where God was.
Exodus 20:20-21 (ESV)

When Moses gave the people the Lord's Ten Commandments and they saw the resulting thunder and lightning, they trembled in fear. In their minds, they could still remember the scary thunder and lightning during the plagues that God had poured out on Egypt. Thus, they had a human reason to be afraid. But Moses told them to fear not the thunder but the One who controls the thunder.

All of nature is controlled by God, and He certainly can decide where lightning bolts will land. God does everything for a purpose and does not waiver in His decisions. He blesses those who bless Him, and it blesses Him that you follow His Law faithfully. His truth, His standard for living, is not to harm you or oppress your life but to protect you from sinfulness and shameful ways. The Law is there to keep a safe boundary around you. The Ten Commandments are the basic rules and regulations for you to follow—a starting point. In a nutshell, God is to be obeyed above all others; you do not have to agree with someone else's command to act in sinful ways. If your parents, spouse, or friend wants you to do something that goes against God's Law, you do not have to do it. You do not lie for anyone. You do not steal for anyone. You should never use the Lord's name in vain. He is holy, and He will hold you accountable.

God had Moses draw near to the thick darkness, and Moses was with God. Moses trusted God's leading. *Are you hiding from the knowledge and wisdom of God because you are too afraid to face the darkness?* God wants to grow your faith in His Holy Law.

Day 207

Your Highest Priority

The Lord made a covenant with them and commanded them,
"You shall not fear other gods or bow yourselves to them
or serve them or sacrifice to them but you shall fear the Lord,
who brought you out of Egypt with great power
and with outstretched arm.
You shall bow to Him and to Him you shall sacrifice."
2 Kings 17:35 -36 (ESV)

The Lord has made a covenant with you through the blood of Jesus. You are not a slave to sin any longer, but you have been bought with Jesus' work on the cross. You are now a servant of the Most High. *Is your service toward the Lord your highest priority? Do you think before you speak so the love of Christ can flow through you?* God wants you to pause; He wants you to include Him in your decision-making process, even in those millisecond decisions you tend to make without regard for Him. God wants your all, your best, not for you to focus on your outward looks but to follow through with what He instructs you to do, through His Word and your prayer life.

If you do not run to God, what are you running to? This illustrates one way people today worship idols. Idols can be not only something you can touch, but anything you put before God in your life. In this verse, the people feared and served their own gods. Today is no different. People today let the culture around them influence their behavior in ways that God disapproves of. Do not be confused; your follow through and integrity, your behavior and obedience, your entire life should reflect the ways of Jesus—how He acted and responded to those around Him. If not, you will miss the blessings He has planned for you. Or you may find yourself in despair, taking the wrong paths. God does not let sin slide. He might be giving you mercy for now because He is a merciful God, but you might want to start looking deep within and see the areas in your life that need to be more in line with God's way of living before it's too late.

Day 208

Honor His Holiness

Do not call conspiracy everything that these people call conspiracy;
do not fear what they fear, nor be in dread of it.
But the LORD of hosts, Him you shall honor as holy.
Let Him be your fear and let Him be your dread.
And He will become a sanctuary and a stone of offense.
Isaiah 8:12-14a (ESV)

Are you looking at the world through the understanding of God's Word and His intentions for this generation? The prophet Isaiah had a God-centered focus and a close relationship with God. But the culture around Isaiah was in moral decline. Therefore, Isaiah's messages and visions from God were ones of punishment and redemption. God-fearing people were taken into captivity because of the sins of the people they lived among. While these people were brought into slavery, God had a message of hope and redemption for those obedient to His Law.

Your situation can look dire, like there is no way out, no freedom to be found, but God has an escape plan for you. God wants you to find the end of yourself so you can find the beginning of Him. God wants you to lose your way so you can find His way.

Isaiah prophesied that Jesus would come into this world and bind the brokenhearted (Isaiah 61). Jesus is the answer for all the world's sin problems. The people around you may be sinning in ways that negatively affect you; their sin problems can become your problems. Clearly, the sins of abuse directly impact those who have endured it. The alcoholic in the family can destroy your trust; you may have to clean up the messes left behind. You might have to carry some of their weight, *so why not press into God and ask Him to give you the strength to deal with the stress they keep bringing you? Why not ask God for wisdom on how to help them through the maze of their messes?* God expects you to have patience with sinful people, and you are an example for Christ in all situations. Respect and fear the Lord with awe and integrity, and He will show you how.

Day 209

Heaven Is the Goal

I tell you, my friends,
do not be afraid of those who kill the body
and after that can do no more.
But I will show you whom you should fear:
Fear Him who, after the killing of the body,
has power to throw you into hell. Yes, I tell you, fear Him.
Luke 12:4-5 (NIV)

If you have ever been in a life and death situation, you are probably aware of the difficulty of this verse. When someone is beating you, or putting you in pain every day, it may seem a difficult pill to swallow, even impossible, to not fear that person. Christians in the world today are persecuted, beaten, and imprisoned for their belief in Jesus Christ. Jesus is fully aware of those who persecute you, and Jesus will judge them. He has a special place in heaven for those who have been martyred.

The book *Hearts of Fire* is a compilation of persecuted Christians' testimonies that tell of extreme abuse and harsh environments where evil rages; yet each story highlights God's protection through the torment. Someone may have the ability to beat the life out of you, but only God can send a person to hell. Only God can protect you eternally. God is your only hope to get out of the situation alive, and He is your only hope when you step into heaven.

God does not want you to overly focus on what is happening around you; God wants you to focus on Him. Physical pain can seem to take over your whole life, and God knows how long He will let it go on. But God knows how to cause all things to work together for His good. *Can you trust Him through the process, even if it means you will step into heaven sooner than you had planned?* To be absent from the body is to be present with the Lord (2 Corinthians 5:8). That is the end goal. Nothing on earth is as precious as your time you will spend in the glory of God.

Fear Only God

Day 210

Complete Allegiance

And I say to you "I AM the LORD your God;
you shall not fear the gods of the Amorites
in whose land you dwell." But you have not obeyed My voice.
Judges 6:10 (ESV)

The first of the Ten Commandments says, "You are not to have any other god before God" (Exodus 20:3). You are not to make an allegiance with anyone other than Jesus. You are not to obey any other spirit, but be led by the Holy Spirit. You are to obey the voice of God, and put that obedience above every other thing you do in this life.

God gave specific instructions to His people, but they failed to follow through completely. They did what they thought best, but they were wrong. God says in Deuteronomy 20:16-17, "In the cities of these peoples that the LORD your God is giving you for an inheritance, you shall save alive nothing that breathes, but you shall devote them to complete destruction, the Hittites, and the Amorites, the Canaanites, and the Perizzites, the Hivites and the Jebusites, as the LORD your God has commanded." Yes, it sounds harsh, but our holy God will punish sin. These "-ites" were people who worshipped many false gods, yet God wanted His people to live in the land. God wanted to turn an area from sin into His dwelling place, just like He wants to do with you.

God knew if His people did not completely destroy the enemy, these "-ites" would work their way into their daily lives, leading them down a slippery slope of sin. Because spouses influence one another so greatly, God says it's vital to marry another Christian. In today's verse, God's people did not completely destroy the ones God had told them to. He gave such a harsh command for He could see what would happen later. He knows your bad choices and where they will lead you: to places He never intended you to go. *Honestly, ask yourself, what small sin are you refusing to completely destroy? What are you tolerating that you should banish from your life?*

Fear Only God (vertical side text)

Day 211

Overcome Temptation

*Consider Him who endured from sinners such hostility against Himself,
so that you may not grow weary or fainthearted.
In your struggle against sin you have not yet resisted
to the point of shedding your blood.
And have you forgotten the exhortation that addresses you as sons?
My son do not regard lightly the discipline of the Lord,
nor be weary when reproved by Him.
For the Lord disciplines the one He loves
and chastises every son whom He receives.
It is for discipline that you must endure. God is treating you as sons.
For what son is there whom his father does not discipline?*
Hebrews 12:3-7 (ESV)

Holy, perfect Jesus left His home in heaven to come to earth as a humble, helpless baby to teach you how He genuinely wants you to live, and He came to die on a cross for you. Jesus had the whole eternal picture in mind, and He was confident that Father God had an entire plan for history. *Do you have the eternal perspective God wants you to have? Do you see lost people and grieve for their souls?* Jesus knew His time on earth was short. He never wasted a day; every day, He did the will of His Father. And through His time on earth, He gained a new perspective on what it was like to be born in the flesh with a sinful human nature.

Yet on earth, only Jesus could resist sin. He was the perfect sacrifice, punished for your sins on the cross. And now because Jesus overcame the cross, you can overcome temptation. By His stripes you are free from sin. By the power of the Holy Spirit, you can be pure, but if you choose to disobey the Word of God, you are sinning, and God will allow some situations to steer you back on track. If you have accepted Jesus, He took your punishment of eternal separation from God, but you can be certain that if you do not fear the One who holds your destiny in His hands forever, you will have a fear in hell you will never overcome.

Day 212

Glorify God in All You Do

Son of men, do not be afraid of them, nor be afraid of their words,
though briers and thorns are with you and you sit with scorpions.
Be not afraid of their words, nor be dismayed at their looks,
for they are a rebellious house.
And you shall speak My words to them,
whether they hear or refuse to hear, for they are a rebellious house.
Ezekiel 2:6-7 (ESV)

The prophet Ezekiel was given the task of prophesying both judgment and hope. His people had been deported out of their homes and sent to live in a place full of rebellious pagans. God's people had acted no different than the pagans they lived amongst. God punishes sin, with consequences for living in sin. God wants and deserves to be respected and honored above all. Your identity in Christ depends on who you identify with.

Do you blend into the culture of pagans around you? Do you identify with God's perspective on how you carry on in this world? Are your words filled with cussing, or with kindness? Is your identity found in the peace of God, or is your identity stuck in proving you are right, even to the point of anger? God wants you wrapped up in an identity of who God says you are—glorifying God in all you do, no matter what you watch or listen to. Would Jesus watch violence on TV? Would He choose to listen to negative music? The answer is obviously "no." So, when you choose not to glorify Him, you are sinning, and you need to seek out the things that please Him. Your heart will follow when you choose to obey. Your identity depends on it, and that is where true hope is found.

Day 213

Suffering for Christ

. . . without being frightened in any way by those who oppose you.
This is a sign to them that they will be destroyed,
but that you will be saved—and that by God.
For it has been granted to you on behalf of Christ
not only to believe in Him, but also to suffer for Him.
Philippians 1:28-29 (NIV)

To live is Christ, to die is gain (Philippians 1:21). What a comforting truth and promise. The most important aspect of your identity in Christ is your faithfulness to Him. Certainly, you will endure extremely difficult situations; pain in this world is impossible to escape if you are doing the work of Christ. He knows the evil hearts and intentions of those who try to drag you down and take you under. He knows that some people are filled with so much rage that they spew hate on everyone around them. But God will deliver you out of the situation. It could be on earth, it could be in heaven, but you can count on His deliverance over your suffering.

Are you seeking the comfort of the world or the comfort of Christ? Is your identity wrapped up in knowing that suffering for Christ will not go unnoticed in the eyes of the Lord? (Revelation 6:9-11). Jesus suffered on a cross, carrying the world's sin. The greater good is that we who follow Jesus follow Him to an eternal deliverance. Jesus suffered so you could know Him purely. *Can you suffer and allow it to bring you closer to God and not pull you away?* Your suffering is to bring you to Him. Leave it at the cross. Jesus defeated the world's sins on the cross, and by the power of the cross in and through you, you can withstand the suffering. Your identity lies not in being a victim but in the victory in and through Christ. For God is with you through your suffering, and He is with you when you praise Him in the storm.

Day 214

Heal Through Forgiveness

I pray that you may be active in sharing your faith
so that you will have a full understanding
of every good thing we have in Christ.
Philemon 6 (NIV)

This letter was written to Philemon, a Christian man who had been betrayed, and God had sovereignly put Paul in place to see the betrayer come to accept Christ as his personal Savior. Paul wanted to send this man back to the one whom he betrayed, and so he wrote Philemon a letter, asking him to forgive and restore the disloyal servant. So, how does this letter relate to you?

Christ, who redeems and changes a person's motives, has the authority and power to ensure you will be with the right people at the right time for God's will to prevail. Sometimes that means someone will be persuaded to forgive or act in a God-honoring way. It's no accident that Paul met the man who had betrayed his friend, or that God showed kindness and forgiveness to the betrayer.

This story in Philemon is all our stories; we have been both betrayers and betrayed. Thank God, He came to save sinners. We as Christians are to forgive others as God has forgiven us. It's all in the power of the cross, not in the power of yourself to forgive your betrayer. Jesus died on a cross so your sins can be forgiven and so you could be resurrected in Jesus. You are living in the power of Christ now, and your identity should be in the work of the cross, the forgiveness of sins.

Are you judging people that God did not intend for you to judge? Do you identify with God's saving grace? It's poured out from a never-ending well to all who believe. One of the best ways you can share your faith in Christ is to find resolution with people. Seek out those God wants you to forgive. If your faith and identity are wrapped up in His forgiveness, you will recognize what God did for your sinful heart, and He wants His people to heal together through forgiveness.

Day 215

A Healthy State of Mind

*Whoever listens to Me will live in safety
and be at ease without fear of harm.*
Proverbs 1:33 (NIV)

What are you listening to? What are you feeding your mind? Garbage in, garbage out. It's a fact: you are what you listen to. *Do the lyrics of a song build you up and encourage you or tear you down? Do the songs you listen to acknowledge God almighty or the mighty dollar?* Melodies stick in your head, and you chant them back to yourself all day. It's also a fact: God inhabits the praises of His people; He is right there, sending Satan away when you listen to God-inspired music. Fear and praise cannot stand in the same place. God wants to direct your thoughts into a healthy state of mind. He wants you to be grateful for the blessings you enjoy, but when you choose to listen to negative sources, your mood and focus change.

When life is hard and stressful, Christian music can lighten your spirits, but worldly music feeds into your fleshly desires and offers mind-numbing, carnal answers for the pain you feel; it entices you to look for healing in all the wrong places. Coming under agreement with negativity will not make the situation any easier. *Do you identify with worldly music, or do you identify with Christ-focused music that glorifies God and allows His Word and truth to wash over you? God speaks through Christian music . . . are you listening?*

Day 216

Rejoice Knowing the Law

*Go your way. Eat the fat and drink the sweet wine
and send portions to anyone who has nothing ready,
for this day is holy to our Lord.
And do not be grieved, for the joy of the Lord is your strength.*
Nehemiah 8:10 (ESV)

The prophet Ezra had just read the Law of the Lord to the people, and they grieved. They understood the wrongs they had committed with truly repentant hearts, but God did not want them to mourn their new knowledge. God wanted them to rejoice that they had found the Law and could walk in it from that point on. God will remind you of His ways when you stray, and He wants you to repent and do things differently, but He also does not want you stuck in the grief or regrets of past sin. He wants you to move past the grief into a place of joy and strength from Him. If you choose to listen to His instructions, He will bless you.

The people whom Ezra addressed had no idea what he was going to teach them the day they learned the Law of God. This illustrates one fabulous reason to sit under the teaching of a pastor; you do not know what teaching you are going to receive when you attend church, but God always has something He wants you to hear. He wants to teach you something new.

Will you allow yourself to grieve your wrongs for a short time so you can repent and find the joy of salvation? There is a time to celebrate with a repentant heart. There is a time to get over all the sin, all the errors you have made, and set your face toward the joy found only in God. You are to be obedient, you are to be faithful, and you are allowed to have fun. God allows people to drink wine, but God does not want to see His people as drunkards, always chasing the next fun time. God's joy is eternal; fun is momentary. *Is your identity in the joy of the Lord? Have you found His everlasting joy?*

Day 217

Love Is the Treasure

Jesus said, "Do not be afraid little flock,
for your Father has been pleased to give you the Kingdom.
Sell your possessions and give to the poor.
Provide purses for yourselves that will not wear out,
a treasure in heaven that will not be exhausted,
where no thief comes near and no moth destroys.
For where your treasure is, there your heart will be also."
Luke 12:32-34 (NIV)

Has God placed certain desires on your heart? Jesus cares about what is on your heart and whether they line up with the things of God. What are the believer's treasures that are stored in heaven? They are things the world may not consider precious or priceless: seeking those who are lost and pursuing a heart-transforming life. God is relational, and He wants you in relationship with Him and others. God does not want you chasing money, and none of the money is yours; God has provided it for you. God put you in a place to minister to the people around you. God put you in a position to make X amount of dollars. *Are you spending His money wisely? Are you being a good steward of the money He has allowed you to have? Do you tithe, do you sponsor a child, do you financially help ministries that equip and spread the gospel of Jesus? Do you spend too much time and money on what you will wear, what flashy jewelry will catch the lights? What overpriced car you will buy? How about the home you live in . . . do you really need it decorated with the newest styles?* God has promised you riches in heaven you cannot even comprehend. *Are you identifying with "the Joneses" or are you identifying with the Servant Christ, who left heaven to serve the poor in spirit?*

Day 218

God Is with You

Be strong and courageous and do it.
Do not be afraid and do not be dismayed,
for the Lord your God, even my God, is with you.
He will not leave you or forsake you,
until all the work for the service of the house of the Lord is finished.
1 Chronicles 28:20 (ESV)

Have you felt abandoned by someone close to you? Does someone you see all the time not know how to be present with you? Have you felt alone for so long that you are certain no one really cares? God wants you to know that you are never alone; He sees every tear, He hears every cry, and He is with you always. If you do not feel close to God right now, chances are that God didn't move away from you but that you put separation between yourself and God. God wants your whole identity enwrapped in the fact that He is always with you. He is always watching you, and you have a calling on your life. You have a ministry that God wants you to grasp and own. He has a tender place in life where He wants you to flourish. It's key you know that your identity in Christ is covered with a sovereign plan, and God's plans get accomplished. He can use you in His plan, or if you turn and walk away, He can find someone else courageous enough to take His hand, go where He leads, and take action according to His Word.

Can you be certain that your identity in Christ is covered by a love so strong that you cannot be separated from His love? Things you do may put a sinful wedge between you and God, but God is always watching His children, regardless of how stupid we act. God is gracious when we are not graceful. God is kind when we are bitter. God is love in a world filled with hate. God is not finished with you until the day He brings you home to Him in heaven. Your identity in Christ is one of boldness. Lean into Him, display your faith in His goodness, and give Him glory every day by speaking His truth into your fear.

Day 219

My Heart Will Not Fear

The Lord is my light and my salvation—whom shall I fear?
The Lord is the stronghold of my life—of whom shall I be afraid?
When the wicked advance against me to devour me,
it is my enemies and my foes who will stumble and fall.
Though an army besiege me, my heart will not fear;
though war break out against me, even then I will be confident.
One thing I ask from the Lord, this only do I seek:
that I may dwell in the house of the Lord all the days of my life,
to gaze on the beauty of the Lord and to seek Him in His temple.
For in the day of trouble He will keep me safe in His dwelling;
He will hide me in the shelter of His sacred tent
and set me high upon a rock.
Then my head will be exalted above the enemies who surround me;
at His sacred tent I will sacrifice with shouts of joy;
I will sing and make music to the Lord. Hear my voice when I call
Lord; be merciful to me and answer me.
My heart says of You, "Seek His face!"
Your face, Lord, I will seek.
Do not hide Your face from me, do not turn Your servant away in anger;
You have been my helper.
Do not reject me or forsake me, God my Savior.
Though my father and mother forsake me, the Lord will receive me.
Teach me Your way, Lord;
lead me in a straight path because of my oppressors.
Do not turn me over to the desire of my foes,
for false witnesses rise up against me,
spouting malicious accusations.
I remain confident of this:
I will see the goodness of the Lord in the land of the living.
Wait for the Lord; be strong and take heart and wait for the Lord.
Psalm 27 (NIV)

Do these words resonate with your heart? Are you confident in Christ like David was confident in God? When things go awry, do you freak out or panic, or do you call on God and seek His face? David had sure confidence in God because he understood the God he served. He knew that God is always faithful, and that his own faith could remain steadfast if he remembered God's character. Like Paul in the New

Testament, David also knew that revenge belongs to God (Romans 12:19). It's God's place to punish those who sin against Him. *Can you confidently hand over your enemies to God and allow Him to do what He thinks is right? Can you accept His punishment?* It's not your place to punish someone who hurt you, but it is your privilege as a child of God to take your burdens to the Lord. Your identity lies in the freedom of the cross, not the chains of revenge. *God can teach you to be free and live for Him; can you take heart, take Him at His Word, and wait for the Lord to act in His sovereign ways?*

Day 220

Tune into the Spirit

When the Spirit of Truth comes, He will guide you into all truth.
John 16:13 (ESV)

Only a holy God knows the whole truth. There are three sides to every story between two people: person A's side, person B's side, and God's side. *Can you accept that your perception is not "spot on" all the time?* Since God knows the heart and mind of each person, He understands how our perceptions are clouded. He knows we do not see clearly because we are blinded by the sin-soaked world. And He also knows how a situation would turn out if people trusted His whole truth. God's Word is something you bet your life on, literally and eternally. *Why won't you trust His Word in each moment every day?* God's Word is designed to guide you in ALL truth, moment by moment. The Holy Spirit is the Spirit of Truth, and this Spirit is alive and active.

Are you tuned-in to the Spirit? Do you feed your Spirit with the Holy Fire—with spending time with the Lord and trusting every word of the Bible—which burns away the things not of God? If not, then you are telling God you are better equipped to handle your life situations. *But if so*, then your flesh becomes obedient to the Holy Spirit living inside you, and He will guide you in all truth, in all situations of life. *And if so*, you will truly bear and enjoy the fruit of the Spirit: love, joy, peace, patience, kindness, goodness, faithfulness, and self-control. The truth is, spending time with God daily, talking with Him, and trusting His Word will make all the difference in your faith life and in your ability to cast all your fear upon Him.

241

Day 221

Fortified

Heaven and earth will pass away, but My Word will not pass away.
Luke 21:33 (ESV)

"Your Word, Lord is eternal; it stands firm in the heavens."
Psalm 119:89 (NIV)

In today's world, things are not made to last. They are made to dispose of and throw out, to consume and trash. In our global media, we are constantly bombarded with incentives to buy new stuff that might outlast the older stuff. We are used to things breaking down and then we "need" a new one, but God's Word has stood the test of time. Nothing in God's Word ever needs replacing, but often it does get used out of context. Only God's Word has true power that transcends time, through each generation, through each century and millennia. No other book has been translated into so many different languages, no other book is outlawed like the Bible, and no other book has been held in such great and high regard.

The Holy Bible is not just a book but compiled with sixty-six books of God's instruction, love, law, and peace. His words have eternal power, and the Word of God stands forever. You can bury your fears in the Word of God because His eternal plans will never perish. If you trust His every Word, you will see eternity in the Living Word: Jesus.

Are you allowing Satan to distract you with activities and pursuits that keep you away from the Word of God? Satan does not want you to spend time in God's Word because he knows you can use it as a weapon against him; he cannot stand up against the power of Scripture. When the Word of God is not breathing into your daily life, Satan can lie to you about who you are. But, if you keep close to the Word, God will build you up in your true identity and you will hear the lies of Satan clearly. You can distinguish Satan's fiery darts and put up a shield of truth before you. If you first know and believe God's Word, you can stop Satan in his tracks.

Day 222

We thank God constantly for this,
that when you received the Word of God,
which you heard from us,
you accepted it not as the word of men but as what it really is,
the Word of God, which is at work in you believers.
1 Thessalonians 2:13 (ESV)

At the whisper of the Word of the Lord, demons flee. By faith in the Word of the Lord, people live freely in Christ. The Word of the Lord is powerful—not to be taken lightly. Godly friends, people who read and trust God's Word, are key to your walk of faith; they will build you up in Christ, sharing how the Word is changing their perception, reactions, and love toward others.

People who spend time with Jesus, talk about Jesus. Jesus interacts with each person differently, and we learn well when we see things from a different perspective. The same Bible verse can impact two different people in two different ways. It can speak to each one personally, and they can see the verse from different angles. Neither of them has to be wrong.

You are not to distort God's Word to fit into your agenda, but the Word can speak uniquely into your life. For example, two people hear the same verse; God knows the first needs to hear a good Word on the Spirit of faith, and the other on encouragement. Both may find what they need in these next verses: "So, we do not lose heart. Though our outer self is wasting away, our inner self is being renewed day by day. For this light and momentary affliction is preparing for us an eternal weight of glory beyond all comparison . . ." (2 Corinthians 4:16-17). God's Word illuminates our hearts in different ways. Some days, a verse can jump off the page and sink deep into your soul. So, reading the Word daily proves vital as your heart reacts to that day's passage. If you choose to forgo God's Word that day, you could miss instructions God needs you to hear. You do not know the disasters that lie ahead, but God does. *Are you choosing wisely?*

The Word

Day 223

Applied Knowledge

Every word of God proves true;
He is a shield to those who take refuge in Him.
Proverbs 30:5 (ESV)

The Word of God impacts people profoundly when they genuinely "walk the walk." God's Word is our instruction on how to live in the boldness of Christ, a life without fear. Metaphorically, the Word becomes "a lamp unto my feet" when I apply the Word to my daily decisions. God never changes, which means His Word never changes as well, and what He did for the prophet Ezekiel, He can do for you. For all who truly believe that Jesus died and rose again to redeem their souls, God has imparted with the Holy Spirit and gave us each equal access to the Spirit's power. Ezekiel took God at His Word and obeyed God's instructions. So, the lessons we glean from Ezekiel, or anywhere else in the Bible, apply to our lives. The prophets of the Bible took God at His Word and trusted His Word to guide their lives. God protected Daniel in the lion's den, and as you trust Him, He will protect your soul from calamity; your salvation in Christ will always be your sure hope and future. Ezekiel did not shrink back when God instructed him to "make Jerusalem realize how disgusting her practices are" (Ezekiel 16:2), and you have the same calling on your life. You are not to stand idle and do nothing about the evil in your homes, churches, and schools. Wherever God has you, bring light into the situation, not agree with the darkness. He will call you out of your comfort zone and give you a bold testimony of faith.

Ask yourself regularly, *is God's Word my foundation for how I live? Do I consider the ways of the Lord? Am I lying to myself about anything? Have I tested His ways and compared my ideas to His instructions?* God Word says to live without fear . . . *are you willing to prove it?*

244

Day 224

Accomplished Purpose

*For as the rain and the snow come down from heaven
and do not return there but water the earth,
making it bring forth and sprout,
giving seed to the sower and bread to the eater,
so shall My Word be that goes out of My mouth;
it shall not return to me empty,
but it shall accomplish that which I purposed,
and shall succeed in the things for which I sent it.*
Isaiah 55:10-11 (ESV)

God has sent His Word to you, and it will not return void. Anytime you choose to sit under the teaching of God—whether reading the Word or daily devotionals, or listening to pastors and ministers—it's not like other forms of communication, sometimes going in one ear and out the other. God's Word is alive and active, interacting with you while the Gardner is watering your faith.

Are you bold enough with Christ to ask Him where you are parched and where you need Him to water your soul with His truth? He has something to say about where you are today. His Word is nourishment that will soften your bitter heart and move you in His direction. God wants you to flourish with His beauty, which radiates brightly when you let His rain fall into the crevices and wounds of your heart. Some people respond frantically when they think they are not doing "it" right, but having a growing, life-changing faith in God is really simple: God will accomplish His purpose in you. He will succeed at transforming your heart to be in alignment with His. His calling on your life starts in the Word of God and ends there as well. Your eternal home is with the Living Word of God: Jesus. Jesus created you for His good purpose, and all you need do is follow through with reading His Word, believing every word. When you believe the Word of God, you will live the Word of God. When you live the Word of God, you begin to sprout forth and help others to transform as well. And *that* is living out a growing, vibrant faith that brings abundant joy.

Day 225

Fertile Soil

*"All men are like grass,
and all their glory is like the flowers of the field.
The grass withers and the flowers fall,
because the breath of The LORD blows on them.
Surely the people are grass. The grass withers and the flowers fall,
but the Word of our God stands forever."*
Isaiah 40:6b-8 (NIV)

What is your legacy? What do you hope will be your mark on the world? God created each and every baby in a mother's womb to be born on earth and do something for Christ at that moment and time. History is comprised of an endless string of people's lives, and God placed each person there; He spoke your soul into existence. If you are covered in the blood of the Lamb, then you are part of the Word of God and in His Book of Life.

Grass is not redeemed but wastes away, fertilizing what is to come. When God blows on you, He does not want you to waste away. *What is your glory?* If it's anything other than God, it proves worthless—just as worthless as a flower with no petals. The beauty is gone, but the seed is left for rebirth. If you choose to let Jesus, the Living Water, quench your soul, then you can be strengthened in the fertile soil of God's Word. You need God's Word and His glory to hold onto so you don't get blown into the wind toward the Lake of Fire. Believe in Jesus, the Living Word, today, accept Him into your heart, and daily drink of God's Word, which never withers nor falls.

Day 226

The Deceiver

But I am afraid that as the serpent deceived Eve by his cunning,
your thoughts will be led astray
from a sincere and pure devotion to Christ.
2 Corinthians 11:3 (ESV)

As the author of this verse as well as thirteen letters we read in the Bible today, Paul knew what it was like to be bold for Christ. Paul was beaten, whipped, tortured, and brutalized because he wanted everyone to know the power of the cross. Paul spread the Gospel of Jesus far and wide, regardless of the danger. So, for him to say "I am afraid" in this verse is a big deal; he was afraid not of man, but for the state of people's souls. Paul understood the gravity of eternal life, as well as how Satan operates. Satan is the deceiver; no one lies more than he. The people to whom Paul was writing did not have a Bible like you and I, and thus they could be deceived much more easily. Since we have the Bible to teach us, we are without excuse.

Do you have the fear of God deep enough in your soul to understand that not having Christ proves a fearful way to exist? God places a holy fear in your heart to prompt you to move in other people's lives. It's your calling, your job if you will, to spread the Gospel, just like it was Paul's purpose as well. All you need to do is share your story with others, thanking God for His love and joy in your life. He will do the rest!

Have you given thought about the ways Satan operates? Have you taken the time to consider Satan's attributes and what he stands for? Satan has wanted God's glory all along, in fact, for thousands of years. So, I'm sorry to tell you, but Satan is much craftier at his art of evil than anything you could ever dream of. People underestimate Satan's cunning ways, his ability to distract you and turn your eyes from Jesus. *What are you devoted to that might be a detraction? Why not decide right now to worship Him moment by moment and thus bring Him all the glory?*

247

Day 227

The Father of Lies

It is God who never lies; however, Satan is the father of lies.
God is not man, that He should lie or a son of man,
that He should change His mind. Has He not said, and will He not do it?
Or has He spoken, and will He not fulfill it?
In Jesus there is no sin;
however, the devil has been sinning from the beginning.
God is love and His love covered your sin.
Titus 1:2, John 8:44, Numbers 23:19, 1 John 3:5, 3:8, 4:8 (Paraphrased)

It sounds so simple, but whom will you trust: Satan or Jesus? God has a plan for you, but so does Satan. God wants to bring you healing, self-worth, peace, and the love of Christ while Satan wants the exact opposite for you. Satan loves gossip, plants the seeds of lies between friends, and wants you to take pride in your accomplishments. God wants you to know with humility that He will empower you with strength and knowledge that can come only from above.

Satan brings his victims into the darkness, encouraging abuse, anger, and sexual misconduct. Satan lies to you about your healing, promising a carnal way out of your pain; after all, it's been a hard week and you deserve one more drink. But God's way says, *you don't have to lie to yourself anymore.* It's okay to feel the pain; it's natural to grieve; it's unhealthy to bottle your feelings. God is the great Comforter, and He will show you how to live righteously. God's Word does not change, and once you are sealed with the Holy Spirit, nothing can separate you from the love of Christ. Nothing!

Day 228

Let Humility Win

Pride goes before destruction, and a haughty spirit before a fall.
Proverbs 16:18 (ESV)

We live in a world that prides itself on an abundance of accomplishments. People spend endless time on social media to see what everyone else did that weekend, but that only gives a glimpse of what they want you to see, not the full story. Is it prideful to put all your activities online? No, but the addiction to feel self-gratified by the appearance of your own and others' lives is. It's also a sin to boast about the blessings God has given you. God has a lane for you to run in, and it is a perfect fit for you.

Can you learn to be comfortable in your own skin? Or have you become too comfortable and seem to think everyone should see your every curve? Every moment you can choose to be humble and confident in who God created you to be, or you can be proud of what "you" have accomplished. Pride is telling God your way is better than His way. Pride is boasting how good you are at something . . . when, in fact, you are nothing without Christ; He gave you your skills and your achievements. Christ gave you the strength and knowledge to be good at something. Apart from Christ, you remain in your prideful sin.

Satan's sin of being prideful, wanting to be as powerful as God, was the true original sin. In the same way, anything you put before God becomes prideful, and pride is a form of idolatry. God is warning you to recognize that all your healing, all your success, all your blessings are because of Him. As all good things come from above, God alone should be the pride of your heart.

Day 229

Deal with the Friction

In your anger do not sin.
Do not let the sun go down while you are still angry,
and do not give the Devil a foothold.
Ephesians 4:26-27 (NIV)

When your anger boils against someone and you don't want to reconcile, *how do you think Jesus feels?* Do you think He is in heaven saying, "You deserve to be upset and hold onto your unforgiveness"? He certainly is not. In fact, Jesus has a lot to say about unforgiveness. As the saying goes, "It's easier to get mad than sad." Satan wants to drive a wedge between you and your family, friends, coworkers, and fellow students while God wants the exact opposite for you. God wants you to use your differences to mix with people different than you. The friction you feel in those heated moments should be a time to learn about things from a different perspective. That's how you will grow to be more like Jesus. That's how you learn to love the way God intends.

What in your past can you still not shake off? What is holding you back? Do you still feel hate toward anyone when you think of them? Anger often stems from unforgiveness and bitterness. Unresolved hurts from the past will catch up with you. God wants you to be honest with yourself about the pains of life. He wants you to pour out your heart to Him. God wants to be your peace, but peace is ripped away when the emotions of anger take over. Peaceful talks tend to have a better outcome than angry fits of rage. Satan loves to lie, saying, "You deserve to be angry with someone that hurt you; they do not deserve your love." But God says, "Don't let the sun go down while you are still angry." God wants you to deal with the issues that cause you to become angry so they lose their foothold on you. We cannot show love and kindness through anger, and in our anger, it's easy to sin. But in the love of Christ, reconciliation and peace are possible—and are awaiting you.

Day 230

Thís Is Your Confidence

No temptation has seized you except what is common to man.
And God is faithful;
He will not let you be tempted beyond what you can bear.
But when you are tempted,
He will also provide a way out so that you can stand up under it.
1 Corinthians 10:13 (NIV)

This verse offers proof that God will not let you be tempted to sin without providing a way out—another avenue to take, another choice you can make. But, contrary to what you may have heard about this verse, He may at times give you more than *you* can handle. And that's the key word: *you*. Because He does not let you struggle and suffer alone. He does not leave you to handle it by yourself. When you feel you cannot take another breath because the pain of life is so thick, God becomes your Breath of Life. When your heart is so heavy that you cannot bear the weight any longer, God is your strength. And He will bear the burden of your complicated situation.

Have you built a stone fortress around your heart so you can stay safe and unhurt? God calls His children to Himself so He can be their Mighty Fortress. All you have to do is believe and pray, asking Him to do what He promises. God promises that when the temptation to sin besieges you, He has a way out. And likewise, He has a plan for you to stand up under the difficulties of life. God does not intend for you to be crushed and broken over all your heartache. God is in control, and for those who love Him, He works all things for good; this is your confidence.

Are you completely stressed out dealing with your lot in life? God promises a way out to freedom. *He wants to be your cornerstone, but is your heart too heavy to lift your eyes to see His plan?* God knows every choice you make can be obedient to His ways. In God's holy eyes, you have no excuses. Nothing in life, no obstacles, will force you to sin; honesty is the only option. And, He will always be your refuge, your safe haven, when life seems more than *you* can bear.

Day 231

Release the Shame

Do not be afraid; you will not suffer shame. Do not fear disgrace;
you will not be humiliated. You will forget the shame of your youth
and remember no more the reproach of your widowhood.
For your Maker is your Husband—The Lord Almighty is His Name—
the Holy One of Israel is our Redeemer;
He is called the God of all the earth.
Isaiah 54:4-5 (NIV)

Are your emotions tangled and inflamed over your disgrace and shame from the ways you have been wronged? Are your emotions raw over the loss of a loved one who left the earth too soon? Time does heal wounds and puts things in perspective, but life can be agonizing. Looking to the future, you may think you'll never see the light at the end of the tunnel. When emotions are tender and today's pain seems too harsh, hearing the promises of God can be hard. They may seem like a pipe dream, going up in smoke to sicken you. But God is not there to scorn you but there to give you hope. God is your Redeemer, whether in your pit of despair, in your day of jubilation, and most of all, eternally. God is your only Hope, and you must learn to know the promises of God so that—in your times of raw emotions—you can know Him as your confidence, today and forever.

Some days, God's eternal promises are all you need to stand confident in this crazy world. But for other days, you will need to hide His words in your heart; then you can recall the blessed promises of Jesus in those moments in the dark. In hindsight, you can learn; you can laugh; you can bravely live your time on earth; and then you can reach your eternal home, where no sin and shame exist. God will not forget the people who choose to live for Him. He loves you so much; you are the bride of Christ. God has endless compassion for you, today and eternally. Release your raw emotions to Him.

Day 232

The Spirit Searches Everything

You will receive power when the Holy Spirit has come upon you.
Acts 1:8 (ESV)

We impart a secret and hidden wisdom of God . . .
As it is written, "What no eye has seen, nor ear heard,
nor the hearts of man imagined,
what God has prepared for those who love Him."
These things God has revealed to us through the Spirit.
For the Spirit searches everything, even the depths of God.
For who knows a person's thoughts except the Spirit of God?
Now we have received not the spirit of the world,
but the Spirit who is from God,
that we might understand the things freely given us by God.
And we impart this in words not taught by human wisdom
but taught by the Spirit,
interpreting spiritual truths to those who are spiritual.
1 Corinthians 2:7, 9-13 (ESV)

What beautiful promises! You have a hidden wisdom, and it is by the power of the Holy Spirit. God has imparted your Spirit with a force that has the power to change everything about you. God gives you understanding through the work of the Holy Spirit; it is not your task to figure out everything on your own. God wants you to figure things out with Him.

Are you aware of all the different ways the Spirit of God interacts with you? Can you recognize His voice? Can you feel His nudging as you read the Word of God? As an active Spirit, the Spirit within you comes alive through the Word of God. *Have you asked God to awaken your Spirit, to overflow with the Spirit of truth in your life and in the lives of those around you?* You cannot access your spiritual bank if you have neglected asking God to awaken your Spirit. *Have you learned the need to ask God daily to empty you of yourself and ask Him to fill you up in His Spirit?* When you ask the Spirit to burn bright in your day, you slowly recognize the hand of God in your daily walk. Your Spirit yearns for connection with God, who wants to take you to a deeper level with Him, but you first have to awaken your Spirit so you can build your spiritual muscles.

Day 233

In Line with God's Righteousness

What the wicked fears will come upon him,
but the desires of the righteous will be granted.
Proverbs 10:24 (NASB)

When God looks at you, He sees your heart. God understands whether you have a selfish ambition or a humble desire. You can lie to yourself all day long, but you are the fool, not God. When you have a wicked intent, God is warning you that your fears will come upon you. But when you seek to do things in line with God, then His desires become yours, and those He always grants.

Can you see the wickedness in your selfish desires? Have you learned to be self-aware? Can you talk to God about the desires of your heart and ask Him to make His desires, your desires, without getting overly emotional every time? God wants to shape us into the image of His Son, Jesus Christ. So, in every situation, His desires for you are aligned with those of your Savior, Jesus. He knows if your desires are evil, self-serving, worldly, or based in your pride; He knows that they may sound good, but in His wisdom, He may have something even better in mind for you—something with eternal consequences that you can't even see.

For not everyone who says to Jesus, "Lord, Lord, will enter the Kingdom of heaven, but the ones who do the will of my Father who is in heaven" (Matthew 7:21). If your heart is fixed on greed, pride, arrogance, and sexual sins, then there is much to fear because your heart is not right with God, and God is not Lord of your life. God promises the power of the Holy Spirit will change you to do His will. The sanctification process causes a person's heart to become aligned with God's righteous plan; God blesses His beloved children and knows what is best for you. God's promises are trustworthy. *Can you trust Him through the process as He makes His desires your own?*

Day 234

Mercy Granted

Do not fear the king of Babylon, of whom you are afraid.
Do not fear him declares the Lord, For I AM with you,
to save you and to deliver you from his hands.
I will grant you mercy,
that he may have mercy on you and let you remain in your own land.
Jeremiah 42:11-12 (ESV)

Today's verse is the same promise God gave to Jeremiah earlier. In Jeremiah 1:19, God says, "They will fight against you, but they shall not prevail against you, For I AM with you, to deliver you." Now Jeremiah is called "the weeping prophet" for a reason. God had this man pronounce the destruction upon the Jews. He was beaten, thrown in a muddy cistern, abandoned, called a liar, imprisoned several times, and taken into captivity. His life proved extremely difficult, but his heart broke for the things of God and he respected the instructions of the Lord.

Jeremiah followed through with God's plan, and when he was captured by the Babylonians, he was treated with favor. He was not set free but no longer in chains. All the people who truly listened to God's voice and placed their trust in His promises were called "the remnant" of God's people. God put a huge test of faith before them, and He blessed those who believed His words. Jeremiah was prophesying over a people who left a legacy for today's believers to follow. "For I AM with you, to save and deliver you," God says in today's verse. You can count on this promise. God is with you in every battle you face; His mercy is a river that never dries up. Regardless of the world pressing you down, God is here to build you up in Christ, sustaining and strengthening you. *Who are you most afraid of? What evil and torment have they caused?* God knows, and He promises deliverance and mercy. *Can you rely on His promises when life becomes a dark, difficult road? Will you try to control the situation so you block God from doing His handiwork, or will you rely on God to save you at the perfect moment, for His good and glory?*

Day 235

Living the Right Way for God

An anxious heart weighs a man down, but a kind word cheers him up.
A righteous man is cautious in friendship,
but the way of the wicked leads them astray.
The lazy man does not roast his game,
but the diligent man prizes his possessions.
In the way of righteousness this is life; along the path is immortality.
Proverbs 12:25-28 (NIV)

Do you understand what God means in this verse by "a righteous man" and "the way of righteousness"? As you live for Christ, are you seeing examples of God's righteousness as you read His Word? Actually, God's Word is His righteousness, or the way for a "righteous person" to live, because His Word shows you how to live in this world His way. Simply stated, His righteousness is "right living," or trusting His promises and doing His will out of love for Him.

God has imparted you with everything you need to stand separated from anxiety and laziness. Anxiety wreaks havoc on your health, both physically and spiritually. Anxiety over a situation usually means you are not trusting God in that place, or that tragedy and emotions are overwhelming you. Ask yourself if you are letting God rule or letting anxiety have full control. God intends for you to enjoy peace, and God's Word can be peace to your soul. God's Word can cheer you, strengthen you, and give you hope when you trust His promises.

God also wants you to take extra care when deciding whom to hang out with because He loves you so much. He wants people to build you up and hold you accountable. Those not following Christ will boost your anxiety and lead you astray. And don't be lazy about your own healing; it often takes effort and tenacity on your part, but in the process, He will give you peace. Seek to live according to His Word, and rest in His promises as you do; then His righteousness will be yours as you place your hope in Jesus.

Promises

Day 236

Take Him at His Word

*Because Joseph her husband was a righteous man
and did not want to expose Mary to public disgrace,
he had in mind to divorce her quietly. But after he had considered this,
an angel of the Lord appeared to him in a dream and said,
"Joseph, son of David, do not be afraid to take Mary home as your wife,
because what is conceived in her is from the Holy Spirit.
She will give birth to a son, and you are to give Him the name Jesus,
because He will save His people from their sins."*
Matthew 1:19-21 (NIV)

Joseph heard the Word of the Lord and believed God—He believed God could do what He said He would do. Before God chose him to be the earthly father of Jesus, Joseph was already "right" with God; he was a righteous man. Joseph had such a close relationship with God that he could recognize the angel as God's blessing who brought instructions to follow. Certainly, God's plan sounded crazy by human standards, but remember, just like He gave Joseph, God gives us dreams to follow.

Do you need to start believing in the dreams God is giving you? Joseph's belief in God changed the whole course of Satan's plan. The act of obediently believing the Word of God has blessed us up to this generation and many more to follow. Hear this: believing God is the most important thing you can do. It's also the most honest thing you can do because if you honestly believe that Jesus died for your sins, your faith can and will wash away all your blemishes. Jesus is a man of His Word, and if you choose to believe and take Him at His every word, then you, too, can change the course of Satan's plans. *Are you doing your part? Are you believing God completely, or are you taking God for granted?* Your dream of being completely restored in Christ is possible if you choose to believe in the full power of the cross.

Day 237

Little by Little

You may say to yourselves,
"These nations are stronger than we are. How can we drive them out?"
But do not be afraid of them;
remember well what the LORD your God did to Pharaoh
and to all Egypt. You saw with your own eyes the great trials,
the signs and wonders, the mighty hand and outstretched arm,
with which the LORD your God brought you out.
The LORD your God will do the same to all the peoples you now fear.
Moreover, the LORD your God will send the hornet among them
until even the survivors who hide from you have perished.
Do not be terrified by them, for the LORD your God, who is among you,
is a great and awesome God.
The LORD your God will drive out those nations before you,
little by little. You will not be allowed to eliminate them all at once,
or the wild animals will multiply around you.
But the LORD your God will deliver them over to you,
throwing them into great confusion until they are destroyed.
Deuteronomy 7:17-23 (NIV)

In today's verse, God is asking you to remember well what the Lord your God has done for you. *Have you ever given thought to starting a "prayer and blessings" journal?* It's a beautiful thing to write out your prayers of gratitude and petitions; then you can look back and have a reference point to remember all the answered prayers. You will see the way God moved in situations, and this will help you build confidence that God is involved in the details of your life. Little by little, God rearranges your life; little by little, God drives out the enemies. Some days you are your own worst enemy, but God can set your mind straight.

When will you stop with your excuses? Are you using your lack of self-respect and heart issues as ways to divert God's plan for you to get in line with His perspective? Little by little, God wants to correct your perspective to be aligned with His. When Christians doubt themselves, it can affect their perspective of God, which leads to doubting God. *If you do not believe that God is faithful and will do as He promises, how can He thwart your enemies? How can God do a miracle in your life if you do not believe?* Believe that God can and will confuse the plans of the enemy. Nothing and no one are stronger than God; believe in this confidence.

Day 238

Authority Given

When Jesus entered Capernaum, a centurion came to Him,
imploring Him, and saying,
"Lord, my servant is lying paralyzed at home, fearfully tormented."
Jesus said to him, "I will come and heal him."
But the centurion said,
"Lord, I am not worthy for You to come under my roof,
but just say the word, and my servant will be healed.
For I also am a man under authority, with soldiers under me;
and I say to this one, 'Go!' and he goes,
and to another, 'Come!' and he comes, and to my slave,
'Do this!' and he does it." Now when Jesus heard this,
He marveled and said to those who were following,
"Truly I say to you,
I have not found such great faith with anyone in Israel.
I say to you that many will come from east and west,
and recline at the table with Abraham,
Isaac and Jacob in the kingdom of heaven;
but the sons of the kingdom will be cast out into the outer darkness;
in that place there will be weeping and gnashing of teeth."
And Jesus said to the centurion,
"Go; it shall be done for you as you have believed."
And the servant was healed that very moment.
Matthew 8:5-13 (NASB)

Jesus came to earth with an eternal plan from God, not acting on His own accord but only as God instructed Him to do (John 12:49, John 14:31). Jesus is second in the Trinity, the Son. Learning obedience from the things He suffered (Hebrews 5:8), Jesus was fully man and fully God; His flesh had to be completely obedient to God's will. Father God, who is Spirit (John 4:24), gave authority to Christ to do the work of Father God. All authority was given to Christ (Matthew 28:18), and believers who follow Christ have been given the Holy Spirit (John 14:26). Under the authority of the Trinity and by the power within, we can believe that God will do as He says He will do. All authority on earth has been given by the Father (Roman 13:1), and by Father God's design, there is a chain of command. He is in the top three positions, but you intermarry with His Spirit in the third position. You have the authority over Satan; He does not have authority over you. *Do you live your life like you believe in the authority God has given you over Satan?*

259

Day 239

Do Not Complicate It

Do not be afraid any longer, only believe.
Mark 5:36 (NASB)

When you look and process these few words of Jesus, you see how simple and deep they are. God does not want you to complicate this message. In today's verse, the circumstances of the father whom Jesus addressed were terrible. This father was just told his daughter had died, but he was standing in the presence of Jesus, the One who gives life. When you stand in the presence of God, you can bring your terrible situations to Him, but you must believe and stop fearing all the outcomes that could happen. Believe that God will breathe new life into the terrible situation. God can bring anything back from the dead, but you must believe first. The father in Mark 5 believed and his daughter was brought back to life.

What are you so afraid of when you do not believe it will get better? What are you so afraid of that keeps you from hope and faith? God is bigger than anything you will ever face. God is stronger than any stronghold in your life. Your mind can be free of the negativity; your conscience does not have to haunt you. God knows what you have done. *Are you comfortable hiding from yourself? Are you comfortable in the dark? Are you afraid of the light and what it might reveal?* God knows, *so why are you not honest with yourself or with Him?* Believe that God can heal all your fears. You do not have to know how God will remove them; you just have to believe that He will. Redeemed children of God believe in the wholeness of Christ. For in Christ, we are free indeed . . . *can you believe it?* Your mind and heart depend on it.

Day 240

Child Arise

Someone from the ruler's house came and said,
"Your daughter is dead; do not trouble the Teacher anymore."
But Jesus on hearing this answered him,
"Do not fear; only believe, and she will be well."
And when He came to the house, He allowed no one to enter with Him,
except Peter and John and James,
and the father and mother of the child.
And all were weeping and mourning for her, but He said,
"Do not weep, for she is not dead but sleeping."
And they laughed at Him, knowing that she was dead.
But taking her by the hand He called, saying, "Child, arise."
And her spirit returned, and she got up at once.
Luke 8:49-55 (ESV)

Your miracle of healing is possible, regardless of who makes fun of you, laughs at you, or puts you down. The people in this verse laughed at Jesus because they "knew" she was dead. *What in your life feels so dead that you doubt it will ever come to life? Has the depression taken such a deep root that you doubt you will ever relax in who God created you to be? Or have you numbed your feelings for so long that you doubt you can ever really be alive in Christ?* God wants to resurrect your deadened heart, to put life back in your soul. Of utmost importance to God, your spirit dwells with the Spirit of the Lord. You have life in you that can raise you from the dead. Christ can take your beaten-down path and make the ground flourish with new life. For God alone can raise someone from the dead, and God alone can change your despair to joy.

In your waking moment, can you believe that God's mercy is new every day? God wants to awaken your soul to be ablaze for the things of Jesus, but first God wants to make you alive all the way down to your core. No matter how hard your heart gets, if you repent and believe God, He will turn things around and will soften your heart. It's okay to ask God to help you with your unbelief (Mark 9:24). When you come to Jesus with an honest heart, He will honestly answer you.

Day 241

Chosen for His Glory

Jesus said, "Did I not tell you that if you believed,
you would see the glory of God?"
John 11:40 (NIV)

You were chosen to show God's glory. Those who believe in the Lord are all chosen for His glory. If we believe He is who He says He is, in His Word, and we abide in Him, prayerfully walking this life out with God, then we will see the glory of God. This is a promise from Jesus. *Did He not tell you who you are in Christ through His Word? Has He not told you that you have the power of the Holy Spirit within you, and with this power, you can withstand all the schemes of the Devil? What are you not believing that God has said in His Word?*

What you believe in Christ is what you will produce. Your lack of belief will throw your life into confusion and turmoil that was not intended for you. Knowing your identity, as a child of God, should be vital for you. God does not condone laziness; He expects us to study His Word and search for His hand, but for some things we do not need to search long and hard. Believing God is not something you have to put much effort into. Accepting the Word at face value will catapult your life into a holy lane of trust, dependent upon His solutions and believing it with all your heart. The power you have through the Holy Spirit is so strong that you can barely wrap your mind around this truth, but all you have to do is believe. God knows how to love you exactly in the ways you need. Let the power of God allow you, through the Holy Spirit, to trust His steadfast love.

Day 242

Believing Jesus

Persecutions I endured; yet from them all the Lord rescued me.
Indeed, all who desire to live a godly life in Christ Jesus
will be persecuted,
while evil people and imposters will go on from bad to worse,
deceiving and being deceived. But as for you,
continue in what you have learned and have firmly believed.
2 Timothy 3:11b-14 (ESV)

Are you willing to be persecuted, laughed at, scorned, or much worse for your faith in Christ? People can be offended by Christ because they do not want to put their trust in Him. It's a fragrance of death to them (2 Corinthians 2:16). Due to their pride, they do not believe they need a Savior to rescue them from their sins, and thus they may lash out at your faith and hope in the Lord. *Can you stand firm in your faith against such oppression?*

God chooses whom He rescues from the grip of Satan, but He also chooses whom He will not pursue (Romans 9:1-23). God has mercy on whom He wants to have mercy. So what's the key to unlock His mercy? It's actually simple: believe that Jesus rescued you from your sin problem and that He is your atonement for your sins. Your faith is a beautiful thing!

To be a chosen child of God is so amazing, but on the flipside, living this life without hope in Christ is horribly distressing; those who reject Christ, those whose minds do not want to accept Him, are eternally dying in their inner being. And that reality can cause a person to act out in anger and persecute those who have the hope of heaven eternally with God. Realize what is happening when others mock you and pray for their hearts to turn to the Only Hope they have.

263

Day 243

Broken Over Sin

I got up from my humiliation, with my tunic and robe torn.
Then I fell on my knees and spread out my hands to the Lord my God.
And I said: My God, I am ashamed and embarrassed
to lift my face toward You, my God,
because our iniquities are higher than [our] heads
and our guilt is as high as the heavens.
Our guilt has been terrible from the days of our fathers until this day.
Because of our iniquities we have been handed over,
along with our kings and priests, to the surrounding kings,
and to the sword, captivity, plundering, and open shame, as it is today.
But now, for a brief moment,
grace has come from the Lord our God to preserve a remnant for us
and give us a stake in His holy place.
Even in our slavery, God has given us new life and light to our eyes.
Though we are slaves, our God has not abandoned us in our slavery.
He has extended grace to us in the presence of the Persian kings,
giving us new life,
so that we can rebuild the house of our God and repair its ruins,
to give us a wall in Judah and Jerusalem.
Now, our God, what can we say in light of this?
For we have abandoned the commandments.
Ezra 9:5-10 (HCSB)

God had commanded the Jews of Moses' time to completely destroy the people of the land. They disobeyed, and the people of Ezra's time were feeling the negative effects. The Holy Race was no longer holy. Ezra was broken over their sins but aware of why things were happening. A person cannot live without fear controlling his or her life if not living the life God intended. Purity is the only way to a life free from fear—purity of heart, soul, and mind, in complete obedience to God's direction. Yet, no one can do this, for we all have sinned and fall short of the glory of God (Romans 3:23), but we can depend on God doing what He promised: He will rescue you from your sins if you repent. Cry out to the Lord. *Are you broken over your sins and wrong doings? Does it impact you and grieve you that Jesus felt your sin on the cross?* The price He paid on the cross was not cheap or easy. *Do you respect the price He paid for you to be rescued?*

Day 244

Long for His Perspective

O Lord be gracious to us; we long for You.
Be our strength every morning, our salvation in time of distress.
Isaiah 33:2 (NIV)

What do you long for? Do you long for a hot, quiet bath? Or maybe a cigarette or your favorite cocktail? Perhaps deep down, you long for healed relationships? Do you long to stand in the woods or next to the ocean, far from the pain you're experiencing right now? Or just perhaps . . . do you long for God to come in and rescue you, right where you are? God might not rescue you until you are ready to long for His perspective. God wants to be first, but you must train yourself to stay focused on Him. God sees your faith and responds accordingly. God sees you right where you are, no matter where you are. He knows the hurtful words that sting your heart. He knows the depression you hide with a smile. He knows what you long for and exactly what you need.

Where is faith in these moments? God knows the best way to rescue you out of every situation you put yourself in and when you need to be rescued from the grip of Satan. Even Jesus said to Peter, "Get behind me Satan" (Matthew 16:23). If Peter, an apostle of Jesus, needed to be rescued from carrying out Satan's plan, we certainly do as well. Peter had just confessed that Jesus is the Christ. He put all his trust in who Jesus said He was, but a little later Jesus started to explain that He was heading for the cross, and Peter tried to rebuke Jesus. By human standards and in Peter's mind, the cross made no sense, but today we live in the freedom of the cross. You put your faith in the cross for your eternal salvation, but God's forgiveness is new every day. What Jesus did on the cross rescued you from being Satan's pawn, but if you do fall for his schemes, Jesus is always there to rescue you. He is never late. Put your faith in His rescue plan, today and every day.

Rescue

Day 245

Fixated on Christ

I love You, O Lord, my strength. The Lord is my rock, my fortress,
and my deliverer; my God is my rock in whom I take refuge.
He is my shield and the horn of my salvation, my stronghold.
I call to the Lord, who is worthy of praise,
and I am saved from my enemies.
Psalm 18:1–3 (NIV)

What is your focus in this life? What has your mind become fixated on? The Bible teaches that we are to fix our eyes on Jesus, and the rest will be given to us. God's rescue plan for you might include you letting go of some things that consume much of your energy and mind. *Are you fixated on your worry or on your worship and praise to God, thanking Him for the ways He has already blessed you, no matter how small they may seem? Are you fixated on your sadness and fear, or on praying and seeking God's solution?*

Praising the Lord in the storm will rescue your attitude and perception over the fears in your life. When you praise the Lord, Satan will flee. He hates the praise of the Lord. When your soul reaches out to God with praise, no matter what you are going through, He will show you how to change your mindset, your decision-making, your friendships, your reactions to stress, your responses to others, your lack of self-control, your doubts and temptations, your apathy for time in the Word and prayer, your fear in sharing your testimony . . . any area that needs transformation. And while it may then seem like a do-it-yourself rescue, He will be gripping you tightly on His rescue mission. God has given you the power to do what you cannot do on your own. He will show you how and give you the courage to latch onto Him to escape some difficult storms, *but are you willing to accept His call, His ways, as He pulls you to safety? Do you love God enough to change?*

Day 246

Compassion in Your Heart

Defend the cause of the weak and fatherless;
maintain the rights of the poor and oppressed,
rescue the weak and needy; deliver them from the hands of the wicked.
Psalm 82:3-4 (NIV)

Do you make it a habit to defend the oppressed? Do you stand up for the things of God? Jesus said, "We will always have the poor." He knew that people will be hungry and starving till He comes back again, and He left it as our duty and task to feed the poor. If you need a place to start, sponsoring a child is a fabulous way to do this.

Has God opened your eyes and let you know about a population that is weak and oppressed, placing compassion in your heart toward them? The work God has done in you can lead you to rescue someone out of a hard place. There are hurting people all around. *What does God do to your heart when you think about the various ways you could defend the cause of those suffering?* God wants you to love everyone around you, not just the ones easy to love. God sends His people to do His work, and many times this work can rescue a person in despair. He wants His children not to just take blessings and move on but to be the hands and feet of Jesus. He wants you to join Him in making this world a better place. God wants you to express how He has pulled you through a tough time. God wants you to share yourself with those hurting. *What are you complaining about?* You might be the answer to the problem. Even if no one knows you are the one taking on the small details for Christ, God knows what you are doing. You are doing what He instructed your heart to do.

Day 247

Trust Is Essential

*". . . I will rescue you on that day," declares the Lord;
"you will not be handed over to those you fear.
I will save you; you will not fall by the sword
but will escape with your life
because you trust in Me," declares the Lord.*
Jeremiah 39:17-18 (NIV)

What particular day did you endure that changed you forever? Is there something that happened in those moments? And now do you seem not to know how to get back to your old self, your former ways? Has your sense of safety been stolen from you? God's ways are higher than ours. He understands what you have been through, and He understands how things have changed you. Not all change is good; sometimes we take the wrong turn and end up in a dark alley. But some bad things that happen to you are not your fault. The abuse and neglect you've endured are not punishment for your transgressions. Jesus said in John 9:3-4, "Is was not that this man sinned, or his parents, but that the works of God might be displayed in him. As long as it is day, we must do the works of Him who sent Me . . ."

God's glory can shine out of your darkness. The things that broke your heart and crippled your mind are not in vain. God wants you to see His glory amidst the pain you feel. Till Jesus comes back, we will have evil people, and we must live with that reality. But there's a rescue plan for us: when we seek the hope of Jesus in the dark, we can feel His presence. In these moments, God has much to teach and show you, but you must be open to receive. Too many people close off Jesus when hurt, but this is exactly when you need Him to rescue you—rescue your mind from becoming too depressed or shut off from the world. Trusting God is a key facet of being a Christian. Through trust, God can rescue you from the dark places in your mind, your financial burdens, and the abuse you endure—anything Satan throws your way. *Is your trust in Christ growing?*

Day 248
Ask for Help

*The LORD is close to the brokenhearted
and saves those who are crushed in spirit.
A righteous man may have many troubles,
but the LORD delivers him from them all.*
Psalm 34:18-19 (NIV)

God does not promise a perfect, easy life. But He promises to be close to you when you are broken and crushed. His love will never leave you nor forsake you. God is not close to the high and mighty, the prideful ones who think they have it all together. God is not close to those who choose to reject God when life gets difficult. But God is close to those who know they need Him and are humble enough to ask for help. He wants to use your brokenness to draw you closer to Him. He can use your terrible situation and turn it into a miracle.

Are you believing God in the midst of your troubles? When the rubber hits the road, are you busy focusing on your wheels peeling out, or are you searching for God in order to gain traction on the trajectory of your miserable state? You can easily miss God's rescue plan if you focus your attention too long on your problem instead of focusing on the only One who can rescue you. Life can change in a second; all it takes is one phone call, one diagnosis from a doctor, or a betrayal of a trusted friend or spouse . . . but God is there. He does not leave the scene when life gets hard. He leans in and gets close to you.

Are you leaning into God as He leans into you? Can you not feel His presence in the midst of the heartbreak? Have you asked Him to show Himself to you? God will rescue you from the loneliness of the heartbreak if you lean into Him as He remains close to you. He has not gone anywhere. *Can you yield to His way of rescuing you?* He has a plan to deliver you from this.

Sovereign

Day 249

All You Need

It is the Lord who goes before you. He will be with you;
He will not leave you or forsake you. Do not fear or be dismayed.
Deuteronomy 31:8 (ESV)

How lonely do you feel? Do you yearn for someone to truly understand you? No one on earth will ever understand exactly how your trauma impacted you. But God does. He understands you better than you know yourself. He knows exactly why you fear the things you do, and how to comfort you when you seek His presence amidst your fear and confusion. God did not allow your pain so you would grow cold towards Him, but so you could experience your need for Him.

As you have seen, He will go to great lengths to show you that He is all you need and to give you an avenue, a platform if you will, to share your story with others. Know that your testimony in Christ is built on healing through the love of Christ. And also know this: God loves you so much, He sovereignly watches over you every moment. Time is not the same for God as it is for you and me. We are confined to a 24-hour day, but God is not. He is not bound by the laws of physics but can go before you as no one else can.

Before you walk into a storm, God already sees you walking out of it. Jesus knows everything about you—including your response to every scenario you could face. You have no secret, no motives, that He does not know. He wants you to follow Him and have confidence in His authority over everything. Even the wind obeys the voice of the Lord. You cannot outrun Him or hide from Him. You are never alone—even when you feel like no one listens or sees you. *Why not ask God to ignite your Holy Spirit in a way that makes it evident that He is with you?* With a thankful heart, praise the ever-present God who is not far off but right in front of you, guiding you along.

270

Day 250

Constant Battles

But the Lord says to Moses, "Do not fear him,
for I have given him into your hands, and all his people, and his land.
And you shall do to him
as you did to Sihon king of the Amorites, who lived at Heshbon."
Numbers 21:34 (ESV)

Life is often one battle after the next. As soon as you have figured out how to live with one challenge, another one comes to light. It can be easy to wonder if you will ever catch a break or if you will always be at war with your mental state. *Will you ever really be able to relax with so many challenges you face?* As soon as one wound starts to heal, another is exposed. *Are you wondering when you can take a break from the heartaches and complexities of life?* Perhaps you feel like you are having to stuff your brain with too much information, too many important concerns, too many responsibilities . . . and it leaves you feeling fearful and overwhelmed. All of that diminishes the power of God's true sovereignty over your life. God wants you not to fear but to trust that He placed you in this battle. God wants your relationship to be built on trust—for you to trust Him with all your heart. But how do you build trust? You remember His faithfulness of the past. You remember His evident love for you. And God shows you how to trust Him more through the battles of life.

Are you fighting a battle against the sovereignty of God? You cannot win that battle, but if you put your trust in His sovereignty, then you can be free not to fear all the battles you are facing. God wants to teach you something in every struggle, in every clash and heartbreak. Remember His faithfulness, how He helped you in the past, and allow your confidence in Him to grow. He is in control of the battles you face today, and He will be with you every moment.

Day 251

Acts of God

> *And the Lord said to Joshua,*
> *"Do not fear them, for I have given them into your hands.*
> *Not a man of them shall stand before you"*
> *. . . The Lord threw down large stones from heaven on them,*
> *and they (the enemies) died.*
> *There were more who died because of the hailstones*
> *than the sons of Israel killed with the sword.*
> *At that time Joshua spoke to the Lord and he said in the sight of Israel,*
> *"Sun, stand still at Gibeon, and moon, in the Valley of Aijalon."*
> *And the sun stood still, and the moon stopped.*
> Joshua 10:8, 11b-13 (ESV)

Some insurance policies exclude compensation for certain "acts of God" or "forces of nature." Why? Because God's power in nature can prove so extreme, affecting the world in ways no one can imagine. If you want to be humbled by God's power, think about His sovereignty over nature. When Hurricane Katrina hit New Orleans, God was in control. People helped people in unexpected and significant ways. Though the natural disaster was devastating to many, though much did not make sense, God knew how everything was going to play out. He knew how He was going to protect and provide, encourage and support, and draw thousands closer to Him in faith.

Notice the first line of today's verse says, ". . . for I have given them . . ." God has already decided the outcome and already has a plan for your struggles. When God decides something, He always follows through. There is no Plan B with God. He has control over every resource and can bring down hailstones on the enemy yet keep His children's eternal destiny safe. If you believe with your whole heart that God will reveal His glory through your trial, be prepared to see miracles happen. The outcome may not be what you prayed for, but good things will come from it. Though you may feel like you're getting pelted by hailstones, God knows where each one will land. *Can you accept that maybe God is showing you His sovereign authority?*

272

Day 252

God's Design

Do not fear, for the hand of Saul my father shall not find you.
You shall be king over Israel, and I shall be next to you.
Saul my father also knows this.
1 Samuel 23:17 (ESV)

In this verse, Jonathan is talking to his close friend David, trying to encourage him not to fear Saul's anger and vengeance. Actually, the prophet Samuel had already told Saul that the kingdom would be taken from him because he did not follow the full instruction of the Lord (1 Samuel 15:26). God also told David that he would be king over Israel (1 Samuel 16). Even so, God had David and Saul on a cat-and-mouse chase all over the land (1 Samuel 15–29) as Saul tried to track down and kill his presumed successor to the throne. Yet readers can see God's sovereignty play out: Saul's heart, bent on jealousy and revenge, pulled him further from God while David grew strong in faith. David relied on the Word of the Lord while Saul disobeyed Him. As this story illustrates, God may put you in a place of honor, but if you choose to disobey the voice of God and become prideful of *your* accomplishments, God will humble you.

Are you claiming your successes are your own doing? God's sovereignty is all over your achievements; you can accomplish something only because God designed you that way. God gave you every skill; you can do nothing apart from Christ. In the same way, God puts you in places so you can learn—in the best ways designed for you—to trust Him and become more like Jesus.

David trusted God above all; he was the man after God's own heart. David recognized that God was sovereign and chose not to harm King Saul. Knowing God wanted him to be righteous and faithful, David waited for God to elevate him and make him king over Israel. David relied on the Word of God, and nothing on earth could shake his confidence in the Lord's sovereignty over his life. *Will you wait on the Lord in your heartache, give Him your fears, and trust Him today?*

Day 253

Live at Peace

Do not repay anyone evil for evil.
Be careful to do what is right in the eyes of everybody.
If it is possible, as far as it depends on you, live at peace with everyone.
Do not take revenge, my friends, but leave room for God's wrath,
for it is written: "It is Mine to avenge; I will repay," says the Lord.
On the contrary: "if your enemy is hungry, feed him;
if he is thirsty, give him something to drink.
In doing this, you will heap burning coals on his head."
Do not be overcome by evil but overcome evil with good.
Romans 12:17-21 (NIV)

In your flesh, it's easy to want to get even and settle the score. "So and so" was rude to you, so your attitude toward them is rude as well. Someone lied to you, so you feel you have an excuse to be dishonest with them. Bitterness from unforgiveness will not only put you in despair but dampen your relationship with Christ. Jesus said we are to pray ". . . forgive us our trespasses as we forgive others." How you forgive others should be a reflection of how God forgives you —and if it's not, then you can feel an estrangement from your Redeemer. *Is your unforgiveness worth your separation from Jesus?* God knows why you are bitter and refuse to forgive someone who wronged you. God wants you to forgive because He wants you to release them to your heavenly Judge. Chances are fairly good you are not hurting them by being resentful. You are hurting yourself and hurting your relationship with Christ.

Jesus paid the price for all sin. It is His job to judge each person. Forgiving an abuser does not mean you do not hold them accountable and that you cannot seek justice. But it does mean that you trust God's sovereignty over everyone's life. You trust that He will discipline the people that hurt you. No sinful deed goes unpunished. God knows how to direct all people. God knows how to work forgiveness into the lives of sinners, and we all are sinners. Satan wants you bitter, but Jesus' forgiveness is the only thing that makes you better.

Sovereign

Day 254
Trust Not in the Provisions

Fear not, O land; be glad and rejoice,
for the Lord has done great things!
Fear not, you beast of the field,
for the pastures of the wilderness are green;
the tree bears its fruit; the fig tree and vine give their full yield.
Be glad, O children of Zion, and rejoice in the Lord your God,
for He has given the early rain for your vindication;
He has poured down for you abundant rain,
the early and the latter rain, as before.
"The threshing floors shall be full of grain;
the vats shall overflow with wine and oil.
I will restore to you the years that the swarming locust has eaten,
the hopper, the destroyer, and the cutter,
my great army, which I sent among you . . ."
Joel 2:21-25 (ESV)

In today's verse, God sent the swarming locust that destroyed the prosperity of life. *Have you ever lost everything? Have you experienced the uncertainty of where you will get your next meal or where you will sleep? Have you lost the people or family you have loved?* God has been with you through the storms, but He also wants to show you that He is your Provider, your Comfort, your Hope. He wants to strengthen your faith and show you that He is faithful. And consider this: perhaps you had an idol that needed to be destroyed. Your soul is more important to God than anything, even relationships, even the comforts of life. He knows that the pain you now feel is nothing compared to an eternity separated from Him. And He also knows that, through you and your testimony, He can come alongside you to help bring many more into His kingdom.

Will you praise Him, even in your loss and heartache? Although it may be hard to hear, God sovereignly gives and takes away. God wants you to praise Him because you know He is all you need. When you turn to Him in praise, then many can see His glory! And He promises that, in His timing, He will restore the years the locusts have eaten. Maybe that will be here on earth, and maybe that will be in heaven, but He always keeps His promises.

Sovereign

Day 255

Worthless Idols

Like a scarecrow in a melon patch, their idols cannot speak;
they must be carried because they cannot walk.
Do not fear them; they can do no harm, nor can they do any good.
Jeremiah 10:5 (NIV)

This verse almost sounds silly when first read. Who in the world would idolize a worthless object that needs to be carried? *But when was the last time you cried yourself to sleep with a bottle of alcohol or pills? When was the last time you reached for a substance to numb the pain? Do you gamble too much? Do you shop too much? Are you afraid someone will find out how you stuff the pain through the things you idolize? Do you like to sleep in on Sunday mornings instead of going to church?* Yes, even sleep can be an idol if you choose it over what God has instructed you to do on Sunday morning. *Do you honor the Lord's Day?* Idolizing anything made by human hands is foolish. Worshiping creation and not the Creator is also foolish. Yet so many people want to see their creation lifted up for all to see. Many people fight hard to keep a forest they love, but they will not fight for an unborn baby.

Our culture has gotten many things wrong, accepting so many lies that the truth can seem laughable at times. But God is not laughing. One of the expectations He has set for us is that He alone is worthy of praise and fear. *Are you brave enough to ask God what you idolize?* You may be blinded by your idols and cannot recognize what you are choosing over Him. He will go to great lengths to teach you that He wants to be first in every situation. Blessing follows when you put God in His rightful place, but He will sovereignly put you in your place if you choose to fear losing your idols over fearing Him, the Righteous Judge. God alone is good, and He will show you that praising and honoring Him above all will bring you the peace that surpasses all understanding.

Day 256

He Never Gets Side-Tracked

Jesus found a young donkey and sat upon it, as it is written,
"Do not be afraid, O daughter of Zion;
see your King is coming seated on a donkey colt."
John 12:14-15 (NIV)

Jesus fulfilled over 300 prophecies when He walked the Earth. It would be nearly impossible for any human to stumble along and by chance fulfill a few prophesies, let alone 300. Yet, Jesus knew His mission. He never got side-tracked. He stayed focused, and His focus was set on heading toward the cross. In Bible times, a donkey represented a spirit of humility and peace. The people expected Jesus to ride in on a war horse, not a donkey. Yet the donkey symbolized something powerful: Jesus humbly came to restore peace between humanity and Father God. And fittingly, He will come back on a war horse and put Satan where he belongs.

Through this one act of donkey-riding, at that time in *HIS*tory, Jesus fulfills four prophecies. First, He proves He is greater than Abraham, who put all his supplies on a donkey to offer up his son Isaac (Genesis 22). Next, Moses put his children on a donkey in Exodus 4:20, but Jesus's suffering brings us better redemption than Moses. Of course, Zechariah 9:9 is the verse Jesus quoted in today's verse, John 12:15. Lastly, Jesus is the fulfillment to all the Jewish feasts. His triumphal entry was during the festival of the first fruits, Sefirat Haomer. This signifies Jesus is the first to be resurrected from the dead; He is the first fruit of our faith.

God sovereignly does not overlook details; nothing is too small or large for Him to control. Through Jesus' life on earth, God's redemption plan was fulfilled down to every detail. *What small details do you need to hand over to Christ? In your mind, what seems too small to bother God with?* God gives you the little things, the details of life, to see how you handle them; this is how character is built, one building block at a time. *Will you trust Him today with your life's details?*

Sovereign

Identity

Day 257

Glorious Plans with a Purpose

"For I know the plans I have for you," declares the Lord,
"plans to prosper you and not to harm you,
plans to give you a hope and a future.
THEN you will call upon Me and come and pray to Me,
and I will listen to you.
You will seek Me and find Me when you seek Me with all your heart.
I will be found by you," declares the Lord
"and will bring you back from captivity."
Jeremiah 29:11-14 (NIV)

Close your eyes for a moment and breath in the glory of God. The glory of the Lord is tangible. You can sit in the warmth of His golden white glow and breathe in deeply, into the core of your being. Let His glory fill you completely. Then do not move and meditate on this verse. When you sit in the glory of God, feel His love and compassion. God has a plan for your life that has purpose. He sees you in your hurt and sorrow. He will not waste your pain. Release your pain onto Him. He can carry your burdens; He wants you to cry and let it out. With God, you do not have to act like you have it all together. He is the only One who can make you whole. If you hide some of your brokenness, your healing may not be complete; being totally honest with God is for your benefit, not His. He already knows, looking into your heart and seeing the whole truth.

Do you need hope, a sense of belonging? Have you been an outsider, looking in on your own life for so long that you feel disconnected and numb? God wants to bring you back from captivity—the places, emotions, people, and coping skills that are keeping you in bondage. God sees your need to prosper, but you have to give Him your whole heart. Everything that has shredded your hope can be restored in the loving glow of God glory. *In the glory of God, will you allow yourself to know you are significant to Him and that He loves you?* In the glory of God, you will find your identity. Now please reread this day's message from the beginning and do all it suggests.

278

Day 258

The Key to Unlock Your Burdens

When I say, "My foot is slipping"
Your love, oh Lord, supported me. When anxiety was great within me,
Your consolation brought joy to my soul . . .
The Lord has become my fortress,
and my God the Rock in whom I take refuge.
Psalm 94:18-19, 22 (NIV)

In what areas of your life does your foot tend to slip? Do your thoughts and reactions seem to slip back down the slippery slope into increased anxiety and despair? God cannot console what you will not bring to Him. God's love will support you when you turn to Him and honestly bring Him the chains that are bogging you down. God has the keys you need to unlock the burdens of your heart. *How can you find the Lord as your Rock?* By standing on the Word of God— reading it daily, sitting quietly before Him, opening your heart to Him in prayer. When you put Him in charge of your life, then He will help you gain control over your decisions that lead to peace and confidence.

In your walk with Christ, you have an assurance that Satan cannot take away. Satan may try to deceive you, but rest assured you cannot be taken from Christ. You are fully sealed in the blood of the Lamb. You are completely free in Christ. Your identity depends on the work of Jesus, not on yourself. It is God's work to sanctify you; it is God's faithfulness you can trust. Your identity is not your surroundings but in who Christ made you. Your identity needs to surrender to God's identity He placed in you. His Holy Spirit is part of your identity in Christ. Get accustomed to the fire of the Spirit and see all that God intends for you. He alone can understand your deepest sorrows and biggest disappointments. Clinging to Christ, your identity in Christ will shine, confident in who God says you are.

Day 259

Dwelling with You

God is so vast, it is impossible to fully grasp His holy glory. He sits on a throne in heaven, and He sits with you, including the moments when your life lies in the bottom of a pit. When darkness has completely covered your mind and you sit slumped over, feeling crazy and out of control, God wants you to know He is dwelling with you. You may not feel Him because your darkness looms so heavy, but He is there.

Do you know that He will not allow your depression to overtake you? Do you recognize that He is guarding you from the cliff? He is waiting for you to remember Him. Let us go to the Lord in prayer: "Lord, when I find myself in the dark places, please help me remember to pause and recognize You are with me. Teach me O God. I ask You to increase my faith so I experience its peace and know You are with those like me—broken and shattered. God, thank You for knowing my need for You to dwell with me. Your Holy Spirit can teach me to put all my hope in You and Your saving grace. Thank You for that reassurance. Thank You, Lord, for allowing me to rest my spirit in the heavenly places with You. For You made me an immortal being by Your grace. When I step into heaven, my eyes will see what my heart knows. Your perfect plan will bring me safely home to You in eternity. Lord, make me the image bearer You want me to be, regardless of life's difficulties. I love You, Lord. In Jesus' name, Amen." You can talk to God daily in a prayer like this or one completely new, speaking to Him like a friend and pouring out your soul. He loves you, and He will revive you to live this life with joy and for His glory.

Day 260

Rely on God

Keep your life free from the love of money,
and be content with what you have, for He has said,
"I will never leave you nor forsake you. So we can confidently say,
"The Lord is my helper; I will not fear; what can man do to me?"
Hebrews 13:5-6 (ESV)

A poor person can love money just as much as a rich person. Both can be equally anxious to obtain more. Both can feel like more might make them content, but when they have more, it fails to bring contentment. *When you cannot get a job and your money runs out, where are you going to stand? Are you going to stand in fear and hopelessness, or are you going to trust that the Provider has provision for you?* In your trust, you can see the miracles of your gas tank not running out of gas, the $20 bill you just so happened to find on the sidewalk, the neighbor who brings you a meal for no special reason. God works through people in beautiful ways. Also, do not overlook the prompting that God places in your mind so you can be the miracle someone else needs as well.

God knows what we all need. Certainly, money proves an extremely important part of life, and He provides your job and your skills; He also ordains how much money you make. You can be certain He will help you provide for your physical needs, but God cares so much more about you; He does not stop there. He also fulfills your spiritual need for Christ to sanctify you in every area. Your emotional well-being also becomes solid when you rely on God to help you through life. Put your whole heart into trusting God's way of helping you. Your whole identity should be wrapped up in trusting His help, His ability to provide for your needs. *In the moment, how content are you with where God has placed you? He continues to help you daily with your sin problem, so what makes you think He cannot help you with your other fears, like your money woes?* Trust Him!

Day 261

Confronting Troubles

Praise be to the God and Father of our Lord Jesus Christ,
the Father of compassion and the God of all comfort,
who comforts us in all our troubles,
so that we can comfort those in any trouble
with the comfort we ourselves have received from God.
For just as the suffering of Christ flows over into our lives,
so also through Christ our comfort overflows.
2 Corinthians 1:3-5 (NIV)

Have you submitted your heart to the compassion of Christ? Can you even recognize Christ's compassion in your life? You have not because you ask not. It is alright to ask God to show up in specific ways, and He will answer you in a way that you can obviously tell is Him. Yet, it can prove difficult to see God's compassion when you choose not to run to Him when life gets hard—especially when you have stuffed your heart with temporary fixes. God makes it clear He wants to be first in your life. He is the Giver and the Sustainer of life. He should not be an after-thought, but has profound things to teach you during your suffering. Jesus suffered greatly on the cross, and through His suffering, you have the blessing of being saved by grace.

God does not waste suffering; He uses our suffering to shape us into the character of Christ. *God wants to teach you, but are you willing to learn*? During your suffering as well as your moments of pure contentment, He is right there with you. He understands where your mind is focused, better than any human being. *Why not cry out to the Lord when your heart is broken and you feel like you cannot take another breath?* Your healing should be wrapped up in the Healer. Moreover, God comforts you not only for your own benefit but so you can do the same for others. He wants you to share your tips of faith with the people you encounter who are experiencing a season of suffering. He wants you to share what you learn in your personal time with God. And remember, you are nowhere by coincidence.

Day 262

Include God in the Equation

Act with courage, and may the LORD be with those who do well.
2 Chronicles 19:11 (NIV)

God wants you to reflect on your life and think through or consider your habits and actions. And when you do so, you are to include God in the equation, with no fear of doing the will of the Lord. You will do well when you give your healing to God and allow Him to show you how to contemplate what is of God and what is not. Healing is not easy, but being whole in Christ is possible when you act with courage. You are not a coward in Christ. Jesus is courageously bold, and as an image bearer of Christ, you can align your identity with boldness. Fearful people do not reach their maximum, God-given potential. People who are courageous for Christ do well in life, meaning that they are open to receiving God's blessings of peace, joy, love, hope, contentment . . . and the list goes on. Obviously, these blessings can affect every aspect of your life.

God created you uniquely different than everyone else. And yes, you can and should love who God created you to be. Therefore, do not dwell in self-condemnation. *Instead, why not ask God why you look down on yourself? Why do you speak critically to yourself in the mirror, or maybe why won't you even look at yourself in the mirror?* God creates both outgoing people and shy people; both types are perfectly created in the image of Christ. There is nothing wrong with being shy, but it should not prove an excuse for lacking courage. The opposite is true for the outgoing person; being outgoing is not an excuse for you to over-dramatize and make a scene. Satan wants your perspective of yourself to be critical and harsh, but God wants your identity to rest in who He says you are. As a child of God, you have the Holy Spirit alive and active inside you. Have the courage to let His power radiate through you. As a child of God, having supernatural courage becomes your God-given right.

Day 263

Confident in the Word

"Be strong all you people of the land," declares the LORD.
"Work, for I AM with you," declares the LORD of hosts,
"according to the covenant that I made with you
when you came out of Egypt.
My Spirit remains in your midst. Fear not."
Haggai 2:4b-5 (ESV)

The Holy Spirit within you connects you to God, and this connection allows His Spirit to remain in your midst. God has worked for you and does not want you discouraged by the negative influences around you. *Since God is not ready for you to quit, why are you neglecting certain things of God? Why are you not rebuilding the things God is specifically asking you to rebuild?*

In the short book of Haggai, God says to "give careful thought" five different times. While He sits on His throne in heaven, He looks for His children who exhibit integrity, for those who give careful thought and act in love and respect. He watches to see who lives their life completely dependent upon His strength. Just like in Mark 5:30-34 when the woman who is bleeding touches Jesus' garment and He feels His power go out of Himself and into her, God knows when you tap into His power and use His strength. The Bible has much to say about integrity. Your honesty at the heart level proves extremely important to God. He blesses your integrity and wants you to genuinely love other people but is not interested in how good of an actor you are.

Have confidence in doing the Lord's work, for He designed work specifically for you, but in the midst of it, God wants you to remember His covenant. Love the Lord your God with all your heart, soul, and mind, and love your neighbor as yourself. Work like it all depends on you while knowing you can do nothing apart from Christ. God's Spirit will confirm the work you are doing if it conforms to His will, but if it does not, He may let you know in your spirit that you should distance yourself from it. *Does God know you as a person with great integrity?*

Day 264

Taken Out of Context

Your life will be brighter than the noonday;
its darkness will be like the morning.
And you will feel secure, because there is hope;
you will look around and take your rest in security.
You will lie down, and none will make you afraid;
many will court your favor.
Job 11:17-19 (ESV)

The book of Job is known for presenting extreme suffering. Job was one of the most upright people of the day, and Satan wanted to test his faith in God. Why would God allow Satan to do this? It was not to punish Job for a past sin; in fact, God knew Job's heart was full of integrity and that he would pass the test. Instead, God entrusted the test to Job to prove that people committed to God can navigate extreme suffering and keep their faith in a perfect, faithful God.

Job offers an example for each Christian to follow. We can plant our identity in knowing we serve a faithful God who uses suffering to shape our character. What Satan means for evil, God means for good. Job proved that God is good, all the time, and is listening when people dispute this truth with their friends. Certainly, the book of Job can prove confusing if you do not know the end of the book. Job continues to praise God, and God goes on to bless Job for his faithfulness, just as He will do for us, whether on this side of heaven or in heaven itself.

In today's verse, one of Job's friends is accusing Job of sinning; he thinks sin is the reason Job is suffering such agony. Yet, Job's friends are speaking half-truths, putting their words in the wrong context. They want him to repent of some secret sin, not believing God would cause such despair unless sin were the culprit. So, believe this: not all your woes result from your sin. Sometimes the only way to fully understand God's glory is to endure extreme suffering first-hand. *Are you tolerating friends verbally judging you for your suffering?* Know your identity in Christ, put your faith in Him, and give God glory amidst your suffering; He will bless you through it.

Day 265
Build Your Spiritual Muscles

My beloved, as you have always obeyed,
so now, not only in my presence but much more in my absence,
work out you own salvation with fear and trembling,
for it is God who works in you,
both to will and to work for His good pleasure.
Do all things without grumbling or disputing,
that you may be blameless and innocent,
children of God without blemish in the midst of a crooked
and twisted generation, among whom you shine as lights of the world,
hold fast to the Word of life.
Philippians 2:12-16a (ESV)

Working out your salvation necessitates a daily commitment to God. You have to build your spiritual muscles, yet if you get lazy and stop growing your relationship with Christ, allowing the Holy Spirit to work in and through you, you will lapse into spiritual apathy. You can enjoy an extremely close relationship with God and then let distractions get the best of you. You can have good intentions all day long, but unless you make your intentions a reality, you are wasting time.

God wants you to be intentional in everything. He wants your healing, your devotion to Him and love for others, all to be intentional. God does not do things haphazardly, so neither should you. Not by chance do you feel God's presence somedays and feel distant on others. He is always with you, but if you feel separation between you and Christ, it's due to your lack of intentionality with God. When you study God's Word intentionally, you learn God's will and see that during different phases of life, the Holy Spirit highlights different biblical topics for you.

God wants you intentional in your prayer life and thankful in all circumstances. A thankful heart does not grumble. God wants you to bring Him your burdens and speak your mind in prayer, but grumbling is when your complaint comes with anger. Grumbling is a lack of trust in God's sovereignty. God's way is not the world's way, and He wants to change your perspective. *Is your identity wrapped up in pleasing God by being intentional in choosing to live for Him?*

Day 266

Your Role Is Still the Same

You will hear of wars and rumors of wars. See that you are not alarmed,
for this must take place, but the end is not yet.
For nation will rise against nation, and kingdom against kingdom,
and there will be famines and earthquakes in various places.
All these are but the beginning of the birth pains.
Then they will deliver you up to tribulation and put you to death,
and you will be hated by all nations for My name's sake.
And then many will fall away and betray one another
and hate one another.
And many false prophets will arise and lead many astray.
And because lawlessness will be increased,
the love of many will grow cold.
But the one who endures to the end will be saved.
And this gospel of the Kingdom will be proclaimed
throughout the whole world as a testimony to all nations,
and then the end will come.
Matthew 24:6-14 (ESV)

Only God knows when Jesus is returning. But the birthing pains do seem stronger these days. You see the sad state of affairs around the world. Our culture makes celebrities out of people who sin. Politics is a divisive, heart-wrenching free for all. Clearly, lying is now the norm. Human trafficking and abuse are prevalent. Depression seems rampant. Plus, we have one natural disaster after another. All these examples could be the birth pains of Jesus returning. Regardless if Jesus comes tomorrow or 1,000 years from now, your role, your call, is still the same. Your pursuit of a relationship with Jesus should be your number one priority every day. When you spend time with Jesus, you encounter the people God wants you to meet—and then you do what God wants you to do: show off His glory through your testimony of faith. *God has warned us that we will see love grow cold, that we will be hated and betrayed, so why are you surprised when it happens to you? Jesus left you His peace, but are you frantic where God has placed you?* Keep your eyes fixed on Jesus, and God will give you the strength you need. This is part of His plan.

Day 267

Here I Am, Lord

Moses was leading his flock and came to Hebron,
the mountain of God, and the Angel of the LORD appeared to him
in a flame of fire out of the midst of a bush.
He looked, and behold, the bush was burning, yet it was not consumed.
And Moses said, "I will turn aside to see this great sight,
why this bush is not burning."
When the Lord saw that he turned aside to see,
God called to him out of the bush, "Moses, Moses!"
And he said, "Here I am."
The Lord said, "I have surely seen the affliction of My people
and have heard their cry because of their taskmasters.
I know their suffering, and I have come down to deliver them.
Come, I will send you."
But Moses said to God,
"Who am I that I should go to Pharaoh and bring
the children of Israel out of Egypt?"
God said, "I will be with you."
Then Moses said, "If I come to the people of Israel
and say to them the God of your fathers sent me to you and they ask me,
what is His name? What shall I say to them?"
God said to Moses, "I AM who I AM. I AM has sent you.
This is My name forever,
and thus I AM to be remembered throughout all generations.
Go, I promise that I will bring you up out of the afflictions."
Exodus 3:1-17 (ESV Paraphrased)

God has called each person who has trusted in Jesus to a duty that will end someone's suffering and affliction. God is telling you to "go." Moses had excuses for why he should not lead the people out of slavery. *Are you, like Moses, looking at your shortcomings as an excuse not to do what the Lord has called you to?* The Lord may have set you up for an impossible task, but He promised He will go with you, just as He did with Moses. You cannot see God's miracles unless you are willing to turn and look for His Holy Fire among your steps in the wilderness. Just obey in faith that God will give you the words to speak at the right time, and He will give you a way out if the road looks closed. In prayer, God wants to meet you at the "burning bush." He wants you to see Him in His rightful place and with His Holy Fire. He wants to burn away certain aspects to purify you in His sight. He wants to burn away just enough so you can find the end of yourself, allowing Him to truly take over. This is when you can see your miracle, and then God clearly gets all the glory. God is the great I AM; no one is His equal. *What is in your heart that the great I AM needs to fill? Do you have a need for security, love, joy, or acceptance?* Meeting Jesus at the "burning bush," you will find these things your heart desires. *What do you need to surrender to the Great I AM so you can be as bold as Moses and confidently say, "Here I am, Lord"?* This is one of the best things to say after you accept His atonement for your sins.

Day 268

Interrupted Plans

One night the Lord spoke to Paul in a vision:
"Do not be afraid; keep on speaking, do not be silent.
For I AM with you,
and no one is going to attack and harm you
because I have many people in this city."
Acts 18:9-10 (NIV)

Paul was a devote Jew who persecuted the Christians until he met with Jesus on the road to Damascus. Paul thought he was doing the work of God, but in fact, he was doing Satan's work. He needed to be set on a completely different path. Just like this encounter, God interrupted Paul's plans over and over. When Paul and Barnabas went their own way in Acts 15:36-41 . . . interrupted. When Paul thought he was on his way to Rome and ended up stranded on an island in Acts 27:27-44 . . . interrupted. In Acts 18, Paul was interrupted again when he wanted to preach the Gospel to both Jews and Gentiles; God used the abuse Paul endured and the discord in the Corinth synagogue for a good purpose, sending him to preach just to the Gentiles.

Will you obey God's voice when He interrupts your plans and sends you in a new direction? Are you pouting that the good ole days are over, frustrated with where you are now? God has always placed people strategically. God, who creates every soul, knows everything that person will ever do. God could have placed you in any time in *HIS*tory, but He put you here today. That's God's design. We live in a world where people know about Jesus, but many don't learn who He is; thus, they make up wild, unbiblical notions. They do things apart from God's plan because they don't invest the time to know His plan. God wants you not to fear using your voice to express your trust in the freedom in Christ so you can create a spark in someone that will align them with God's direction. Obey God's will and share your voice in a manner that pleases God, edifying, building others up, not tearing people down. Your words have power; keep speaking the truth.

Day 269

Choose Faith Over Fear

See the Lord your God has set the land before you.
Go up, take possession, as the Lord, the God of your father's,
has told you. Do not fear or be dismayed.
Deuteronomy 1:21 (ESV)

When these words were declared, the people of God chose not to listen. Instead, they chose to grumble and rebel. They ended up spending 40 years roaming the wilderness because they chose fear over obeying God's instructions. In your flesh, some people may seem intimidating, scary, and even evil, but you serve a God who is in control. He knows what is happening in the world He created. Nothing is more powerful than God, no one is smarter than God, and no one on earth can so dramatically change the heart of men as God Himself. God had a victory planned in today's verse, but the people chose fear over faith. God wanted them to claim the victory that would come, giving them peace on the other side, but they were too afraid of the land's inhabitants. They did not hold God in awe and respect in faith. God is worthy of your obedience to everything He says to do.

In your life, what land is God wanting you to claim? Where does He want you to start? God wants you to make your job, your family, your schoolwork, your livelihood, or something else your own, clearing out the negative influences, cleaning out the bad habits and ways of treating others, but you have to obey Him and take action. *What about "it" looks so scary that you are afraid to claim it? Does God want you to purge the sinful surroundings you are in? Does He want to move you to an unfamiliar place? Does He want you to look hard at the truth, even though it makes you uncomfortable, so that you can show honesty and integrity in a certain area?* He has a plan for you to obey, but you must make His courage your own to take possession of the land He is giving you.

Day 270

He Is Teaching You

"Do not fear, O Jacob My servant," says the LORD,
"For I AM with you; for I will make a complete end of all the nations
to which I have driven you, but I will not make a complete end of you.
I will rightly correct you, for I will not leave you wholly unpunished."
Jeremiah 46:28 (NKJV)

God wants you to discover that He is the answer to everything, but first He will bring discipline to your life. He might have scattered your loved ones far and wide, but Father God has a purpose in the pain; He knows how to direct your attention to His lessons, His words, His perspective, and His blessings. *Are you faithful with all He is teaching you? Are you sensitive to God's voice?* When you faithfully learn His teachings, He renews you. He restores you to a place that is dependent upon Him and not your circumstances. God put you in your nation or your area because that is exactly where He needs you to be. Your neighborhood might not be as nice or clean as you hoped, but you can come alongside others or do your part on your own to help your neighbors and the community. Perhaps God allows certain things to annoy you so you can either learn contentment or do something about it. God wants you to be thankful in all circumstances. *If you are not, what are you doing to bring improvement?*

Do you bless the Holy Spirit or grieve Him in your conduct? God sees the people who belittle you. *Do you trust that Jesus is disciplining them? Do you pridefully look at the filth of the world and think you are better than your neighbors?* You hold your position in life only because God put you there. *Can you humbly accept where you are? Are you mature enough to know you are saved by grace alone?* Your judgment on those around you will fall back into your lap. God will judge you as you judge others. Lies get exposed, and the truth is, God will set your pride straight if you do not grow in self-awareness through the Holy Spirit and heed His warning.

Day 271

Do What Is Right

For rulers hold no terror for those who do right,
but for those who do wrong.
Do you want to be free from fear of the one in authority?
Then do what is right and he will commend you.
Romans 13:3 (NIV)

How comfortable are you with the idea of people having authority over you? Has someone abused this kind of power in your life? And now you feel resistant to others' authority? When someone distorts his or her authority and has a power trip and control problem over your life, this does not reflect godly authority. It's actually straight from Satan, who wants your vision blurred on authority in the family and the government. We need to follow laws, family rules, and the commandments of God as they are the safe boundaries that God has called you to live by; as you abide by this authority, it can also bless others.

Some people would make their lives easier if they learned to submit to authority. When a cop says stop, you stop, period. But we live in a world where people hold guns, standing on two sides of a street and blocking access, wanting to know why you want to drive down "their" street. Say the wrong thing . . . and where are the cops? This exemplifies the evil in our world. Some people don't care about killing another person. They do not obey the government, and we all suffer for it. People might steal your car and not care about its devastation to you and your family.

God knows we need officers of the law to hold evil men accountable for those who have been violated. God places government protection in our society. You should be thankful He set up our system this way, because had He not, more tragedies would ensue. You may not like the political party in office, but overall, it protects the greater good of law and order. *These rules are for your safety, so why not ask God why you fear them and to help you overcome your fear?*

293

Day 272

Accept Victory

*The Lord said to Joshua, "Do not be afraid of them,
because by this time tomorrow I will hand them over."*
Joshua 11:6 (NIV)

Joshua was about to lead the people of Israel into a battle against many kings. Joshua 11:4 says they were fighting against ". . . a great horde of people, like the sand on the seashore"—thus outnumbered by human standards. God told Joshua that He would hand them over to his army, so Joshua put his faith in God's ability; he chose to obey God's voice. Dependent upon God's direction, Joshua followed through, exactly the way God instructed. Joshua took the land God promised them, engaging in battle to do so, but he was willing to let God use him.

Joshua saw the generation before him, those too afraid to go and obey the Word of God. Joshua had wandered in the wilderness with them, but he was a warrior for God. Thus, God allowed Joshua to bring punishment to the sinful inhabitants of the Promised Land. God wanted them completely removed so the Israelites, God's chosen people, would not become intrigued by the evil practices. God is a holy God, and He will burn away sin. There is a day coming when you will get to rest from all the wars of life, but until then, God wants you to exhibit the confidence of Joshua. God will hand over the oppressors and abusers to Satan, those that refuse to put their faith and trust in our Redeemer. *Have you learned to depend upon God's faithfulness over your life? Will you trust and obey with tenacity as Joshua did?*

Day 273

Jesus Prays for You

Behold, Satan demanded to have you, that he might sift you like wheat,
but I Jesus have prayed for you that your faith may not fail,
and when you have turned again, strengthen your brothers.
Luke 22:31-33 (ESV)

Jesus has prayed that your faith will not fail. Essentially, He has prayed for you to have complete faith in His power, authority, goodness, peace, love, and patience. Satan wants to break you down; in fact, he demanded to have you. But God wants you to put all your faith in Him. *Why do you have a hard time believing God and taking Him at His Word? Has it seemed like the demands and sorrows of life have broken and shattered your heart so you do not see how Christ could ever mend you?* Dear child of God, your confidence should rest solely on Jesus. Satan does not have dominion over you. Jesus has dominion over Satan and over you. God wants you to learn how to resist the Devil's temptations. You will fail repeatedly, but keep trying, relying on the Holy Spirit to guide you.

You can carve out your own path with Christ, but it takes persistence. Your faith cannot grow if you don't cultivate your relationship with Him or if you don't call upon your faith when Satan is shaking up your life. *Satan knows your triggers that can spin you out of control, but have you faithfully asked God to heal your triggers?* When God does so, your triggers can no longer torment you. They no longer do Satan's bidding but, instead, your healing gives proof to God's glorious work in you. *Are you bold enough to ask Christ to reveal and heal your red flags, the indicators that you are still letting fear drive you and not living by faith?*

Day 274

Peace That Surpasses Understanding

By faith Moses, when he was born,
was hidden for three months by his parents,
because they saw that the child was beautiful,
and they were not afraid of the king's edict.
By faith Moses, when he was grown up,
refused to be called the son of Pharaoh's daughter,
choosing rather to be mistreated with the people of God
than to enjoy the fleeting pleasures of sin.
He considered the reproach of Christ greater wealth
than the treasures of Egypt, for he was looking to the reward.
By faith he left Egypt, not being afraid of the anger of the king,
for he endured as seeing him who is invisible.
By faith he kept the Passover and sprinkled the blood,
so that the Destroyer of the firstborn might not touch them.
Hebrews 11:23-28 (ESV)

Moses had extraordinary faith in God, but his parents did, too, not fearing the king's edict. They had peace that surpasses all understanding because God gave them that peace. God also gave them the notion that they needed to hide their beautiful baby boy. Through faith in God's will, you can be confident in what you are doing as well.

Repeatedly, Moses chose faithfully to obey God. Moses was a leader, not because he put himself there but because God elevated him as a result of his faith. *Do you have faith that God will elevate you to where He wants you to succeed, or are you trying to force your way to the top?* Moses did not get to enter the Promised Land, but he kept his faith in God's eternal plan. This side of heaven God does not heal all wounds or answer all prayers with a "yes." *Can you trust that God almighty will make things clear when you step into the Promised Land of heaven? Can you have faith that Jesus' work on the cross was enough for you to forgive the person who tormented and abused you? Can you have faith the unjust will stand before the Just Judge?* Jesus is your Passover, the firstborn of all creation and the first to be resurrected. Only because of the work of Christ can you stand faithfully with God.

Day 275

A Calling on Your Life

Jesus said to Peter, "Do not be afraid;
from now on you will be catching men,"
so they left everything and followed Him.
Luke 5:10-11 (ESV Paraphrased)

Just before this verse, Jesus performed the miracle of catching a huge number of fish, demonstrating He is Lord over creation. Peter responded by falling at Jesus' feet, saying, "Depart from me, for I am a sinful man, O Lord." Peter knew he was sinful—we all are—but he did not yet understand the weight of Jesus' response in today's verse. Essentially, Jesus was saying, "Do not fear your sin, for the great I AM will carry your burden to the cross, and you are going to tell the world about it." Peter was Jesus' first disciple, and He immediately put a calling on Peter's life. Today you have the same calling: Jesus tells us to go into all the world and preach the Gospel.

Do you feel ashamed to admit what has happened to you? Does shame linger over your heart, reminding you of the ugliness of your thoughts or actions? Because God set you free, learn to live in that freedom. God does not want you to fear the fact that you are a sinful human. He wants you to admit your guilt so you can change your ways. One way to change? Ask God to help you be open and tender with people, placing Him in the middle, sometimes as the focus, of your conversations with others. Talking things through with both God and safe people will help you grow, teaching you how to talk about God and all He is doing right there in the mess of life. Sharing the Gospel is not always about going halfway across the globe. Sometimes, it simply means going to dinner with someone or making a phone call. Learning to live through the work of the cross, you can show off your God-given glory. This change in your thought, words, and actions does not become a prideful boast on your accomplishments, but rather your excitement for how God has worked in your life, which overflows to others. Let your words, your cup, overflow today!

Day 276

Make Impossible Possible

The disciples came to Jesus privately and said,
"Why could we not cast it (the demon) out?"
He said to them, "Because of your little faith.
For truly, I say to you, if you have faith like a grain of mustard seed,
you will say to this mountain, 'Move from here to there,'
and it will move, and nothing will be impossible for you."
Matthew 17:19-21 (ESV)

Notice how the Bible says that the disciples went to Jesus privately. Many conversations you have with Christ should be this way: private. When your relationships are falling apart, it should be between you and Jesus first. When you are tired of the abuse and finally decide to leave, it should be Jesus leading you safely out. When you faithfully run to Jesus with your demonic issues, your spirit of depression, your spirit of distraction, He can cast out all that is not of Him. When you faithfully run to Jesus, you do not have time to talk out your issue with too many people. Yes, God puts people in your path so you can learn from them, but running to them first is not option one. People can distort the truth, and people can diminish your faith in God's solution.

Do you have a mountain of problems but only little faith you will overcome them? Jesus can make your impossible possible. Jesus' disciples saw Him perform many miracles, yet still they had no faith to cast out a demon. These disciples' lack of faith is recorded to encourage you. Have mercy on yourself when your faith seems small, and ask God to fill you with His faithful Spirit. When your spirit is full of His Spirit, no room is left for the spirits sent from Satan. Have complete faith that God will redeem your every cell. The disciples, too, had to learn, not fully understanding who Jesus was until after He was resurrected. Today you have the Spirit's power inside you, and your faith can grow first to the size of a "mustard seed," which can move the mountains of heartache in your life, and then stronger still, making the impossible possible, giving Him glory.

Day 277

Sovereignly Placed

"Do not fear, O Jacob My servant; do not be dismayed, O Israel,"
declares the Lord. "I will surely save you out of a distant place,
your descendants from the land of their exile,
Jacob will again have peace and security. And no one will make him afraid,
I AM with you and will save you."
Jeremiah 30:10-11a (NIV)

Has God set you in a distant place? Perhaps it's not your home; perhaps it's uncomfortable. *Have you felt out of place, like you don't belong there? Where does your faith stand in the face of the unfamiliar? Can you faithfully trust that God sovereignly placed you where He wants you to be, where you can learn to trust Him more?*

If you've been wrongly accused and are now being punished for someone else's folly, it can seem like justice for you is out of reach. If so, you may feel dismayed, but take heart; God knows what your heart yearns for. *God wants to save you from feeling distant, but are you seeking His familiar presence? Are you listening faithfully for the saving grace of His voice?* Your family could have raised you in a way that led you astray, but God is faithful to stay the course with His children. He wants to lead you down a straight and narrow path, not one filled with doubt but filled with faith in God's faithfulness. God will restore you on the path that leads you home. Ask Him now to allow you to sense His presence and see Him provide for the details in your life amidst the pain. As you begin to see His fingerprints everywhere and feel His love grow in your heart, you will become faithful in your distant places. He is with you and will bring you peace.

Faith

Day 278

The Righteous Will Never Be Moved

Praise the LORD! Blessed is the man who fears the LORD,
who greatly delights in His commandments!
His offspring will be mighty in the land;
the generation of the upright will be blessed.
Wealth and riches are in His house,
and His righteousness endures forever.
Light dawns in the darkness for the upright;
He is gracious, merciful, and righteous.
It is well with the man who deals generously and lends,
who conducts his affairs with justice.
For the righteous will never be moved;
he will be remembered forever. He is not afraid of bad news;
his heart is firm, trusting in the LORD. His heart is steady;
He will not be afraid, until he looks in triumph on his adversaries.
He has distributed freely; he has given to the poor;
his righteousness endures forever; his horn is exalted in honor.
The wicked man sees it and is angry;
he gnashes his teeth and melts away;
the desire of the wicked will perish!
Psalm 112:1-10 (ESV)

In today's verse titled, "The Righteous Will Never Be Moved," *never* is a long time. *What occurrence or circumstance can you say with certainty will never happen?* In our humanness, we change; we do not stay the same. Certainly, those in Christ are being sanctified, and God is calling you into a new life, a new light. He expects you to change, but He is never-changing, never-failing, always gracious, merciful, and righteous. You are righteous because of the cross, not because of anything you do or say, and you never have to be separated from Christ.

Your faith in Jesus gives you riches not of this world. They are deep-seeded in your soul—eternal. But for now, let His love reach your heart's deepest parts. Your confidence in His healing grows when you experience your heart lifted into God's presence. Being grounded in the never-changing God will keep you steady when bad news comes. *What news are you afraid of getting that it is stopping you from moving forward?* God smiles upon those who have a firm heart of faith in Him.

300

Day 279

*And when He got into the boat, His disciples followed him.
And behold, there arose a great storm on the sea,
so that the boat was being swamped by the waves;
but He was asleep. And they went and woke Him, saying,
"Save us, Lord; we are perishing." And He said to them,
"Why are you afraid, O you of little faith?"
Then He rose and rebuked the winds and the sea,
and there was a great calm. And the men marveled, saying,
"What sort of man is this, that even winds and sea obey Him?"*
Matthew 8:23-27 (ESV)

When you follow Jesus, He will lead you into storms. You can count on it. Jesus was following the will of God, and the will of God brought them right into high winds and pouring rain. Meanwhile, Jesus was sleeping, displaying His complete faith in Father God. He was not worried, but the disciples were anxious and claimed to be perishing. They set their minds on what they thought would happen.

Have you set your mind on a situation's outcome, putting God "in a box"? God is the God of the unexpected. You cannot understand how He will work wonders, but faith is trusting that He will come through. God has a way of bringing you through the downpours, the sorrows of life, but you need faith that He will keep you safe. Just as Jesus was sleeping through the storm, confident God would keep Him safe, you can have the same confidence. You can rest in the safety of God when the waves come crashing.

Why are you afraid of the storms of life? Why can you not relax in the peace of the Lord? When your faith in Christ's promises grow, you will see God stop the waves from crushing you, but if you do perish, a glorious day of celebration in heaven awaits. Death is the door to your eternal destination, but until then, God gives you peace amidst the trials. Be still and rejoice in Him today.

Day 280

Eyes Fixed on Jesus

"I will set shepherds over them who will care for them,
and they shall fear no more, nor be dismayed,
neither shall any be missing," declares the Lord.
"Behold, the days are coming," declares the Lord,
"when I will raise up for David a righteous Branch
and He shall reign as King and deal wisely
and shall execute justice and righteousness in the land."
Jeremiah 23:4-5 (ESV)

Jesus is the Righteous Branch, and the days have come; you get to live out the blessed promise of Jesus. You belong in the Tree of Life through the work on the cross. *Who grafted you into the family of God?* Jesus Himself. Your nourishment comes directly from the Source, and He will not forget anyone. He hears everyone who turns to Him and cries out to Him to save them from their sins. When your sins break you, you are gaining a godly perspective, and God is watching. He will deal wisely with you, not wanting to hurt you in times of testing but to shape you and build character in Him. God wants you to have deep roots in the soil of the Righteous Branch.

When Jeremiah prophesied these words, he was talking to the remnant of the Jewish people. They were the survivors of the exiled, but are remembered as the faithful ones, choosing to keep their eyes fixed on God. Following God is always a choice, one choice after the next. You choose the redemption of the cross. You choose to be joyous in the Lord. You choose to learn the Word of God. And you choose to do the work of the Word. God gave you free will, but He is testing His people to see who will be the most loyal to Him. God is looking for those who worship Him in Spirit and truth (John 4:24). He has a special blessing for the ones who experience and endure torment but keep their eyes focused on the Giver of Life. You can be one who faithfully does so—and someday you will see that all was fully worth it.

Day 281

Reassuring Love

My sheep hear My voice, and I know them, and they follow Me.
I give them eternal life, and they will never perish,
and no one will snatch them out of My hands.
John 10:27-28 (ESV)

Allow yourself to receive the Gospel into the depths of your soul; nothing is excluded from the washing in Jesus' blood. Do not discredit His grace by continuing to hold yourself down over your past mistakes. You are pure, a new creation! When you trust the work of the cross and don't deny its power, then nothing from your past holds you back. Just realize, anything you put above God is an idol. *Are you making your past an idol by letting it weigh you down?*

Jesus came to speak truth to your life, meaning you have already overcome your past. God already gave you forgiveness. Satan, the liar, whispers past misgivings into your mind to try and confuse you, wanting to discredit Jesus' grace. *Are you tired of listening to the lies? The Shepherd wants to speak truth over your life but can you recognize His voice?* Believing Jesus for your eternal salvation is only the beginning of a beautiful journey. God is holding you, and He wants you to know you can relax when you faithfully follow Him.

Take the next two minutes and complete this activity with Jesus. Close your eyes and ask Jesus to pour His love into you, from the top of your head all the way to your toes, and feel His love, receive His love. Let it pour down your face, down your neck, over your shoulders . . . relax and continue to breath in His love. Feel His love pour over your chest, spilling into your heart. Ask God to mend your broken heart . . . and fill it with

His beauty. Let His love pour over your abs so your gut reactions are filled with His mercy and grace. Continue to feel His love over your hips, embracing the woman or man God created you to be. Let His love pour down your legs, and release all the pent-up anxiety. Let your feet fill up with His love so completely that when you stand, you literally walk in the love of Christ. Lastly, thank God for His reassuring love. Every time you relax in active ways like this with Jesus, you choose to drown out Satan's lies. Focus on Christ's love, and your misaligned attitudes will change, blessing others as you do.

Day 282

Peace in the Name of the Lord

*Let them come to Me for refuge; let them make peace with Me,
yes, let them make peace with Me.*
Isaiah 27:5 (NIV)

Gospel

The only way to make peace with God is to accept His plan for redemption. God's plans for your life might not look the way you expected. Your dreams, your aspirations, may now look out of reach as your life has taken several detours, landing you in a place that looks much different from who or what you wanted to be. God's straight and narrow path does not always feel straight. Sometimes God brings us on a winding, hilly road, but with God nothing is ever wasted. *Are you frittering away time by not trusting God's direction? Are you choosing to rest in God's peace or choosing to let the world weigh you down?*

God uses every moment to teach you something about Himself and how He wants you to walk out this life with Him. He did not call you to a life of solitude but to one of resting at His side, finding His peace, so you can share His peace with others. We live in a chaotic world, and you must carefully navigate many real dangers. In the redeeming love of Christ, you can walk in His strength and protection. God wants you to find the balance between facing your fears and your ability to find peace in the name of Jesus. It might take time to find your sweet spot, but once you do, you will grow confident in sharing your peace that surpasses understanding with others who feel bogged down by the chaos of today.

Day 283

Empowered by the Cross

As for you, the anointing you received from Him remains in you,
and you do not need anyone to teach you.
But as His anointing teaches you about all things
and as the anointing is real, not counterfeit—
just as it has taught you, remain in Him.
1 John 2:27 (NIV)

Back in the Jewish temple and before Christ died on the cross, the Holy of Holies was the place man could stand or bow in the presence of God's glory, but the priests could enter the room only once a year. When Jesus died on the cross, the veil into the Holy of Holies was literally torn, top to bottom. Now, all who believe have access to the glory of God via His Holy Spirit. Jesus promised to leave a Helper, the Holy Spirit, as our anointing. As Christians, we have the glory of God within us because the Holy Spirit lives in us, empowering us through the cross. We are empowered by the work of Jesus as He left us His Spirit to do His work.

God does not need our help, but He allows us to be part of His eternal plan. Jesus could have opened up the sky and announced He is the only way to heaven, but instead, our loving God left us His Spirit so we could be co-laborers with Him. The more you tap into the work of the Holy Spirit, the more you will be moved to walk in the Holy Spirit's strength. The more you face your battles in the Holy Spirit, the more you will see God move on the battlefield. The more you talk with Jesus in the Spirit, the more you will talk with others in the Spirit. *Are you training yourself to tap into the Spirit?* Your anointing is real, and you have no fear in Christ. The God-man, Jesus, faced His biggest fear on the cross. The only time Jesus was ever separated from Father God was there, on the cross. He chose to be separated from God for a moment in time in order for you to be joined with Christ through His Holy Spirit forever.

Day 284

Acknowledge Sin

Blessed is the one whose transgressions are forgiven;
whose sins are covered.
Blessed is the one whose sin the LORD does not count against them
and in whose spirit is no deceit.
When I kept silent, my bones wasted away
through my groaning all day long.
For day and night Your hand was heavy on me;
my strength was sapped as in the heat of summer.
Then I acknowledged my sin to You and did not cover up my iniquity.
I said, "I will confess my transgressions to the LORD."
And You forgave the guilt of my sin.
Therefore, let all the faithful pray to You while You may be found;
surely the rising of the mighty waters will not reach them.
You are my hiding place; You will protect me from trouble
and surround me with songs of deliverance.
I will instruct you and teach you in the way you should go.
I will counsel you with My loving eye on you.
Do not be like the horse or the mule,
which has no understanding but must be controlled by bit and bridle
or they will not come to you.
Many are the woes of the wicked,
but the LORD's unfailing love surrounds the one who trusts in Him.
Rejoice in the LORD and be glad, you righteous;
sing, all you who are upright in heart!
Psalm 32 (NIV)

Are you carrying around a weight that God does not intend for you to carry? Jesus unshackled the burdens of your sins from you. He took your sins down to Sheol; they are tied to you no more. *You now have freedom to live in joy, but are you?* You can experience sweet freedom by speaking up and admitting your iniquities in full disclosure to our merciful God.

What are you trying to hide? What secrets are you keeping? God wants you to acknowledge all in your life that is sinful in His eyes; He wants you to live in the resurrection power of Jesus Christ. Let your heart be filled with the wonder of worship. You can choose joy. Come to Jesus with an open heart and empty hands.

Day 285

Perceive His Voice

*"The LORD your God will raise up for you a Prophet
like me from among you, from your brothers—
it is to Him you shall listen—
just as you desired of the LORD your God at Horeb
on the day of the assembly, when you said,
'Let me not hear again the voice of the LORD my God
or see this great fire anymore, lest I die.'
And the LORD said to me, 'They are right in what they have spoken.
I will raise up for them a Prophet like you from among their brothers.
And I will put My Words in His mouth,
and He shall speak to them all that I command Him.
And whoever will not listen to My Words
that He shall speak in My name,
I Myself will require it of him.
But the prophet who presumes to speak a word in My name
that I have not commanded him to speak,
or who speaks in the name of other gods,
that same prophet shall die.' And if you say in your heart,
'How may we know the Word that the LORD has not spoken?'—
when a prophet speaks in the name of the LORD,
if the word does not come to pass or come true,
that is a word that the LORD has not spoken;
the prophet has spoken it presumptuously.
You need not be afraid of him . . ."*
Deuteronomy 18:15-22 (ESV)

In Acts 3:22-24, Peter quotes some of today's verses, with Jesus fulfilling their prophetic promises. When God spoke these words back in the days of Deuteronomy, He already knew how every person, in their own will, would respond to Jesus. God sees every detail and sovereignly understands every aspect of every situation, including each time you turn and follow His direction, but He also wants you to be careful; not everyone who claims to hear from the Lord is actually hearing His voice. Ask God for discernment; you already have everything within you to walk in His strength. *Do you ask God to reaffirm the direction you're going, or are you listening to too many opinions and not God's voice?* He wants to reaffirm you and show you how He can lead you to repentance; He will guide you to turn from apathy and diligently recommit to searching for His truth.

Day 286

A Daily Choice

This is what the Sovereign LORD, the Holy One of Israel, says:
"In repentance and rest is your salvation,
in quietness and trust is your strength."
Isaiah 30:15 (NIV)

The Gospel message of Jesus proclaims that He came to seek and save the lost, and when He arose from the dead, He performed the biggest miracle of all. Those who have not asked Jesus into their heart are lost while those who have acknowledged Jesus' saving grace have experienced the biggest miracle in their life. That we have been found innocent because of the blood of Jesus is an amazing miracle. That He allows us to rest in His glory and grace is a wondrous one as well.

Jesus took your punishment for all the sin you have committed— or ever will have committed—but you must admit your sin and turn to God to live for Him. Doing so offers so many life-changing benefits: it makes you aware of what you are doing that does not please God, and it helps you correct your wrong choices, preventing you from sinning down the road.

The freedom you find in the Gospel is first eternal, then daily. You have a daily choice to walk in the freedom of the Gospel. God wants to be first in your life and is unafraid to remove whatever has a less-than-purifying effect on you. He is your Bridge, and you can find rest living the life He planned for you. Rest in knowing your "to do" list does not have to be jam-packed. He wants you to take breaks, to breathe in deeply and seek Him in your pause. In the Ten Commandments, God built in a day of rest. *Are you honoring God by keeping one day a week dedicated to resting in Him? Do you feel lost trying to accomplish so many tasks?* God does not want you to overbook yourself, taking on every project. He wants you to relax and enjoy the life He gave you. When you choose to rest in the Lord as a habit, then you know how to tap into His strength the other six days. Sit in His presence today and absorb the Son like you absorb the sun.

Day 287

A Testimony to God's Work

I want you to know, brothers,
that what has happened to me has really served to advance the gospel,
so that it has become known throughout the whole imperial guard
and to the rest that my imprisonment is for Christ.
And most of the brothers,
having become confident in the Lord by my imprisonment,
are much more bold to speak the Word without fear.
Philippians 1:12-14 (ESV)

Christians need to share their testimony of God's work in their lives to spur on someone else's courage. We are to build each other up. One of the best ways to do so is to talk about how God is using you. God wants to use you right where you are, and you can be encouraged when you hear about how God has used someone else in their ordinary life. Paul was in prison when he penned today's verses, demonstrating that you can impact the world for Christ in any situation.

God does not want us to waste our time on things that rust or that moths can eat but wants us to store up our treasures in heaven. What can we store there? Love. We can love others by sharing our stories and telling them about Jesus, who gave us the greatest Love of all. We can love others by giving them a smile, praying for them, and showing a life committed to God's Word.

Jesus left us the Holy Spirit who lives inside you so you can love others as He loves you. The Gospel message is all about love. We are called to be tender, forgiving, loving, and unified. *How are you doing with showing others the love of Christ?* When we exhibit a forgiving heart, others open up when they see they won't be judged. When Christians work in unity, much can be accomplished, but everyone must leave pride at the door and then let God's suggestions fill their minds. Instead of embroiling our differences with anger, we need to use our differences in positive ways. God cannot teach you something new unless you are willing to listen to different solutions. *Are you opening your mind to how God can use you to love others right where they are?*

Day 288

Ministry Battles

But the Lord said to him, "Peace! Do not be afraid.
You are not going to die."
Judges 6:23 (NIV)

For many people, death proves a very real fear. So much so that their fear distracts them from what God has willed for their lives. Allowing fear to control them, some people miss opportunities God wants to give them. Perhaps they are unwilling to drive in certain areas of town, feeling it is too dangerous, yet God wants them there for ministry. Perhaps God is calling them into the military, but their parents are too afraid of losing their son or daughter. Perhaps God is calling them into all the world to preach the Gospel, yet some areas are more dangerous than others, and God wants all peoples to hear His message of love and forgiveness. If they are willing to receive it, God gives His followers a courageous peace about any place He calls them to go.

Is your fear of death or physical harm keeping you from helping the poor and needy? God is calling all of us to certain ministry battles, but He wants us to have a peace, knowing He holds our lives in His hands, the safest place to be. In today's verse, God called Gideon to be a warrior. How did Gideon respond? With anxiety. He felt like he was the weakest member of the weakest clan. While Gideon questioned and objected to God's will for his life, he pressed on and had a face-to-face encounter with God. When Gideon faced his fears with God, God protected Gideon through his battles. Gideon was able to see victory that resulted in peace for the land for forty years. Just like Gideon, you can come face to face with Jesus and face your fears. When you do, you will find your peace. Your blessing of peace will flow freely into your life, benefitting your friends and family as well.

Peace

Day 289

Shadows of Control

*Lord, You establish peace for us;
all that we have accomplished You have done for us.*
Isaiah 26:12 (NIV)

What has stolen your peace? Can you identify tension that has crept in over time? A job you once loved, you no longer like. A task at church that once brought joy is now a tedious weight. An important relationship has become strained. Brokenness seems pervasive, and peace seems elusive . . . but God wants to give you His peace. He does not want you to give yourself all away to wearisome concerns but to spend your energy worshipping Him and following His lead in your life. He does not want you depleted, running on empty, but running to Him, your Comfort and Refuge. When we let God balance our time, rely on His goodness to accomplish His work, and focus on Him moment by moment, He becomes our Peace.

God predestined your life to have meaning and value. You have purpose, and that purpose does not include fretting about how things may go. You have no control over how other people will respond or how they express their emotions. The only person you can control is you, and your time is best spent when you submit to God's will and let Him take control. Trying to control your life, keeping everyone happy, keeping life orderly . . . it can feel overwhelming and steal your joy. But by trusting His plan and placing your hopes in God's promises, knowing He will never leave you, knowing He works all things for good, knowing heaven is real and He brings restoration, you will find peace. It is God who works in you, and the more you let God work in your life, the more peace you will have. *Are your hands clinging to something so tightly as you refuse to let God take hold of it?* Lift it up to God, release your grip, and open your hands in praise to heaven. A life of peace and joy is never about what you do but how much you let Jesus accomplish through you.

Day 290

Fully Dedicated

If you have come to me in friendship to help me,
my heart will be joined to you; but if to betray me to my adversaries,
although there is no wrong in my hands,
then may the God of our fathers see and rebuke you.
Then the Spirit clothed Amasai and said,
"We are yours, O David, and with you, O' son of Jesse!
Peace, peace to you, and peace to your helpers!
For your God helps you."
1 Chronicles 12:17b-18a (ESV)

God's original plan for the Jews was that He would govern them in all their ways. God selected the Jews to be an example to the world, demonstrating what life looked like when fully dedicated to God. But over time, the Jews wanted to be like the nations around them, wanting a king to rule over them. And God let them have their way, choosing Saul as their first king.

At first, Saul wanted to please God, but soon he was doing things his way, allowing circumstances to sway him and not waiting on the Lord for direction. In turn, God told Saul, "Your kingdom shall not continue. The LORD has sought out a man after His own heart, and the LORD has commanded him to be prince over His people because Saul had not kept what the LORD commanded" (1 Samuel 13:14). David was that man, and Saul in his jealousy hunted David down to kill him. But David was focused on God and kept God's law. While David was hiding, God spoke to the hearts of mighty warriors to join forces with David. People can recognize when God is with someone, blessing this person for a task, as reflected in today's verse. The NIV translation uses the word "success" instead of "peace." We fight our battles in the spiritual realm through prayer; we can pray for the Holy Spirit to fight for us. *Are you waiting for a helper in the battles you face? Are you waiting and expecting Jesus to give you success?* Do not be like Saul and cave into men's pressure. Be like David and be at peace with your Helper, who will give you success.

Peace

Day 291

A Heavenly Perspective

As they were talking about these things,
Jesus Himself stood among them, and said to them,
"Peace to you!"
But they were startled and frightened and thought they saw a spirit.
And He said to them,
"Why are you troubled, and why do doubts arise in your hearts?
See My hands and My feet, that it is I Myself. Touch Me and see.
For a spirit does not have flesh and bones and you see that I have."
And while they still disbelieved for joy and were marveling,
He said to them, "Have you anything here to eat?"
They gave Him a piece of broiled fish,
and He took it and ate it before them.
Luke 24:36-43 ESV

Why do you doubt God's promises to you? God does not lie; what He says will come to pass. Sometimes we're like Jesus' disciples in our doubts and distrust. For example, Jesus told the disciples He was going to the cross four different times (Matthew 16:21, 17:22, 20:17, 26:2). But they did not fully believe Him, still unsure He would keep His promises. They did not understand nor have the right perspective. *Have you ever had the wrong perspective but upon learning more or understanding someone's intentions, the whole situation changed?* The disciples had the miracle-working Jesus with them, yet still they could not grasp God's plan. God needed to show His glory through Jesus in ways they could not perceive. In contrast, Jesus lived a sinless life, making Him worthy to bear our sins on the cross. And though tempted, He kept a heavenly perspective, staying obedient to God's plan for His life. He was completely God *and* completely man, so facing the torture of the cross did not prove easy. After Jesus died on the cross and before He was raised from the dead, He was at war with Satan . . . and Jesus overcame. Jesus is the all-powerful Holy One. As an act of worship, remain focused on Jesus, even when your feelings get hurt and people let you down; be obedient to God's ways. Miracles can happen when you ask God for a fresh perspective. Kindness and joy are attainable when you choose Jesus over the world.

Day 292

Intentional Life Lessons

Indeed, it was for my own peace that I had great bitterness;
but You have lovingly delivered my soul from the pit of corruption,
for You have cast all my sins behind Your back.
Isaiah 38:17 (NKJV)

God may allow us to sit in a bitter, corrupt place so we can learn from our bitterness. Sometimes we can learn key life lessons through seeing examples in others' lives, and sometimes it's best to experience and learn firsthand. While we can learn from others' mistakes, a hard, personal lesson and tough love can direct our steps quicker toward God's path and way of living. More than anything, our all-loving, faithful God wants to conform us to the image of Christ; He wants us to find our peace in the life of Jesus. And to help us do so, He may use our bitterness as a tool to show us our ways are hostile toward His plan for us.

God wants to deliver you from your pit of despair, but you have a choice: remain there or surrender your bitterness to Him. Can you surrender halfway? Well, you may try, but He wants your whole heart, and He will never stop pursuing you. *Will you stop running from God and turn around? What one thing are you still holding back? Where is the root of bitterness crushing your soul? Can you recognize where your jealousy resides?* God wants you to name it, releasing your bitterness and jealousy to Him, which will lead you to forgive others as He forgave you. You can have peace only when you trust God's plan of forgiveness for all the sins of the world, not just yours. Remember, Jesus died for all; He paid the price for everyone's sin. And He can change your bitterness to forgiveness when you rest in His saving grace—for all. In other words, He will deliver you from your bitterness when you fully entrust to Him all that has made you bitter. Hand Him your bitterness, trust Him for deliverance, and take hold of His peace. Do it today!

Day 293

Godly Women

She is clothed with strength and dignity,
and she laughs without fear of the future.
Proverbs 31:25 (NLT)

Some women look at the whole chapter of Proverbs 31 and feel deflated, thinking they lack the qualities of God's picture-perfect woman. Certainly, God is flawless and pure, perfect in every way. But He knows we are human and imperfect. And He does not want these verses to put you in turmoil. Instead, think of them as a guide for areas in which you can grow; you cannot reach for something unless you know what you are reaching for.

God wants to sanctify women in their marriages, workplaces, and homes, doing their daily tasks. Yet, He knows we all fall short of His glory and none of us can do His will perfectly. So, do today as God wants for you: give yourself mercy for not being the perfect mom, wife, friend, or follower of Jesus. *Keep in mind that even Adam and Eve essentially had Father God as their parent, yet they still rebelled against Him. How much more will our children, in their flesh, act out against their parents?* Do not be too surprised if your child becomes the Prodigal Son. Do not get stuck in Satan's games, twisting your children's failures to be your fault. Adam and Eve had free-will to question God, and they did. *What makes you think your children will not question your authority?* God loves your children more than you do, and He wants you to trust Him while He builds their faith. Your role is to show them how you love God and put Him first; then you will be the "Proverbs 31 woman," exhibiting the godly qualities of strength and dignity He wants for you. God does not value your attempts to "do it all," but wants your heart and your best. God will clothe you with His strength to raise your family His way. So, find time to laugh, give yourself grace, rest in His Word, and praise Him wholeheartedly . . . He will banish your fear and give you peace.

Day 294

A Better Return

Blessed are those who find wisdom, those who gain understanding,
for she is more profitable than silver and yields better returns than gold.
She is more precious than rubies;
nothing you desire can compare with her.
Long life is in her right hand; in her left hand are riches and honor.
Her ways are pleasant ways, and all her paths are peace.
She is a tree of life to those who take hold of her;
those who hold her fast will be blessed.
By wisdom, the LORD laid the earth's foundations,
by understanding He set the heavens in place;
by His knowledge the watery depths were divided,
and the clouds let drop the dew.
My son, do not let wisdom and understanding out of your sight,
preserve sound judgment and discretion;
they will be life for you, an ornament to grace your neck.
Then you will go on your way in safety,
and your foot will not stumble.
When you lie down, you will not be afraid;
when you lie down, your sleep will be sweet.
Have no fear of sudden disaster or of the ruin that overtakes the wicked,
for the LORD will be at your side
and will keep your foot from being snared.
Proverbs 3:13-26 (NIV)

When you gain understanding and wisdom from above, God does not disappoint. *When you seek to live a peaceful life yet turmoil and stresses keep piling up, do you trust God over those situations? Are you living in fear of your circumstances, which zaps your peace? Don't you desire to trust God with the outcome?* Blessed are those who trust in God and seek His wisdom and understanding. Know God will give you sound judgment, and no matter what, your soul can rest in safety; He will never leave you and will lead you. *Are you looking for Him, for His loving hand and miracles amidst the trials? Are you ready for the next disaster?* It is coming. *Can you trust that God is on your side?*

Day 295

Going to New Heights

*Whoever dwells in the shelter of the Most High
will rest in the shadow of the Almighty.
I will say of the LORD, "He is my refuge and my fortress,
my God, in whom I trust." Surely, He will save you
from the fowler's snare and from the deadly pestilence.
He will cover you with His feathers,
and under His wings you will find refuge;
His faithfulness will be your shield and rampart.
You will not fear the terror of night, nor the arrow that flies by day,
nor the pestilence that stalks in the darkness,
nor the plague that destroys at midday.
A thousand may fall at your side, ten thousand at your right hand,
but it will not come near you. You will only observe with your eyes
and see the punishment of the wicked.
If you say, "The LORD is my refuge,"
and you make the Most High your dwelling,
no harm will overtake you, no disaster will come near your tent.
For He will command His angels concerning you
to guard you in all your ways; they will lift you up in their hands,
so that you will not strike your foot against a stone.
You will tread on the lion and the cobra;
you will trample the great lion and the serpent.
"Because he loves me," says the LORD, "I will rescue him;
I will protect him, for he acknowledges My name.
He will call on Me, and I will answer him;
I will be with him in trouble, I will deliver him and honor him.
With long life I will satisfy him and show him My salvation."*
Psalm 91 (NIV)

Where is your mind dwelling? Are you dwelling on regrets? Are you comparing yourself with others? We must dwell in the shelter of God if we want to find rest. And we cannot find rest by dwelling on the past, dwelling on people's downfalls, or dwelling on skills we don't have. Claim your victory you have in Christ and dwell there. The day Jesus went to the cross, He gave your soul eternal safety. Trusting God daily for your safety is an added bonus. You can learn how to live out this psalm. With each step you take, trust Him and rely on His ability to do everything He says He will do. In trust, you will be reaching new heights with your Lord and Savior.

Day 296

Fireproof

Shadrach, Meshach and Abednego replied to him,
"King Nebuchadnezzar, we do not need to defend ourselves
before you in this matter. If we are thrown into the blazing furnace,
the God we serve is able to deliver us from it,
and He will deliver us from your majesty's hand.
But even if He does not, we want you to know, your majesty,
that we will not serve your gods
or worship the image of gold you have set up."
Then Nebuchadnezzar was furious
with Shadrach, Meshach and Abednego,
and his attitude toward them changed.
He ordered the furnace heated seven times hotter than usual
and commanded some of the strongest soldiers in his army
to tie up Shadrach, Meshach and Abednego
and throw them into the blazing furnace.
So these men, wearing their robes, trousers, turbans and other clothes,
were bound and thrown into the blazing furnace.
The king's command was so urgent and the furnace so hot
that the flames of the fire killed the soldiers
who took up Shadrach, Meshach and Abednego,
and these three men, firmly tied, fell into the blazing furnace.
Then King Nebuchadnezzar leaped to his feet in amazement
and asked his advisers, "Weren't there three men
that we tied up and threw into the fire?"
They replied, "Certainly, your majesty."
He said, "Look! I see four men walking around in the fire,
unbound and unharmed, and the fourth looks like a son of the gods."
Nebuchadnezzar then approached the opening of the blazing furnace
and shouted, "Shadrach, Meshach and Abednego,
servants of the Most High God, come out! Come here!"
So, Shadrach, Meshach and Abednego came out of the fire,
and the satraps, prefects, governors and royal advisers
crowded around them.
They saw that the fire had not harmed their bodies,
nor was a hair of their heads singed; their robes were not scorched,
and there was no smell of fire on them.
Then Nebuchadnezzar said, "Praise be to the God
of Shadrach, Meshach and Abednego,
who has sent His angel and rescued His servants!
They trusted in Him and defied the king's command
and were willing to give up their lives
rather than serve or worship any god except their own God.
Daniel 3:16-28 (NIV)

319

Do you feel uneasy or awkward when people ask about your relationship with God? Do you downplay that relationship with others? Are you seeking to please other people and not share what God means to you? Whose approval are you going for? Shadrach, Meshach and Abednego had one aim—to faithfully trust the Lord. They trusted God and refused to worship false gods. They stood strong, not losing faith, not giving excuses, not feeling ashamed, but boldly demonstrating their reliance on God's sovereign power. They knew that God is in control, so certain that they bet their lives on it. They knew they were eternally safe. The risk of dying in the fire was worth it to them. But God, who loves to show His glory, walked with them in the fire. They were so protected they did not even smell like smoke when they emerged.

God does not promise to keep you out of the fire but promises to be with you in the fire. *What situations are making you feel the heat? What trials have you on fire?* God is a consuming fire and wants to purify you in the furnace. He does not want to burn you. *Can you trust God when the fires rage?*

Day 297

Cross Over

Do not rebel against the Lord. And do not fear the people of the land,
for they are bread for us. Their protection is removed from them,
and the Lord is with us; do not fear them.
Numbers 14:9 (ESV)

The people in today's verse were choosing to grumble and complain, not trusting God's protection. In fact, they were so frightened by the land's people that they thought it wiser to go back to Egypt and become slaves again. *How about your life? Has God given you the desire to loosen the yoke of your bondage, but the road to freedom seems daunting? Are too many friends trying to keep you bound to your past?* You can put substance abuse behind you, but you may need all new friends. You can stop reacting out of anger that keeps strife going, but you may need Bible-believing Christians to encourage you. Negative people breed negative talk. *Are you surrounding yourself with people who trust God's strength to get them through?* The ones who rebel against the Lord are those not trusting His truth or His ways that will bring them to a place of peace.

Peace is found in God alone. To maintain your peace, spend time in prayer abolishing Satan's schemes, not in complaining about God's direction for your life. When you have a complaining attitude, that is sin. The Israelites were complainers, too. God gave them directions for taking the land, promising He would defeat the enemies, but only Joshua, Caleb, and Moses trusted the Lord. Only Joshua and Caleb entered the Promised Land, and the Israelites spent their lives wandering the wilderness. Though they had seen God protect them in amazing ways, they refused to trust His ability to protect them now. *Who is intimidating you, making you too afraid to take possession of the abundance God has in store for you on the other side?* Do not waste your time wandering around. Be intentional and trust the direction that God is sending you.

Day 298

It Is No Surprise

Since therefore Christ suffered in the flesh,
arm yourself with the same way of thinking,
for whoever has suffered in the flesh has ceased from sin,
so as to live for the rest of the time in the flesh
no longer for human passions but for the will of God.
1 Peter 4:1-2 (ESV)

Why does it surprise you when life takes a turn toward difficulties? Why does the stress keep building and the release of stress seem so hard to find? Why do you feel like your peace is gone? God sent Jesus to earth to save the world from sin. In order to put death, sin, and Satan in their proper place, Jesus needed to suffer. Yes, His biggest suffering was when He was on the cross, but during His time in ministry He suffered for the people. In John 11:35, Jesus wept for Lazarus. In Luke 19:41, Jesus wept over Jerusalem. And in Hebrews 5:7-8, "Jesus offered up prayers and supplications, with loud cries and tears, to Him who was able to save Him from death, and He was heard because of His reverence. Although He was a Son, He learned obedience through what He suffered." Jesus can relate to your suffering, sympathizing with you. He understands better than you know. When your loved ones go to heaven too soon, He understands your loss. When your city or country turns its back on you, Jesus sympathizes. When sin is pressing you down and shaking you up, Jesus wants you to pray and cry with Him. Jesus told us in John 15:18, "If the world hates you, know that it has hated Me before it hated you."

God has an earthly mission set up for you, but He wants you to courageously trust His sovereign plan. God does not want you stuck in your feelings or frozen in your fear. He wants you to draw strength from Him to endure the suffering; there is always a sacrifice when sin is erased. *Are you willing to sacrifice your selfishness to accomplish His eternal plan? Can you accept the pain and suffering in this world?* It's part of God's great redemption story.

Day 299

Obeying the Voice of God

Thus says the Lord God of hosts, "O My people, who dwell in Zion,
be not afraid of the Assyrians when they strike you with a rod
and lift up their staff against you as the Egyptians did."
Isaiah 10:24 (ESV)

God was speaking to the remnant of Jews who were carried off to Assyria years before (2 Kings 18:11); they were seized and taken away because they did not obey God's voice. But God had a plan. The captives would return to Israel, but they needed to listen, obey, and trust. In the verses before today's passage, God tells them He will punish the Assyrians. And in today's verse, God reminds them what He did to the Egyptians when the Jews fled from Egypt. God did wild things to the Egyptians, including parting the Red Sea. Indeed, God can do anything that is beneficial for His glory, and He always wants His people to return to Him.

When Israel trusted God, they may have been prosperous, but prosperity brought greed, and they pushed God out. When people exclude God from their lives, He lets them do what they want. Before long, the Israelites looked like the other nations with all their false gods. So, out of love, God sent a message of discipline to call His people back to Him, and they listened to Him again. Many times Israel turned from God, yet each time He called them back. God will do the same for you; no matter how many times you go your own way, God is always there waiting when you repent and trust His voice. *Is your fear from past abuse causing you to lack confidence in Christ? Can you trust His protection in the midst of a verbal attack?* Your life can overflow with righteousness when you fix your eyes on Jesus. God wants to teach you something right where you are, even if you are living with the consequences of past mistakes. God is just and fair, and He sees you right where you are. *Do you see His righteousness and love amidst the hardships?* Call out to Him today.

Day 300

Develop Faith

"Whether the land is rich or poor,
and whether there are trees in it or not,
be of good courage and bring some of the fruit of the land."
Now the time was the season of the first ripe grapes . . .
"We came to the land to which you sent us.
It flows with milk and honey, and this is its fruit" . . .
"We are not able to go up against these people,
for they are stronger than we are."
Numbers 13:20, 27, 31 (ESV)

God wanted to send His people into a corrupt land to purify it; the area's inhabitants were wicked but the land itself flowed "with milk and honey." So, Moses sent out twelve spies to scout out the Promised Land, and ten came back with a report that showed a lack of faith in God. They saw the land was good and fruitful, but they were intimidated by the people's size.

God selected the Jews as His chosen people and separated them from others to give them strength to follow Him. And while they had recently seen Pharaoh's army get swallowed up in the Red Sea (Exodus 14:26), they now chose to be intimidated by life's difficulties. Though the parting of the Red Sea made a way for them when there seemed no way out, they did not build up their faith but chose to live in fear. Living a life courageous for Christ is a choice we all must make.

In the same way, God has separated you; He has called you out of the dark to be a light, but you must have faith that God will fill in the gaps. All your weaknesses are places God can demonstrate His glory through you. God demonstrated His glory when He sent the ten plagues to the Egyptians, yet He kept His people free from harm. God wanted them to exemplify faithfulness, a trust in His ability to sustain them. We don't have to spend forty years wandering in desert places. Trusting God is the most direct way to see Him display His glory. *What about you? Has God shown you His glory, yet today you question your trust in Him as the perfect Heavenly Father?*

324

Day 301

Recorded Misery and Tears

Trust God in times of fear: Be merciful to me, my God,
for my enemies are in hot pursuit; all day long they press their attack.
My adversaries pursue me all day long;
in their pride many are attacking me.
When I am afraid, I put my trust in You. In God, whose Word I praise—
in God I trust and am not afraid. What can mere mortals do to me?
All day long they twist my words; all their schemes are for my ruin.
They conspire, they lurk, they watch my steps, hoping to take my life.
Because of their wickedness do not let them escape;
in Your anger, God, bring the nations down.
Record my misery; list my tears on Your scroll—
are they not in Your record?
Then my enemies will turn back when I call for help.
By this I will know that God is for me.
In God, whose Word I praise, in the LORD, *whose Word I praise—*
in God I trust; I will not be afraid. What can man do to me?
I am under vows to You, my God;
I will present my thank offerings to You.
For You have delivered me from death and my feet from stumbling,
that I may walk before God in the light of life.
Psalm 56 (NIV)

Are you asking God for mercy over the fears that loom before you? Are you trusting His Word when fear grips you? David wrote today's Scripture passage when he was on the run from Saul and the Philistines had seized him in Gath (1 Samuel 21:10-15). By human standards, David had every "right," every justification, to be afraid, but he always placed God in the equation. David understood that he should fear only God, not man; therefore, God was the only One with the power to give him the peace he needed.

In this psalm, we read that God keeps a record of our tears. He wants you to take all your pent-up misery and release it to Him. It's okay to cry in God's presence, and He will comfort you. He wants you to come to Him when your load is too heavy and praise His freedom over your fears. Praise Him for what He will do; you can be sure He has a trustworthy answer to all your fears and misery. And this process proves reliable: bring your fears to God and trust Him with the next step.

Day 302

The Lord Renews Your Strength

Why do you complain? Why do you say,
"My way is hidden from the LORD; my cause is disregarded by my God?"
Do you not know? Have you not heard?
The LORD is the everlasting God, the Creator of the ends of the earth.
He will not grow tired or weary,
and His understanding no one can fathom.
He gives strength to the weary and increases the power of the weak.
Even youths grow tired and weary, and young men stumble and fall;
but those who hope in the LORD will renew their strength.
They will soar on wings like eagles;
they will run and not grow weary; they will walk and not be faint.
Isaiah 40:27-31 (NIV)

God is asking you today's questions: Why do you complain? Why do you say, "My way is hidden from the LORD; my cause is disregarded by my God?" Do you not know? Have you not heard? God is paying attention to everything you do. He has blessed you with His strength, but He requires you to put your hope in Him to renew your strength.

The older we get, the more our bodies break down. Spiritually speaking, the opposite should hold true. The older you get, the more confident you should become that God is working on your behalf. The more confidence you have in the strength of God, the more blessing you will see from Him. Since belief is step number one in any miracle and blessing, you must believe that God will bless you with the strength to do what He has called you to. Stop complaining how weak you feel. Stop complaining that your times are tough, and seek the safety of trust in Him. So evident are His blessings that even scientists have documented that positive people live longer. Positive people tend to trust God's strength when times get tough, but negative people tend to wallow in weak-willed self-pity. So, stop the complacency; banish your weariness! Turn your eyes to Him and choose joy. Rest in His love. Humbly put your hope in the strength God has waiting for you.

Day 303

Slow to Anger

*The Lord is compassionate. Praise the L*ORD*, O my soul;*
*all my inmost being, praise His holy name. Praise the L*ORD*,*
O my soul, and forget not all His benefits—
who forgives all your sins and heals all your diseases,
who redeems your life from the pit and crowns you
with love and compassion, who satisfies your desires with good things
so that your youth is renewed like the eagle's.
*The L*ORD *works righteousness and justice for all the oppressed.*
He made known His ways to Moses, His deeds to the people of Israel:
*The L*ORD *is compassionate and gracious, slow to anger,*
abounding in love. He will not always accuse,
nor will He harbor His anger forever;
He does not treat us as our sins deserve or repay us
according to our iniquities.
For as high as the heavens are above the earth,
so great is His love for those who fear Him;
as far as the east is from the west,
so far has He removed our transgressions from us.
*As a father has compassion on his children, so the L*ORD *has compassion*
on those who fear Him; for He knows how we are formed,
He remembers that we are dust. The life of mortals is like grass,
they flourish like a flower of the field;
the wind blows over it and it is gone,
and its place remembers it no more.
But from everlasting to everlasting
*the L*ORD*'s love is with those who fear Him,*
and His righteousness with their children's children—
with those who keep His covenant and remember to obey His precepts. The
*L*ORD *has established His throne in heaven,*
*and His kingdom rules over all. Praise the L*ORD*, you His angels,*
you mighty ones who do His bidding, who obey His Word.
*Praise the L*ORD*, all His heavenly hosts,*
you His servants who do His will.
*Praise the L*ORD*, all His works everywhere in His dominion.*
*Praise the L*ORD*, O my soul.*
Psalm 103 (NIV)

Are you comforted by knowing God is slow to anger? He sees your situation and has compassion for you. *As God is patient with you, waiting for you to repent, do you perceive this blessing, this love for you?* Praise the Lord that He has removed

327

your sins and cast them into the sea, that they are as far from you as the east is from the west, and He does not treat you as you deserve. He is holy and loves to see your obedience in action, obeying His Word. He will continue to pour blessings out over you, giving you new life. Let your soul be blessed in the everlasting love of God.

Day 304

At the Feet of Jesus

Now as they went on their way, Jesus entered a village.
And a woman named Martha welcomed him into her house.
And she had a sister called Mary, who sat at the Lord's feet
and listened to His teaching.
But Martha was distracted with much serving.
And she went up to Him and said,
"Lord, do you not care that my sister has left me to serve alone?
Tell her then to help me."
But the Lord answered her,
"Martha, Martha, you are anxious and troubled about many things,
but one thing is necessary. Mary has chosen the good portion,
which will not be taken away from her."
Luke 10: 38-42 (ESV)

These verses offer a profound teaching for those of us who try to do too much. From her perspective, Martha was doing the right thing. She opened up her home to Jesus and was making preparations to serve Him a meal, but Jesus said all her busyness was merely a distraction from leaning in to all He wanted to teach her. In Matthew 6:33, Jesus said to "Seek first the kingdom of God and His righteousness, and all these things will be added to you." Mary was choosing to sit at Jesus' feet and learn about His righteousness. Undistracted by her "to do" list, she wanted to soak up as much of Jesus as she could get. Jesus is the Bread of Life (John 6:51), and He was providing her nourishment; she wanted to feed her soul with the goodness of His wisdom.

What is distracting you? What is keeping you away from sitting at the feet of Jesus? Are you asking God if He approves of all you are doing? Are you asking for peace about a decision but instead are feeling anxious? Perhaps you are choosing unwisely. Maybe your time could be better spent at Jesus' feet, seeking His wisdom and peace. He will guide you in how to spend your time. Doing more for Christ is not the goal, but sitting at Jesus' feet, reading His Word with a grateful, hungry heart and a thirst for His truth, will bless your perception in all matters of life.

Day 305

Come Into His Presence

I will sing of Your strength; in the morning I will sing of Your love.
For You are my fortress my refuge in times of trouble.
Oh, my strength, I sing praise to You;
You, O God, are my fortress my loving God.
Psalm 59:16-17 (NIV)

Does every song you listen to glorify the Lord? Have you completely opened your heart to Him during worship? The sound that comes from your mouth is perfect for Him; He created your voice, your sound of singing and praising Him, and to Him it's beautiful. He desires your participation in this wonderful way to give Him praise, whether alone or joined with others in one pleasing accord. Psalm 100:1-2 says, "Make a joyful noise to the LORD all the earth! Serve the LORD with gladness! Come into His presence with singing!" He does not exclude anyone.

Only music can stimulate your whole brain; it touches your mind like nothing else and gets your feet moving. God created it as a powerful gift in your life, and He loves it when you sing worship to Him. Its words and melodies can transport you into God's presence and get His goodness "stuck in your head." You can even use the instruments of sound to gain a heavenly perspective, a sensation of your spirit worshipping and connecting with all those already in heaven with Him. God will move you for what moves Him when you seek His face in worship.

In Job 38:7, we learn that Satan sang together with other angels in God's heavenly courts, but when his pride was exposed, he was hurled from heaven (Ezekiel 28:12-19; Isaiah 14:11-14). *Why do you think the Devil tries so hard to trick and deceive you through the power of music? Why does vulgar, sexualized music entice you to act in dishonoring ways?* At first, Satan's ideas may sound like they could help in hard situations, but God wants to pour truth over you. Let the words and rhythms of Christ-centered music wash over you and uplift your soul as you pour out your praises to God.

Day 306

The Maker's Chosen

Thus says the LORD who made you, who formed you
from the womb and will help you:
"Fear not, my servant, whom I have chosen.
For I will pour water on the thirsty land,
and streams on the dry ground;
I will pour My Spirit upon your offspring,
and My blessing on your descendants."
Isaiah 44: 2-3 (ESV)

The LORD chose you. That in itself is the biggest blessing of all. He did not hand you over to your fleshly desires (Romans 1:24) but saved you from becoming completely foolish. For a fool follows after things God considers unrighteous: gossip, deceit, and strife. Moreover, God called us to teach our children His righteous ways, and He gave us His Spirit to empower us to act in love. As God is the Author of Peace, He therefore wants peace over your home. *Only the fool separates a family, but did you know that God can give you the wisdom to dampen the flames of your family's discord if only you would ask Him?*

Satan knows that if he can tarnish a family's reputation, he can stain the testimony of God's work in that family's life. But what Satan does not understand is the power of Jesus' love. So, keep coming back to the cross when your family acts foolishly. Jesus will pour out His Spirit and stop the fire from spreading further. *Do you know that your yesterday does not have to shape your tomorrow?* Forgive the harsh words toward you, and ask the person to whom you spoke rudely for forgiveness—a simple act with huge impact: your sin released to God, and the sins of others released to the One against whom they ultimately sinned. God knows your family intimately, including all your hot buttons, so lay down your regrets of not raising your family properly. He created you all and knit your family together for a purpose. *Why not pick up the Word and let it have its purifying power?* It's your calling: mom, dad, grandparents, aunts, and uncles.

Day 307

Surviving the Worst Days

If the LORD had not been on your side when people attacked you,
they would have swallowed you alive
when their anger flared against you; the flood would have engulfed you,
the torrent would have swept over you,
the raging waters would have swept you away.
Praise be to the LORD, who has not let you be torn by their teeth.
You have escaped like a bird from the fowler's snare;
the snare has been broken, and you have escaped.
Your help is in the name of the LORD, the Maker of heaven and earth.
Psalm 124 (NIV)

Have you been abused and neglected so long that you question if God is on your side? Have you been lied to so much that grasping the idea of the Holy Word as God's truth seems questionable? Have things happened to you that were so horrific you cannot see any type of blessing that could come out of that nightmare?

On days when terrors seem to surround you, you might not feel blessed, safe, or secure, but God is helping you to survive your worst days. God knows the evil in others' hearts and how they hurt you, committing crimes against you as well as against Him. People can be much more hurtful than you can imagine; they can abuse you, lie, and cheat their way right over you. You may feel stepped on and trampled, but God knows right where you are. He is with you in the darkness, in the pain, and He will bring justice to everyone on the day that they face Him. Nothing He created is out of His control, and He will cause all things to work together for good, to those who love God, those who are called according to His purpose (Romans 8:28). You might have survived the abuse; you may have found a way out. And because of Jesus, you can move forward, not overwhelmed by the torment. God wants to show you His blessings of walking closely with Him while you learn to thrive in the strength of Jesus.

Day 308

A Life-Long Journey

*Being confident of this, that He who began a good work in you
will carry it on to completion until the day of Christ Jesus.*
Philippians 1:6 (NIV)

*Are you completely confident that God, who began the good
work in you, will complete it? Or are you doubting that you will ever
get past the difficulties of healing? Are you looking at the road you
still have ahead of you and it feels daunting? Or are you praising the
Lord for how He will finish what He started?* Do not doubt the
promises of God. Build your confidence in God's promises by
praising the blessings that will come. Praise the Lord for what He will
do, not only asking God for help but thanking Him for His answered
prayer ahead of time.

God wants your complete confidence in Him and His ability to
help you escape the dark, where sin originates. He wants to sanctify
you in His light . . . as you read His Word, move His truth from your
head to your heart, pour out your pain to Him, and obey in faith.
Praise God for not leaving you out in the dark and for easing your
pain—a true blessing. *Do you know that He has chosen you? And that
He wants you to give Him all the praise?* For when you are weak, He
is strong. God's healing path for you will take a lifetime, and the
sanctification process is a life-long journey with the LORD. So, begin
today. Every day God wants you to seek Him, to crave His presence,
to need Him in your life. And for heaven's sake, you really do!
Recognize your need for His blessings every day, for His love and
peace and freedom from fear—and He pours them out to you.

Day 309

A Cheerful Giver

The point is this: whoever sows sparingly will also reap sparingly,
and whoever sows bountifully will also reap bountifully.
Each one must give as he has decided in his heart,
not reluctantly or under compulsion, for God loves a cheerful giver.
And God is able to make all grace abound in you,
so that having all sufficiency in all things at all times,
you may abound in every good work.
2 Corinthians 9:6-8 (ESV)

Do you consider yourself a cheerful giver, or are you stingy? How do you feel when it's time to tithe? How do you react to opportunities to give of your time or money to help the homeless or the elderly, perhaps your neighbor or someone else struggling financially in hard times? Pride is Satan's stamp of approval, for he is the most prideful of all, and he wants to steal the glory of the Lord. *Are you giving Satan room in your life because you are holding onto your things too tightly?* A bigger house and a fancier car may make you "feel" classy or cool, but God wants you to be a good steward of the money He has allowed in your life. God does not call most of us to wealth, but He still calls us to help the poor. Everything God has gifted you with is not for your benefit only; He wants you to share your time in fellowship, and He expects you to share His financial resources that He has allowed you to have—and do so with a cheerful, thankful heart.

Notice in today's verse that God can make His grace abound in you so you can serve and share with others. He can soften and refine your heart so you can clearly see that He is the Provider of all you have. After all, He has created everything and owns everything; all your money is actually on loan from Him! Certainly, He has blessed you with everything you need to do His will. Don't let your ego make you conceited but remain humble toward God's blessings. Draw upon His wisdom and choose to spend His money and resources wisely—all for His glory.

Day 310

Committed to His Glory

*The eyes of the LORD search the whole earth
in order to strengthen those whose hearts are fully committed to Him.*
2 Chronicles 16:9 NLT

Is your life fully committed to God? He sees you and wants to strengthen your heart still more. *Is your identity found in the waters of your baptism?* If you have been baptized, then this act of obedience was symbolic of God washing away your sins and raising you as Christ's faithful servant. God is searching for people who commit their decisions and emotions, thoughts and actions, habits and words—everything in life—completely to Him. *How committed are you?*

In Matthew 3:11, John the Baptist says, "I baptize you with water for repentance, but He who is coming after me is mightier than I . . . He will baptize you with the Holy Spirit and fire." When you get baptized today, it's no different. A priest, pastor, or minister baptizes you with water, but Jesus baptizes you with the Holy Spirit and fire. *Are you on fire for Jesus?* For the fire of Jesus will burn away all your unrighteousness and purify you to live a life of integrity. *Does His water quench your soul?* In John 7:38-39, Jesus says, "Out of His heart will flow rivers of Living Water, and anyone who believes in Him will receive the Holy Spirit." The Holy Spirit is the Living Water that quenches your soul.

Do you do everything for the glory of God? When you learn to drink in your relationship with Christ, it flourishes to such depths that Jesus will spill from your fingertips, glorifying Him in all you touch. One of the easiest ways to think of bringing glory to God is by marveling at nature. God created birds to eat berries and seeds, to migrate from one place to the next, and they do it all to God's glory. How? They don't complain but are obedient to God's design for them. In the same way, your identity should be in who God designed you to be, and by your baptism, you have the ability to give Him all the glory.

335

Day 311

Put Your Weapons Down

For I, The LORD your God, hold your right hand;
It is I who says to you, "Fear not, I AM the one who helps you."
Isaiah 41:13 (ESV)

Anytime the Bible mentions God holding your right hand, let your ears perk up. Why? In Isaiah's time, weapons were held in people's right hand for battle. So, God wants you to put your weapons down, hold tight to Him, and let Him fight your battles. When you identify with trusting Him completely, you let go of the tension associated with always being on guard, ready for an attack. God wants to give you peace and joy, but when you hold onto your personal weapons, you forgo the spiritual weapons in Christ (Ephesians 6:10-18). God will take your hand and walk beside you, easing your fears. When you let God help you, He will keep you from feeling like you need to wave your sword around.

We do not live by our emotions; we live by Truth. However, when our identity is linked to the Truth, then over time our emotions will change. In John 18:10, Peter thinks that using his sword is a good idea, but Jesus rebukes him. Peter wants to take matters in his own hands, but Jesus trusts God's plan. Later, Peter's emotions of anger and insecurity change to confidence in Christ, and God uses Him mightily to build His church.

Jesus also identifies with His calling to the cross. *Do you identify with the cross? Do you recognize the cross as the reason God holds your right hand?* Because of the cross, you can identify with Jesus' characteristics through His Spirit, which empower you to drown out your fears. *What weapons are you holding too tightly? Is your bank account your weapon, your tool to get your way? Is your intelligence your weapon, your tool to manipulate those around you?* God wants you to fight your battles on your knees, letting go of the outcome and reaching for His hand.

Day 312

The Name of The Lord is a strong tower;
the righteous run to it and are safe.
Proverbs 18:10 (NIV)

What do you run to when you don't feel safe? What crutch are you using to hold yourself up? The tides will rise again, but will you allow yourself to be tossed along? God gave you responsibilities to deal with, but He does not want them to overtake you.

In modern day culture, we may not have many strong towers around town, but think about what they represented in the Hebrew world where they were prevalent. They were lookout towers, built solid for protection, and could be seen from miles away. An attacker knew where the people were hiding, but the people also knew the strongest men in town were there to protect the weakest. Think about that in the spiritual realm. God is your strong tower. No one in the world is stronger, and He is looking out for your life. You will find refuge when you run to Him and seek His safety. If you veer off course, He sends you warning signs that you are running toward the wrong things.

Who is your attacker? It's Satan, and he tries to prevent you from running to your Strong Tower. When life gets difficult and the world has taken your peace, Satan sees you running to your Strong Tower and wants to keep you from finding Jesus' safety. Every time you run to Jesus and embrace His hiding place, Satan knows he is defeated. Finding your way to the Strong Tower is not hard but natural and effortless when you practice putting God in His proper place. For God alone is worthy of being high and lifted up. You may have to run for your life to escape the danger, you may have to leave some things or even people behind, but God has given you the strength to outrun the Devil's devious plans. Turn to God today, ask Him for keen eyes to see Him clearly, immerse yourself in His Word, and cry out to Him in repentance and faith. He is there!

Day 313

The Fortunate

*He executes justice for the fatherless and the widow
and loves the sojourner (landless people), giving him food and clothes.*
Deuteronomy 10:18 (ESV)

God has a special kind of love for the ones that society considers less fortunate. God loves to come alongside the brokenhearted and lonely. He can hold your hand when you miss your father, your child, or spouse's hand in yours. God can comfort, provide security, and provide in times of great loss, whether it's fellowship, finances, or renewed hope. God's perfect design, before sin entered the world, was an established relationship between a husband and wife and a father and child. God had specific roles for the men. He had roles that protected and provided for the women and children. God created women to complement their spouse and fill in the areas that men overlook. Men provided the meat through hunting while women collected the wood for the fire, worked in the veggie fields, and found the herbs and spices to make the meat taste better. Everyone came to the table doing his or her part, and the whole meal was better because of it. All the tasks complemented each other.

God knows what is missing in your life, has compassion on your broken heart, and promises you justice. He designed men's bodies to be stronger than women's. This in turn makes a woman dependent upon a man for certain things. God also designed men to be the spiritual leaders in the home, giving spiritual guidance, love, wisdom, and companionship. God knows your loss is both spiritual and physical, He sees where you are, and He wants to bring people alongside you to help you. *Are you pushing people away who want to help you in your brokenness?* No one on earth can completely replace the person you have lost, but God can raise people up to help you along in your time here and now.

Day 314

Financial Blessings

Hear this, all you peoples; listen, all who live in this world,
both low and high, rich and poor alike:
My mouth will speak words of wisdom;
the meditation of my heart will give you understanding.
I will turn my ear to a proverb; with the harp I will expound my riddle:
Why should I fear when evil days come,
when wicked deceivers surround me—
those who trust in their wealth and boast of their great riches?
No one can redeem the life of another
or give to God a ransom for them—
the ransom for a life is costly, no payment is ever enough—
so that they should live on forever and not see decay.
For all can see that the wise die, that the foolish and the senseless
also perish, leaving their wealth to others.
Their tombs will remain their houses forever,
their dwellings for endless generations,
though they had named lands after themselves.
People, despite their wealth, do not endure;
they are like the beasts that perish.
This is the fate of those who trust in themselves, and of their followers,
who approve their sayings. They are like sheep and are destined to die;
death will be their shepherd
(but the upright will prevail over them in the morning).
Their forms will decay in the grave, far from their princely mansions.
But God will redeem me from the realm of the dead;
He will surely take me to Himself.
Do not be overawed when others grow rich,
when the splendor of his house increases;
for they will take nothing with them when they die,
their splendor will not descend with them.
Though while they lived they count themselves blessed—
and people praise you when you prosper—
they will join those who have gone before them,
who will never again see the light of life.
People who have wealth but lack understanding
are like the beasts that perish.
Psalm 49 (NIV)

The name of this psalm is, "Why Should I Fear in Times of Trouble?" *Are you as confident as David was when he wrote this psalm? What fears overtake you when evil is knocking on your door? Are you afraid your money is going to run out and you won't be able to provide for your family at the level you had hoped?* This psalm should bring you reassurance that God will provide for your needs. Your trust should not be the money in your back account; your reassurance should be in the One who is the Provider.

"My God will supply every need of yours according to His riches in glory in Christ Jesus" (Philippians 4:19). In God's economy, the faithful will seek souls and more souls for the Kingdom of God. Everything you own on earth will not get to go to heaven with you, but the ones you brought to Christ will be there rejoicing with you. In heaven, all live without fear. But here on earth, the days to come are our hope. Nothing troubling you today is outside of God's protection. He will bless you when you trust His provision.

Day 315

God Is Our Fortress

God is our refuge and strength, a very present help in trouble.
Therefore we will not fear though the earth gives way,
though the mountains be moved into the heart of the sea.
Though its waters roar and foam,
though the mountains tremble at its swelling.
There is a river whose stream makes glad the city of God,
the holy habitations of the Most High. God is in the midst of her,
she shall not be moved. God will help her when morning dawns.
Psalm 46:1-5 (ESV)

This psalm is written for the here and now moments. God is our refuge and strength, and you can count on Him when troubles come roaring toward you. God is right here, a very present help in the midst of all that gives way and makes you tremble. He is not far off in heaven, looking down with apathy or disdain. *Have you asked Him to help you know this deep in your heart?*

If you want to live a bold life in Christ, then faith in your identity in Christ becomes extremely vital; your identity in Christ is the springboard for working out the life God designed for you. But, if your identity in Christ rests not on God's promise that He is your strength and refuge, then you are choosing a lackluster, lukewarm faith. If you choose to find your strength in your knowledge and ability to make things happen, then you are declining a miracle of God.

Who or what can you count on? Is your confidence in material things, in what you can touch and see? Or is your identity found confidently in faith that He is your strength through every difficulty? How is God your strength? By trusting His power and letting Him do what only He can. God is in control, and nothing happens without Him knowing it—nothing! He can use every trial and hardship in your life to show His glory . . . if you submit your will to His during the situation's unfolding. If He seems absent, maybe you are not really seeking Him in the midst of your troubles. God does not want to be an afterthought, but wants to be your initial thought. Seek His face today.

Day 316

Your Spirit Can Be Whole

*Now may the God of peace Himself sanctify you completely
and may your whole spirit and soul and body be kept blameless
at the coming of our Lord, Jesus Christ.
He who calls you is faithful; He will surely do it.*
1 Thessalonians 5:23-24 (ESV)

Are you busily working at being a Christian, getting burned-out, or are you living out your faith, trusting in God as your hope and joy? By faith you draw close to God and discover supernatural peace. By faith you receive the blessings of grace and the wondrous reality that all things in life, including your trials, are working for your good and for God's glory.

You cannot work your way to heaven; instead, heaven must come down to you. *Are you busy for Christ but hiding a heart that's drained of passion?* God will give you an expanded heart for the things He wants you to do. He will give you the perseverance and stamina to do the ministry work He wants you to accomplish. If you are drained, maybe it's because God is not sustaining your efforts; maybe He wants you to go in a different direction. God looks at our heart and knows where we have a heart problem. He knows exactly why you feel stagnant. *Is your identity in being the best volunteer at church, or is your identity found in the work of Christ?* God does all the work. *Are you taking up responsibilities that God does not intend for you to carry?* People with a calm, pure heart have complete faith in the Faithful One (Hebrews 11). It's not by works we are saved but by faith in Christ. When you lay down *your* plans and *your* will, submitting to what God has planned, then your spirit, and His Spirit within you, can be refreshed. He wants to mold you into a unique representation of Jesus. Don't try to sanctify yourself. The work of the Holy Spirit will do it. Draw upon His strength to make you faithful in seeking Him out with your whole heart. Then peace will follow as you build confidence that God will completely heal your soul.

Day 317

Peacefully Listen

A soft answer turns away wrath, but a harsh word stirs up anger.
A hot-tempered person stirs up strife,
but a person who is slow to anger quiets contention.
Proverbs 15:1 and 18 (ESV)

Those who find their identity in Christ should be known as His image-bearers; they should exemplify God's characteristics as Jesus did, being slow to anger and abounding in love (Exodus 34:6), meaning we should imitate this behavior. When was the last time you screamed at someone, got your way, and thus created peace? Probably never. Perhaps the initial conflict or disagreement seemingly ended, but not the bitterness and resentment still brewing underneath. *Was a bridge of strife built instead of a bridge of peace? How long did you let that bridge be the wedge between the two of you?* Christ forgave us, so we should forgive others; yet, so many have a hard time letting go of their anger.

God wants us to live out our lives in peace, demonstrating love toward everyone. He does not exempt a group of people from His redemption plan, but expects us to love and bring peace to our environment. Satan loves chaos, bitterness, and unforgiveness. And when you allow your anger to get the best of you, you are being duped by Satan's desires—a sure sign of sin in your life. *How tolerable are you of others' opinions, especially when theirs are unlike yours?* God wants us to peacefully listen to one another; anger and peace cannot stand in the same space. You can choose to seek God when your anger starts to flair and to claim the peace He has for you in that moment.

God designed us to feel anger but tells us not to sin in our anger; we should not let anger control us. He designed us to rely on His peace that surpasses all understanding—submitting to God's ways and speaking to one another in love. You will find that your identity in Christ is filled with peace when you imitate Him during conflicts and rest in His mercy.

Day 318

Established Position

*If a ruler's anger rises against you, do not leave your post;
calmness can lay great errors to rest.*
Ecclesiastes 10:4 (NIV)

Do not leave your post—a wise truth. But do you know what that means for you today? Maybe it means that you should stand tall for God and His ways. *Are you running away from challenges He wants you to face?* In today's world, people are calling evil "good" and good "evil." Christian values are diminishing from our culture and government. All around us, things are changing, and at times it seems that, just maybe, this is the environment of the last days. Prophecies are being fulfilled. Jesus could be here any minute. *What does all this really mean for you and me?*

God has warned us, so we should not be surprised by all the world's sin. Yet, to watch the acceleration of sin in our culture can seem astonishing. *What about things in society that are wicked in God's eyes?* We are not to tolerate them. *What about the election of our leaders?* Voting for the voice of God is your responsibility. The government shapes our future, and it's sending us in a sinful direction. The year 2020 was a tipping point, it seemed, and many became angry to the point of burning and looting cities. *Do you now see clearly what God wanted to teach you that year?* You must pick a side, either standing on God's Word and doing what He instructs, or faltering by not standing up for His ways and teachings. Certain things are sinful, regardless of what society tells you. Sin is sin; there is no grey area. You stand with God, or you fall with society—it's your choice. People are filled with anxiety because they do not live under Jesus' umbrella. When Jesus lives in your heart, He gives you peace, wisdom, and discernment to discuss difficulties with a positive outcome. Rely on God to help you remain calm as you explain your stance. He will give you the peace you need when you stand up for Christ's position.

Day 319

Value God First

Are not two sparrows sold for a penny?
And not one of them will fall to the ground apart from your Father.
But even the hairs of your head are all numbered. Fear not, therefore;
you are of more value than many sparrows.
So, everyone who acknowledges Me before men,
I also will acknowledge before My Father who is in heaven.
But whoever denies Me before men,
I also will deny before My Father who is in heaven.
Matthew 10:29-33 (ESV)

People find their personal value in many places. By looking at a person's home, you might see if they value its curb appeal. Others value their clothes and how they dress or their car. But often you can't see what people value most. Such as love of family. Children. Friends. Freedom. Marriage. Or faithfulness to God. Where we place our value proves important.

If you value God first, He will change your heart and your intentions to value the things He thinks are important. Where you place your identity changes as well. Certainly, people should value their job, their kids, their relationships, but not find their value in those things. Your value lies in your Creator, who knows the exact number of hairs on your head. He created you for the exact place you are right now. Find your value in who God says you are, which is "wonderfully made" (Psalm 139:14). *Where do you look for your self-worth? In the mirror? Do you see your shame there from something in the past? Do you feel like no one sees you or cares?* We serve a God who sees everything He created and values it all—but He values His people the most. You are so valuable to Jesus; He paid the price for your sins. *Do you feel you lack a personal quality?* Fear not, because God created you for a specific purpose in this hour. He values you right where you are, and He created you to have the precise qualities needed to love and serve others—and to get the job done He has planned for you.

Day 320

Merciful Success

*Your servants and Your people, You have redeemed
by Your great power and by Your strong hand.
O Lord, let Your ear be attentive to the prayer of Your servant,
and to the prayer of Your servants who delight to fear Your name.
And give success to Your servant today,
and grant him mercy in the sight of this man.*
Nehemiah 1:10-11 (ESV)

God has sovereignly placed everyone in your life, including those who bring you strife. Jesus says in Matthew 5:44 that "we are to pray for those who persecute us." Why would God want us to love our enemies and pray for them? Because He wants us to value what He did on the cross. He wants us to model His plan of forgiveness.

Sometimes we see other people's sin that they cannot see; when it comes to sin, people often have blind-spots. But your prayers could open their spiritual eyes. Plus, the time you spend in prayer for your enemies will soften your own heart. Look at Jesus as an example. One of Jesus' twelve disciples did not hold Him in holy fear but chose to hand Jesus over to the people that put Him on a cross. Jesus knew Judas would betray Him yet He still loved him, treating him the same as He did the eleven faithful disciples. *Can you do the same, following Jesus as your role-model for how to treat your enemies?* God may test you to see if you will follow His commandments, even through difficult situations and people. *Do you fear what the storms will bring? Do you make excuses that keep you from following God's instructions?* He is sovereign, over not only your life but the people's lives who bring you grief. God can change people's hearts while you cannot . . . but your prayers for them could. You will always have difficult people around you, but you will not be here on earth forever. *Do you fear your Judgment Day as much as you fear the people bringing you difficulties?* God wants to remind you that you are redeemed and protected by His hand.

Day 321

In Light of Eternity

"I, I AM He who comforts you;
who are you that you are afraid of man who dies,
of the son of man that is made like grass.
And have forgotten the LORD, your Maker,
who stretched out the heavens and laid the foundations of the earth,
and you fear continually all the day
because of the wrath of the oppressor,
when he sets himself to destroy?
And where is the wrath of the oppressor?
He who is bowed down shall speedily be released;
he shall not die and go down to the pit,
neither shall his bread be lacking. I AM the LORD your God,
who stirs up the sea so that its waves roar—
the LORD of hosts is His name.
And I have put My Words in your mouth and covered you
in the shadow of my hand, establishing the heavens
and laying the foundations of the earth,
and saying to Zion, 'You are My people.'"
Isaiah 51:12-16 (ESV)

Who in charge of our eternal destination? God alone. Things on earth can seem like the biggest of issues, but in reality, they are small and insignificant in light of eternity. *The great I AM wants to comfort you, but are you letting Him? God is asking you today, "Who are you that you are afraid of man who dies?" Are you forgetting the power of God? Is it not evident in your life?*

The questions to ask yourself today continue, for God alone can heal your soul, and He alone is worthy of our praise. *What places in your life have you put above God? What is continually nagging you? What is your mind fixated on?* God restores our mind when we put God first in all situations. Do not cower; God has called you to stand tall because He is on your side. Fear of doing the right thing can feel challenging, but when you tune in to God, you learn to trust that He is the only one worth trusting. He will empower you to work through your fear. No one can overcome fear unless he or she fears only God. *Will you trust Him with your fears today? Will you give Him the praise, the awe and respect and worship, that only He deserves?* He alone will bring you peace.

Day 322

Proclaim His Truth

So have no fear of them, for nothing is covered that will not be revealed,
or hidden that will not be known. What I tell you in the dark,
say in the light, and what you hear whispered,
proclaim on the housetops.
And do not fear those who kill the body but cannot kill the soul.
Rather fear Him who can destroy both soul and body in hell.
Matthew 10:26-28 (ESV)

In these verses, Jesus is instructing His apostles before He sends them out to minister to the physical and spiritual needs of the Jews. The Holy Spirit had not been poured out yet, so Jesus extends His power through them. This now stands as the Christian's instructions from Jesus, all which can be found throughout Matthew 10. After Jesus was resurrected, He left us the Great Commission (Matthew 28:19): to go out into the world and preach the Good News. He also left the Holy Spirt with us so that we, too, can be an extension of Jesus' power.

Jesus does not want His followers to be surprised when they are persecuted or the focus of friction and discord. People will not always want to hear about Jesus, but Jesus wants us to keep talking about Him. God wants to work in your life in a way that will exhibit that He is Lord and Savior. He wants to prove to you that He is who He says He is, and then He expects you to talk about it, to share your story and not fear what people may think or say. *Do you place your loyalty to your friend over your loyalty to God?* If so, you have things backwards. Through His power, you do not have to fear people's reactions. If you lie about the Truth, you are gaining a false sense of security. In the Ten Commandments, the ninth clearly says not to bear false witness (Exodus 20:16). God wants you to proclaim His Truth, to build your life around doing things honestly. *What are you lying about out of fear?* God wants you to speak honestly and be honest with yourself as well. *Are you afraid of the Truth?* The words of your testimony should be the honest truth.

Day 323

Motivated Healing

You who fear My Name,
the sun of righteousness shall rise with healing in its wings.
Malachi 4:2 (ESV)

Satan uses fear as a tool because he knows how fear can steer some away from doing God's will. Yet, God calls His followers to do fearful things. He tells us to not fear His will but to fear Him, respect Him, and do what He tells us. Don't fear the outcome of God's request unless you choose not to obey His voice. Don't let fear allow you to miss the blessings He has for you!

Jesus came to seek the lost, and He calls us to do His work on earth. Thankfully, He also left us His powerful Holy Spirit to call on anytime, day or night. If you completely believe that God's Word is complete Truth, then you are left without excuse; you don't need to let fear control you. His Spirit will help you act in confidence, with calmness and conviction. Someday you might need to confront your fears by confronting a boss or a spouse who seems to think it's okay to talk to you in a demeaning way. There is a time to speak up, and a time to keep your mouth quiet. *Do you stand up for yourself in a gracious way, or yell at people?* While Christians are not called to be pushovers, God wants us to stand up for ourselves, for justice and righteousness, in a way that brings Him glory and honor. And He will give you a holy nudge when it's time to move forward.

Ambassadors of Christ have to learn to not allow their feelings of anger, bitterness, and depression control them, but to set healthy boundaries and confront these issues with our God. We can't control our negative behaviors until we practice doing things God's way. You can learn how to be patient and loving at all times, but it takes perseverance. God has partnered with us, and what a privilege that is! *What fears are you allowing to dictate your relationship with God?* Let Him heal you His way because it's the only way to get to the root of the fears you have inside.

Day 324

Love and Serve the Lord

No one shall be able to stand against you.
The Lord your God will lay the fear of you and the dread of you
on all the land that you shall tread, as He promised you.
Deuteronomy 11:25 ESV

Deuteronomy chapter 11 is about loving and serving the LORD; these two things go hand and hand. If you love the Lord, you will serve Him. By letting God's instructions dictate how you live, you will discover that you are serving Him. Anytime you love someone, you want to get to know him or her better. The same is true when you love God: you want to study and know all His characteristics, and then you come to a place where you love Him deeply and know He is worthy of your complete dedication. When completely dedicated to God, you fear only Him, and He puts the rest of the world in the correct perspective for you.

To keep a godly perspective, you must ask Him to direct your thoughts and actions in every way. Since sin separates you from God, God wants you to be careful to follow His commandments. He knows what will happen when you are not careful: sin creeps in. God does not expect you to be perfect, but He expects you to do your best as you lean on Him. God wants you to hold fast to Him, to trust Him with your life. His Word is clear that He expects you to be holy, to obey His Word, to glorify Him by your words and deeds. He wants you to treat people with love and respect, and as you do, you will see Him acting in little and big ways around you. God does exactly as He promises, but often He will test you to see where your loyalty lies. *Do you fear your surroundings? Or are you being loyal to God all the days of your life?* Each day is another day that God has a purpose for you. *Do you fear what will happen today?* God will keep you safe when you tread into the fearful land with Him. If it's a place where God wants you to do His business, then do not get mixed up in the evil and wrong attitudes there. Keep your eyes on Him, and He will bring peace.

Day 325

Reverent Humility

*For I resolved to know nothing while I was with you
except Jesus Christ and Him crucified.
I came to you in weakness and fear and with much trembling.
My message and my preaching were not with wise persuasive words,
but with a demonstration of the Spirit's power,
so that your faith might not rest on men's wisdom, but on God's power.*
1 Corinthians 2:2-5 (NIV)

The work of the Holy Spirit is powerful, but pride can bring it to ruin. We are called to be humble. *Why?* Because those who are humble know that all good things come from above. The humble know they have joy in their lives because God has blessed them. The humble also know that when they lack anything, they can pray and trust that God's provision will provide, even when there seems to be no way. *God can supply everything you need spiritually, emotionally, and physically, so where is your faith? Do you have faith that your job is putting you in the right position, or do you have faith that God put you there?* Nothing you have is the result of your hard work; nothing you treasure is because you worked your tail off. Regardless of how tirelessly you have labored, all is in vain unless you recognize that God put you where you are.

Paul was confident, not in himself but in God. He humbly knew that God would supply him everything he needed to win souls for Christ. Paul knew what it was like to be hated and beaten. Yet, he did not fear talking about the power of God because he trusted that the Holy Spirit would empower him. Paul feared only God, and because of that holy fear, he was able to do exactly what God called him to do. Our walk on earth is not supposed to be safe and comfortable. *Are you letting pride ruin the work of the Holy Spirit in your life? Which of your messages will be a lasting testimony?* Satan is prideful, and it will bring him into hell forever. Fear only God because He can ignite your Spirit and empower you to do His will.

351

Day 326

A Word to the Wise

The Lord your God fights for you, just as He promised.
So be very careful to love the Lord your God.
Joshua 23:10b-11 (NIV)

Joshua was warning Israel's leaders not to serve the land's false idols but to cling to the Lord and follow Him wholeheartedly. God had sent Israel into a land full of wicked people, but He did not want them to imitate their wicked practices; He wanted Israel to live their lives completely dependent on Him and nothing else.

And He wants the same for you! Anyone who puts their trust in the One True God becomes set apart from those who do not have His Spirit living in them. God's sanctification process for your life sets you apart from your culture. Thus, Christians are to be careful not to blend into the world but to trust God fully as He protects them. God wanted the Israelites to be His witness, examples of a faith-filled life. Just like them, your pure dependence on God leads to Him fighting your battles for you. As a strong warrior, Joshua knew his strength came from God, and he looked to God for guidance before each battle. What was true then is true today, and through this verse, God is warning you, beseeching you, to be careful to love Him and not the world. *Why do you think God is telling you to be careful to love Him? What are you doing with your time and money? What in the world is drowning out your dedication to God?* The world and Satan want to grab your attention and put a wedge between you and God, causing you strife; some battles are self-inflicted and a result of bad choices. God calls you to repent and turn right around, doing things His way. Don't complicate a simple idea. Jesus gave you your eternal life on the cross, but He also covers your life in freedom as you choose His way moment by moment. He has promised He will fight for you, so keep your heart open and seek to always love Him. His promises are *always* true.

Protection

Day 327

Found in Jesus

The LORD is my shepherd, I lack nothing.
He makes me lie down in green pastures,
He leads me beside quiet waters,
He refreshes my soul.
He guides me along the right paths for His name's sake.
Even though I walk through the darkest valley,
I will fear no evil, for You are with me;
Your rod and Your staff, they comfort me.
You prepare a table before me in the presence of my enemies.
You anoint my head with oil; my cup overflows.
Surely Your goodness and love will follow me all the days of my life,
and I will dwell in the house of the LORD forever.
Psalm 23 (NIV)

In this passage, notice how much Jesus does for you. He makes you lie down in green pastures, a peaceful, sunny place; you don't take yourself there. Only in Jesus do you find peace and rest, not in the world nor in your own strength. You must choose to follow Him to see the quiet waters He has for you. By trusting His protection, Jesus will steer you from things that could have drowned you.

What is your perspective when life gets hard? Do you blame God for leading you into the dark valleys, or do you lean into His protection while you are there? God says He will lead you on the right paths, so the dim place you find yourself may be His path of righteousness for you. And consider this: you can be a light for Him there and not blend into the darkness; if He has you there, it's an opportunity to do good. Consider it an honor to work hard for God; He sees you! He has prepared a table for you in the presence of your enemies. So, He provides for you through it all, regardless of how many foes are banging down the door. God is there protecting you. *Why not ask Him to reveal to you all He has for you on your journey?* He will protect your heart if you trust in His goodness and not in your circumstances. And yes, you will dwell forever in His house—the best promise you will ever receive. The Lord truly is your Good Shepherd.

Day 328

Restored Hope

*Fear not, Jacob My servant, nor be dismayed, O Israel.
For behold, I will save you from far away,
and your offspring from the land of their captivity.
Jacob shall return and have quiet and ease,
and none shall make him afraid.*
Jeremiah 46:27 (ESV)

How far off does complete healing appear to you? What holds you in captivity? What is circling in your mind that you cannot seem to stop? God knows, and only He knows how it dictates and destroys certain areas of your life. God knows the lies you keep telling yourself, and God says, "You shall return to Him and you shall have quiet and ease, without fear." *Are you resisting? Do you know how to make the pain go away?*

God's Truth lies in the Bible, not hidden from you. For every lie that Satan tells you, God has written the Truth about it in His Word. When Satan whispers, "You are not worthy," God says, "I have a plan for you" (Jeremiah 29:11). When Satan says, "You are unloved," God says, "I love you so much I consider you My child" (1 John 3:1), When Satan says, "You are not smart enough or strong enough," God says, "You can do all things through Christ" (Philippians 4:13). Satan will rob you of your peace if you do not know what God says about you. When you understand who God says you are, you can stand protected from Satan's lies.

So do not be dismayed, O child of God. He can restore your hope when hope seems lost. God alone has the keys to your freedom from all the fears taunting you. Your role is to place your trust in the protection He is providing you. Rest in the love of Christ when your heart feels too heavy, and God will lighten your heaviness.

Protection

354

Day 329

Divinely Sustained

You are a shield around me, O LORD;
You bestow glory on me and lift up my head.
To the Lord I cry aloud, and He answers me from His holy hill.
I lie down and sleep; I wake again because the Lord sustains me.
I will not fear the tens of thousands drawn up against me on every side.
Arise, O LORD! Deliver me, O my God! Strike all my enemies on the jaw;
break the teeth of the wicked. From the Lord comes deliverance.
May Your blessing be on Your people.
Psalm 3:3-8 (NIV)

The abuse and mistreatment can build a fortress around your soul, causing your confidence to wane that God is shielding you. *Do you have the survival skills to get through each begrudging day but are burned out each step?* The hope of protection can seem lost when in the midst of those who are not on your side. *How can one persevere through constant abuse?* Verbal abuse can make your mind feel like God's Word is overly harsh. A father's abuse can make Father God look intimidating, confusing the Truth of a loving God who disciplines His children. No standard of truth in your home can make God's Word seem like it's not the standard for living. Satan likes it when abuse happens; he knows it can dwindle our faith and make us feel like God does not care. *If He is sovereign, then why is He allowing this to happen? Have you asked yourself that question?* Satan asked Eve, "Did God really say . . .?" in Genesis 3. Satan twist things and makes us question God.

God does not want you to experience abuse; it breaks His heart also. We are not designed to live in abuse; we are designed to love. When people try to prevent you from living dependent on God and want to be the ones in control of your life, then you have clear indication that He wants you to step back or away from these people. God wants to deliver you from your enemies and that could mean you need to remove yourself completely from the ones abusing you. *Is your Protector asking you to leave the abuse?*

Day 330

Take Courage!

Immediately Jesus made His disciples get into the boat
and go on ahead of Him to Bethsaida,
while He dismissed the crowd. After leaving them,
He went up on a mountainside to pray.
Later that night, the boat was in the middle of the lake,
and He was alone on land. He saw the disciples straining at the oars,
because the wind was against them.
Shortly before dawn He went out to them, walking on the lake.
He was about to pass by them,
but when they saw Him walking on the lake,
they thought He was a ghost.
They cried out, because they all saw Him and were terrified.
Immediately He spoke to them and said, "Take courage!
It is I. Don't be afraid."
Then He climbed into the boat with them, and the wind died down.
They were completely amazed, for they had not understood
about the loaves; their hearts were hardened.
Mark 6:45-52 (NIV)

Jesus had just fed the 5,000 men, plus woman and children, when He sent His disciples into a storm. Though they were scared, God's purpose was to show Jesus' glory. He wanted them to understand who Jesus is. Every miracle Jesus performed when He walked the earth pointed to the fact that He was in control of everything. Nothing lies out of His hands.

If Jesus can turn a few loaves and fish into a meal for thousands, and if He can tell the storm to stop and it does so immediately, then why have you hardened your heart to the thought that God can provide the perfect miracle for your storm? The disciples were getting to know Jesus, but their hearts were hardened in areas that Jesus wanted them to soften. In order to be receptive to the work and teachings of Christ, one must first have a pliable, moldable heart. *In what area of life is your heart rigid and unyielding? Are you receptive to His teaching? Is God doing miracles around you, yet you still do not believe in His security and protection?* Jesus can prove who He is. Jesus can see where you are heading, and He just might have sent you straight into the storm so He can show you His strength and you can learn to rely on His protection. *Why not stop resisting and start listening?*

Day 331

Jesus Has Swallowed Up Death

O Lord, You are my God; I will exalt You and praise Your name,
for in perfect faithfulness You have done wonderful things,
things planned long ago. You have made the city a heap of rubble,
the fortified town a ruin, the foreigners' stronghold a city no more;
it will never be rebuilt. Therefore strong peoples will honor You;
cities of ruthless nations will revere You.
You have been a refuge for the poor,
a refuge for the needy in their distress,
a shelter from the storm and a shade from the heat.
For the breath of the ruthless is like a storm driving against a wall
and like the heat of the desert. You silence the uproar of foreigners;
as heat is reduced by the shadow of a cloud,
so the song of the ruthless is stilled.
On this mountain the Lord Almighty will prepare a feast of rich food
for all peoples, a banquet of aged wine—
the best of meats and the finest of wines.
On this mountain He will destroy the shroud that enfolds all peoples,
the sheet that covers all nations; He will swallow up death forever.
The Sovereign Lord will wipe away the tears from all faces;
He will remove His people's disgrace from all the earth.
The Lord has spoken. In that day they will say,
"Surely this is our God; we trusted in Him, and He saved us.
This is the Lord, we trusted in Him;
let us rejoice and be glad in His salvation."
Isaiah 25:1-9 (NIV)

You can trust God's protection all the time because God knows the beginning to the end. He is the Alpha and the Omega; nothing is before Him, and nothing is behind Him. All people must meet Him in the present time. He knows what lies ahead on your journey, and He knows how to build your character so your life can reflect His ways. Through your life, God moves in subtle ways. He slowly opens your mind to His perspective and tests your character throughout the process, not to harm you but to build you up. His faithfulness is perfect, and His plans for you started at the exact moment that He ordained. *Are you questioning God about where your mind has wandered? Or are you diligent with your brain health and staying focused on the things of God?* God brings your mind to a place of recognizing the strongholds confronting you, at the exact moment that Jesus planned for you to find freedom from them. Jesus has swallowed up death forever, and one day we will stand face to face with Him. That will be amazing! He is the only reason we have freedom today. Rejoice and be glad that Jesus has already protected you from hell, and rejoice daily, knowing you can *always* trust His protection.

Day 332

Helpful Friendships

Stay with me; do not be afraid, for he who seeks my life seeks your life. With me you shall be in safekeeping.
1 Samuel 22:23 (ESV)

Though one may be overpowered, two can defend themselves; a cord of three strands is not quickly broken (Ecclesiastes 4:12). In other words, fellowship can lead to protection. God puts people in our lives to help one another and to help us grow to be more like Christ. We are to build each other up, encourage one another, give each other wise counsel, enjoy the good times, and walk through the hard times together. The buddy system we were taught in school is still a good idea when ladies want to enjoy a girls' night or when taking a hike through the woods or secluded area. The noise and movements of two people conversing keeps most of the wild animals away, providing protection from surprise attacks. The same should be our experience when we metaphorically walk through the hills and valleys of life; when we share our thoughts and feelings with someone, listening and encouraging with wise, biblical counsel, we keep Satan at bay.

Satan does not want you to voice your fears, but God does. God wants you to release them with honesty and forthrightness. Words have power, and when the Holy Spirit is ready for you to verbally release the things that make you afraid, then someone else can be there to listen, and the emotions can drain, causing your fear to lose its power. *Are you allowing Satan to keep you in the dark by not talking about the things you fear?* God will protect your heart to endure the Truth when you reveal your heart to someone. *Why not ask God for help in doing so today?*

Day 333

Forgiven Guilt

The steward replied: "Peace to you, do not be afraid. Your God
and the God of your father has put treasure in your sack for you.
I received your money."
Genesis 43:23 (ESV)

The steward in this verse was most likely an Egyptian speaking to Joseph's brothers. We know that Joseph, a dedicated follower of God and a Jew, held a high position in Egypt and worked directly under Pharaoh. We don't know the steward's background, but here's the important point: Joseph's brothers were scared, and these words were a comfort and relief to them; hearing "peace to you" and the mention of their God reassured them in the face of grief. In Genesis 42:21, their guilty conscioues were revealed, and they thought perhaps their past was catching up to them. You might remember that, years before, they had sold their brother Joseph to a caravan of slave traders that happened to be headed straight to Egypt (Genesis 37:28); people with a guilty conscious often tend to think the worst of things. Instead of holding a grudge against his brothers, Joseph was orchestrating events in order to see his beloved younger brother and father again.

Joseph's love for God is apparent throughout his life. He credits God for all his blessings, many which came through his slavery and then imprisonment. The Bible never records Joseph doubting God's sovereignty. Instead, Joseph brings his best to the worst of places. Although his brothers had sold him into slavery, he does not retaliate. And when his brothers stand before him and he tests them, their fears are brought to light. Joseph's heart was broken by what his brothers had done, but that does not stop him from forgiving them and providing all they need to survive. Regardless of the pain people cause us, we are not to act out. We are to live peaceably with our fellow brothers and sisters, not in fear of past sins. The debt has been paid. *Is your guilty conscious holding you prisoner in a way God does not intend? Are you living in the sovereign forgiveness of Jesus?*

Day 334

Made Strong

*"Like emery harder than flint have I made your forehead.
Fear them not, nor be dismayed at their looks,
for they are a rebellious house." Moreover, He said to me,
"Son of man, all My Words that I shall speak to you
receive in your heart and hear with your ears."*
Ezekiel 3:9-10 (ESV)

What does God mean when He says, "Like emery harder than flint have I made your forehead?" How about this: God created you to withstand the blows this world throws at you. God created His people to withstand the test and trials of their times. God's people are not to be weak or feeble but to "be strong, have courage, and do not fear." God knows the rebellious people you will encounter, and He created you to listen to *His* Words over theirs. Reading and listening to God's Word will strengthen you and train you up to deal with the people assailing you.

Everyone knows people who are rebellious, who choose not to listen to God or put their faith in Him. Rebellious people can be hurtful, twist everything you say, and take your words out of context. *Who is giving you the evil eye when you walk by? Who thinks they are better than you? Do you allow these people to bring you down? Do you know how to 'let go and let God'?* God knows the people that are rebelling against Him, and He will deal with them.

People sin against God and hurt people, but God has given you the strength to handle them. He knows how you will react when they hurt you, yet He wants you to receive His Word down in the deepest part of your heart. He wants you to hear exactly what He has to say. He has sovereignly placed rebellious people in your life for a reason, but it's not to torment you; it's to build your faith in His sovereignty and quiet your overly emotional reactions. God is telling you to "toughen up." You don't need to be easily affected and overly sensitive about everything done or said to you. You can be tender without being full of drama, and yes, you can have faith without fear.

Day 335

The God of Confirmation

. . . the LORD said to him,
"Arise, go down against the camp, for I have given it into your hand.
But if you are afraid to go down, go down to the camp with Purah,
your servant, and you will hear what they say,
and afterward your hands will be strengthened
to go down against the camp."
Judges 7:9-11 (ESV)

The man in this verse was just about to go to war with the Midianites, but Gideon's 300 men were scared to fight them. God knew that Gideon and his men needed courage to do what He had called them to do. In the same way, when you feel scared about the path God has set you on, you should know there is nothing wrong with asking God to confirm what He has told you to do. God wants you to have confidence, which He can strengthen when He answers specific prayers. When Gideon went to hear what the Midianites were saying, behold, he heard about a soldier's dream. The dream seemed to mean that God was going to hand over the Midianites to Gideon's army, which was just an example of one of the many miracles that God performed for them.

Are you building your faith in the miracle-working God? God asked Gideon to have only 300 men go into battle against a huge army, but that's how miracles happen. When you face the impossible, know that nothing is impossible for God. And He wants you to know that He caused the miracle, not wonder if things just worked themselves out. God is the "somehow" when things somehow happen miraculously, so be confident that your sovereign God made it happen. God can put thoughts into the minds of people and He can give them dreams; either way, God can change a heart of stone into a heart of compassion. And He can confirm to you the ways He moves and works in your life so you know things are from Him and not your adversary. *Are you afraid to go where God is calling you?* He has a way to give you courage, so just ask.

Day 336

Despite Feelings

Despite their fear of the people around them,
they built the alter on its foundation and sacrificed burnt offerings
to the Lord . . . For seven days they celebrated with joy
the Feast of Unleavened Bread.
Because the Lord had filled them with joy
by changing the attitude of the King of Assyria,
so that he assisted them in the work on the house of God,
the God of Israel.
Ezra 3:3, 6:22 (NIV)

When God's people disobeyed Him, they were sent off as slaves; but God always redeems His people when they humble themselves, acknowledge Him, and repent. This passage details the first time the Jews returned to rebuild the temple in Jerusalem, and they started with the altar. This proved important, signifying that the people had placed their worship of God as a first priority; God always wants our heart right with Him and wants to be the only One worthy of our worship.

The Israelites were afraid of the people in the neighborhood, and rightfully so. These people wanted to do the Israelites real harm. Yet, despite their feelings of fear, the Israelites did the work God called them to do. In turn, due to their obedience, God eventually changed the attitude of the Assyrian King, and they were protected from him. Confidence in God's sovereignty is often built just like the temple, one stone at a time. Our lives need to be built on the confidence of who God says He is and who God says we are in Christ. Sometimes God will knock down your altars so you can start over, beginning anew. God knows what you hold onto that enslaves you, and He is willing to knock down whatever is keeping you from being fully invested in your worship and sacrifices for Him. Your surroundings don't matter as much as God's sovereign protection. *Can you see places in your past life torn down as you disobeyed God? Have you gone your own way, becoming a slave to those things not of Him?* He wants you to celebrate your freedom over sin, but you must first submit to God's sovereign rule in your life.

Day 337

Nothing Is Impossible with God

The angel said "Do not be afraid, Mary,
you have found favor with God.
You will be with Child and give birth to a Son
and you are to give Him the name of Jesus."
For nothing is impossible with God.
Mary said "I am the Lord's servant."
Luke 1:30-31, 37, 38 (NIV)

Mary was chosen to be the virgin mother of Jesus, and God knew she would accept the role's challenges. Saying "yes" to God's sovereign plan, she would experience both great sorrow and joy. Pregnant as a young teenager, she became a social outcast. Yet, she got to see the bond grow between the last prophet to live, John the Baptist, and Jesus the Messiah; they were cousins.

This family must have had extraordinary passion for the ways of God. Yet, Joseph's first reaction to leave her due to the pregnancy must have left her emotionally broken and confused. Perhaps this confusion turned to joy when the angel visited Joseph, reassuring him, and he obeyed and stayed with her. Then after Jesus' birth, they had to flee their home twice to reach safety. All her days as Jesus' mother, she bore both pain and joy, right up until she watched Jesus die on a cross. Mary didn't realize all she had said "yes" to when she told God she would be His servant, but she followed wholeheartedly. She believed God could do the impossible, and she was blessed as the only woman to experience it all. She served as the human vessel to carry the blessed Christ in her womb, and He grew in wisdom and stature as the world's Savior and Messiah. She was able to prompt Jesus to perform His first miracle, turning water into wine, using her mother's intuition; even Jesus needed a loving mother at his side. As Mary's legacy, God blessed her as an example of motherly love for all the generations to come. God sovereignly gave us our mothers to be honored and loved. *Have you accepted your responsibilities in your family? Are you serving God faithfully in that role?* You can serve God faithfully by raising your children to love our Lord.

Day 338

Repeated Promise

The Lord appeared to Isaac the same night and said,
"I AM the God of Abraham your father,
Fear not, for I AM with you and will bless you
and multiply your offspring for My servant Abraham's sake."
Genesis 26:24 (ESV)

When you look at Genesis chapter 26, you see that we are similar to Isaac in many ways. First, Isaac had no idea of the historical life he was leading, no idea of the plans God had for him. God planned for Isaac to be the father of Jacob, whose sons would lay the foundation of the twelve tribes of Israel. In the same way, we have no idea how God will use us as parents and grandparents to see the role our children will play in the foundation of Christ.

When God has a plan for your life, He will work it out. He did so with Isaac; He will do so for you. But you must trust Him. Despite all of Isaac's shortcomings, including lack of trust and fear controlling his decisions, God still used him to do exactly what He had planned. In Verse 2, the Lord appears to Isaac, telling him to stay in the land and that He will be with him and bless him. Yet, in verses 6 and 7, Isaac fears the men there. He is looking down at his situation, not up at God, not taking God at His Word. *Can you see these tendencies in yourself?* In verses 11 and 12, God's plan through Isaac is bigger than Isaac's fear, and God protects Isaac and blesses him richly. So much so that by verse 17, he becomes too rich for the land and is told to leave. By verse 22, he finds land for his household, which brings us to today's verse, the second time God tells him to "fear not." By verses 28 to 32, you can see that the Lord had been with Isaac, blessing him with water and full protection again; God works in the details. What He did for Isaac, He will do for you. *Are you looking down at your situation or up at God? Do you fear that God's sovereignty will put you in a hard place?* Despite your shortcomings, God can use you, just as you are.

Day 339

Purpose Through It All

*Do not lose heart or be afraid when rumors are heard in the land;
one rumor comes this year, another the next,
rumors of violence in the land and of ruler against ruler.*
Jeremiah 51:46 (NIV)

Do not lose heart when the president is not who you wanted. Do not lose heart when the school board is not filled with people of your same ideology. Do not lose heart when your HOA president does not make the changes to your neighborhood that you wanted done. Do not lose heart when God replaces the pastor you loved with someone new. Do not lose heart when your boss is hard to handle. God already designed these people to win and overcome certain obstacles.

God designed people to have a certain position in life; can you accept that and move on? Or does it consume your thoughts? Does it make you angry? God knew every terrible king that would rule over the Israelites; yet, He did not stop them from becoming king. They certainly became examples of actions and attitudes we should avoid in our own lives, but we should not fear the direction people will go. Each person is responsible for him or herself, but God gives strength to those who depend on His ability to control everything this world has against them. You will hear rumors of things people did that make you uncomfortable, but do not lose heart. Keep doing what God has called you to do. But also know that God never calls us to a place of abuse. Satan does that. It's your job to be confident that God is sovereignly in control of all the people that hold a high position in your life. He has a purpose through it all. One of the great mysteries of God is that He does use the evil in this world for His good, somehow, in some way.

Day 340

Say, What?

Do not be anxious how you are to speak or what you are to say,
for what you are to say will be given to you in that hour.
For it is not you who speaks,
but the Spirit of your Father speaking through you.
Matthew 10:19-20 (ESV)

Have you been worried about what to say to a person over a touchy situation? Do you choose not to share your faith in Christ because you do not know what to say? In these verses Jesus is telling His apostles not to worry about what to say. Certainly, the original building blocks of the Christian faith were dependent upon what they said. And Christians are to pass the torch of faith along from one person to the next by our words, but God does not leave us to our own devices. God works through us. He will give you the words to say, so do not fear the "what if" scenarios and faithfully believe God will do all He has promised. Trust and obey, and God will give you the words. He gave you free will, and He will not force you to submit to His sovereign plan. Yet, your life can find peace if you choose to hand over your will and start doing His will.

What does turmoil over a project sometimes mean? Perhaps that you are not following the will of God. When God sends things your way, His peace and assurance often come, too. Through the power and leading of the Holy Spirit, you can faithfully trust His will in your life. God can equip you for the correct response. God will give you the holy nudge about when it is time to speak up and correct some wrongs. But you must seek God's direction if you want to be led by His sovereign plan. You must have a conversation with God about the touchy situation before you speak to the person involved. *Will you ask God today to awaken your senses and ignite your Holy Spirit?* Then when the time comes, He will guide you to have the conversation despite your fear. When you speak up and step out in faith, God will direct your steps.

Day 341

Trusting His Will

I have heard the groaning of the people . . .
I AM the Lord and I will bring you out from under
the burdens of the Egyptians,
and I will deliver you from slavery to them,
and I will redeem you with an outstretched arm
and with great acts of judgment. I will take you to be My people,
and I will be your God and you shall know that I AM the Lord your God
who has brought you out from under the burdens . . .
I will bring you in the land that I swore to give to Abraham,
to Isaac, and to Jacob. I will give it to you for a possession.
I AM the Lord.
Exodus 6:5-8 (ESV)

In these verses, God says "He will" seven times. God will do what He promises and never leaves you. In fact, He is so close to you that He knows exactly what is weighing you down. *Are you believing He will redeem your every burden? What have you accepted as your cross to bear? What if your view changed to realize your burdens should bring you closer to God, not pull you away?* For His grace is sufficient for all the thorns in your life. For when we are weak, He is strong.

Satan may have been lying to you for a long time, saying things like, "You will never get over this, the emptiness is too deep, the pain is too woven into the fabric of who you are." But God wants your complete confidence in Him and His power to redeem you from the burdens you carry. Right now, you can stand up and dust yourself off. There is a time to cry and mourn, but also a time to let go and let God redeem you from your burdens. God wants His people tender, but in reality, we live in a harsh world. And some of our concerns are the same as His. He wants your heart to break for the things that break His as sometimes you are the God-given answer to correct some wrongs. But no matter your burdens, God wants you to tell Him whatever has imprisoned your heart. *What has you enslaved?* God wants you to be honest with Him; then, He can redeem you and show you His great acts.

Day 342

Watching Closely

But you, take courage! Do not let your hands be weak,
for your work shall be rewarded.
2 Chronicles 15:7 (ESV)

These words were so encouraging to Asa, a king of Judah, that he took courage and destroyed the idols from all the land. The land's people were worshipping false gods, putting their faith and trust in something made from human hands. *Are we doing the same today? What idols or things you can hold in your hands are standing in the way of your deeper faith?* God wants you to disallow these idols in your life and give Him your full attention. He also wants you to place your identity in Him, find joy in serving Him, and not worry about not receiving others' praise.

Do you feel overlooked by others? Might you be looking for the approval of people instead of God? Don't let Satan twist the things you love to do. You might love to bring people together, making the plans and preparations, but sometimes Satan asks, "Who calls *you* and extends an invitation? Who really appreciates your efforts?" Or you might work with people who don't notice what you do, perhaps at church or in a ministry, and Satan says, "Your part is insignificant, certainly not special." Well, God says, "I know your heart and understand your thoughts." *He gave you the desire to do what you love, so why are you even listening to Satan's negativity?* God never overlooks you because He never leaves you. He wants you to destroy your idols of self-worth, self-promotion, and self-esteem. He wants you to humbly come to Him and receive your identity in Christ, where your flesh is buried and your Holy Spirit rules. When you learn to put down your idols and come to Him with open, empty hands, He will receive and reward you. Perhaps not in the timing or area you imagined, but your reward is coming. God wants you to do all things for Him, not other people. Do not doubt your gifts are from God or that He knows your good intentions. Listen to God's whispers; He wants you to be His servant. *Can you accept serving Christ without recognition? Can you remain patient for His reward?*

Day 343

The Way

They will see the glory of the LORD, the splendor of our God.
Strengthen the feeble hands, steady the knees that give way;
say to those with fearful hearts,
"Be strong, do not fear; your God will come,
He will come with vengeance;
with divine retribution He will come to save you."
Then will the eyes of the blind be opened
and the ears of the deaf unstopped.
Then will the lame leap like a deer,
and the mute tongue shout for joy.
Water will gush forth in the wilderness and streams in the desert.
The burning sand will become a pool,
the thirsty ground bubbling springs.
In the haunts where jackals once lay,
grass and reeds and papyrus will grow.
And a highway will be there; it will be called the Way of Holiness.
The unclean will not journey on it;
it will be for those who walk on that Way;
wicked fools will not go about on it.
No lion will be there, nor will any ferocious beast get up on it;
they will not be found there. But only the redeemed will walk there,
and those the LORD has rescued will return.
They will enter Zion with singing;
everlasting joy will crown their heads.
Gladness and joy will overtake them,
and sorrow and sighing will flee away.
Isaiah 35:2b-10 (NIV)

Jesus is the Way: the only way into heaven. And that's why the early Christians were called "the Way" as well. They pointed the only way to Jesus, the only way to eternal life. Is there a backup plan for your redemption? The answer is no. When you follow the Way in this life, when you take to heart His Word, He will redeem your heart and soul. He will also come to save you and bring you justice. As today's passage declares, "Be strong, do not fear; your God will come, He will come with vengeance; with divine retribution He will come to save you." *Do you feel like you want to take vengeance on the person who wounded you?* Believe God will act justly with that person. Believe He will intervene on your behalf at the perfect moment you need His redeeming love to rescue you. *What are you clutching onto that God does not intend for you to carry? What bitterness do you need to release so God can show you that He always keeps His promises?* He wants you to be filled with love and peace in this chaotic world. But you can do so only by following His Way, His Word, into His Holiness. Vengeance is not yours. Taking matters into your own hands and retaliating does not please God. You can spin in the wrong direction if you choose to let bitterness and unforgiveness take root in your heart. You find joy when you let God be God, when you let Him show you His Way to peace and the prosperity of eternal life.

Day 344

Believe He Will Provide

Blessed is the one who considers the poor!
In the day of trouble the Lord delivered him;
the Lord protected him and keeps him alive;
he is called blessed in the land;
You do not give him up to the will of his enemies.
The Lord sustains him on his sickbed; in his illness
You restore him to full health.
Psalm 41:1-3 (ESV)

Some of the most grateful people I've ever met have been poor. They depend on God to provide when it seems they don't have the means to feed their families. They experience miracles, like finding a $20 bill on the ground at the perfect moment, an empty gas tank that seems to go for miles, or just the right person bringing a meal or lending a hand. In many low-income neighborhoods, it's common to see people helping out neighbors when disaster strikes.

God allows the poor to see His miracles in amazing ways because they believe He will provide. I know because I was raised poor, and I thank God for all the times people came to my family's rescue. It is our duty, as an act of obedience in the name of Christ, to come alongside people, to lend a hand or serve a meal. God wants you to take part in people's miracles. You can redeem a little child's day by providing for his or her family when life brings them down financially. God may have given you riches or a little extra to bless someone's life. *Are you looking for opportunities to be the hands and feet of Jesus? Have you ever consider sponsoring a child?* You can come alongside God and partner with Him to help feed the poor. You can be the miracle in someone's life sent by God. You can help redeem their faith in their desperate situation. So, take God at His Word and be blessed today: "Blessed are you who consider the poor."

Day 345

Purifying People

For the grace of God that brings salvation has appeared to all men.
It teaches us to say "No" to ungodliness and worldly passions,
and to live self-controlled, upright, and godly lives in this present age,
while we wait for the blessed hope—
the glorious appearing of our great Savior, Jesus Christ,
who gave Himself for us to redeem us from all wickedness
and to purify for Himself a people that are His very own,
eager to do what is good.
Titus 2:11-14 (NIV)

Are you eager to do good? Do you live like Christ will appear at any second? God will redeem you from all wickedness when you step into heaven with Him. Until then, you live in a corrupt world, tainted by sin, but you are not of this world; you are different. The people not living for Christ have worldly desires that make them greedy for personal gain. Yet, God wants you to live for His good purpose. Humbly, God wants you to live putting other people's needs before your own. In fact, He gives you directions on how you are to live in this present age. In the process, Jesus Himself is purifying you. Over time you will recognize how God has helped you change your attitude to align with His character. Your redemption is a process with God that will build your faith in His ability to work in your life.

Do you have a situation that needs healing, and unless God comes in and breathes His redemption on the situation, your fears might become reality? What are you waiting on? Where are you placing your hope? Is God trying to teach you to say "no"? Jesus will redeem every soul who admits he or she is a sinner in need of His redemption. And He will redeem each part of your heart, soul, and mind that was destroyed due to someone's wickedness poured out on you. Build your faith now while waiting for His blessed hope. This world and its suffering are momentary. The wickedness you have endured will not last forever. Your hope lies in healing through Jesus.

Day 346

At Your Point of Need

Fear not you worm, you men of Israel! I AM the one who helps you,
declares the Lord; your Redeemer is the Holy One of Israel.
Isaiah 41:14 (ESV)

In the Bible, the worm is a symbol of weakness and insignificance, a representation of who we are when separated from Christ. However, when Jesus redeems your life, He helps you right where you are. God does not expect people to get themselves together before they come to Christ. He is not asking you to figure out how to live your life sober before you come to Him. God is not waiting for you to figure out how to be a better person. He wants you to come to Him exactly as you are. There is no need to cover up or clean up before lifting your eyes or hands to Him. He just wants you to reach out to Him covered with the dirt, mire, and broken glass where you lay shattered. He wants to clean you up right in the middle of the mess.

The great I AM is your helper, ready to meet you at your point of need. The I AM statements in the Bible show us the character of God, which is to help and redeem you. It is who He is. God's character does not change, but He wants to change your character. *What in your life is making you feel weak or insignificant? What is draining you?* God declares He will help and redeem your weaknesses. He will give your life significance. *Are you seeking God's redemption when your emotions get the best of you?* People may make you feel insignificant, but God places great worth on the people He has redeemed. As a child of God, you are accepted right where you are. God will clean you up if you allow His Word to minister to your heart, right there in the mess where you lay.

Day 347

Back on Course

*Even if you have been banished to the most distant land
under the heavens, from there the Lord your God
will gather you and bring you back.*
Deuteronomy 30:4 (NIV)

Many times, God repeats in His Word, "Even if you . . . then I will." God promises us so many times that He will redeem us, even when we follow our own hearts and go astray. He remains so faithful because humans tend to go astray on a regular basis, and God keeps calling us back to Him. God will redeem you every time you stray from Him. For many people, a slight distraction in the beginning can easily become a roadblock. A few fun weekends gambling with friends can turn into a habit. A few too many of anything occasionally can turn into an ongoing practice. If you don't know how to hurdle these obstacles, remember God; He will redeem you. Ask God to show you where the roadblocks are, regardless of how far off you have wandered. Regardless of what you have done, God is faithful; He can redeem you and bring you back on course.

What roadblock is keeping you from God's promise? In what areas do you need to repent? Even if God has sent you into a valley, you can ask for forgiveness and turn back to Him, but it's up to you to accept His redemption plan. Our days are numbered, so as long as you have breath, seek His redemption. Only Jesus can redeem your soul in a way that will make it completely whole.

Day 348

Fearless Integrity

*Now my daughter, do not fear. I will do for you all that you ask,
for all my fellow townsmen know that you are a worthy woman.
And now it is true that I am a redeemer.*
Ruth 3:11-12a (ESV)

Are you a worthy person? Not worthy in a prideful kind of way. But in a God-honoring way. *Are you worthy to be called a Proverbs 31 kind of woman, or a wise Proverbs 2 kind of man? Do you seek to be wise from God's wisdom? Has God redeemed your perspective as to why on earth you are here, to serve Him, showing love to others? Do you extend unexpected kindness to people?*

The theme for the book of Ruth is kindness and redemption. It exemplifies for us the Truth that when we choose to live our lives with humility and kindness toward others, God will redeem our hardships. We are called to love, regardless of the difficulties we face. Naomi, Ruth's mother-in-law, knew great loss. Her husband died, and ten years later her two sons died. A widow without sons living in a foreign land back in 1010 BC, as Naomi now was, faced scorn and shame. How would she support herself? Who would protect her? Her plight as an outcast was now a big deal. Her only hope, she thought, was to return to her home village and hope she could survive somehow. Ruth, the daughter-in-law, was from a Moabite family who "believed" in God but also followed false gods. In Ruth 1:16, Ruth decides to follow the one true God when she decides to stay with her mother-in-law. She makes a vow, a public profession of faith—just as we are called to do when we humbly accept the redemption of our sins by the power of Jesus.

God sovereignly placed those two women together to depend on each other through love and labors so His redemption story could be exhibited for the world to see. God sees us when our challenges look daunting, and He expects us to faithfully trust He will send in a Redeemer. We are to do the work; we are not called to sit by on idle. Our faith is active. In faith, Ruth went to the fields to glean the wheat, recognizing her need for mercy. She acted in faith and just "happened to come" to the field owned by the man she would marry. When we face our worries, God builds our trust in His ability to redeem us from all our fears.

Day 349

Clothed in Righteousness

Then he showed me Joshua the high priest standing
before the angel of the LORD,
and Satan standing at his right hand to accuse him.
And the LORD said to Satan, "The LORD rebuke you, O Satan!
The LORD who has chosen Jerusalem rebuke you!
Is not this a brand plucked from the fire?"
Now Joshua was standing before the angel,
clothed with filthy garments.
And the angel said to those who were standing before him,
"Remove the filthy garments from him."
And to him he said, "Behold, I have taken your iniquity away from you,
and I will clothe you with pure vestments."
And I said, "Let them put a clean turban on his head."
So, they put a clean turban on his head and clothed him with garments.
And the angel of the LORD was standing by.
And the angel of the LORD solemnly assured Joshua,
"Thus says the LORD of hosts:
If you will walk in my ways and keep my charge,
then you shall rule my house and have charge of my courts,
and I will give you the right of access
among those who are standing here.
Hear now, O Joshua the high priest,
you and your friends who sit before you,
for they are men who are a sign:
behold, I will bring My servant the Branch.
For behold, on the stone that I have set before Joshua,
on a single stone with seven eyes, I will engrave its inscription,"
declares the LORD of hosts,
"and I will remove the iniquity of this land in a single day.
In that day," declares the LORD of hosts,
"every one of you will invite his neighbor
to come under his vine and under his fig tree."
Zechariah 3:1-10 (ESV)

There is a battle between God and Satan for your soul. But anyone who turns to the saving grace of Jesus will be saved, and the battle has already been won. Jesus is the fulfilment of these passages. Jesus Christ is the Branch, and you have been grafted into the Kingdom of God. Yet, you must come under His authority. If you walk in His way and keep His charge, then

378

your covenant of peace in Christ will prove a sure-footed step. Before you came to Christ, you were soiled with dirt, but Jesus cleansed you from your sins and clothed you in righteousness—the only One who can do so. You are cleansed by His work. Once filthy, you are no longer. *Satan was there to accuse the high priest of his past sin, in the presence of God. Why do you think you are any different?* Satan loves to accuse Christians of their past sins, but God rebukes Satan and wants to remind you that your sins have been paid for by the blood of Christ. Satan wants to keep you bogged down by his lies and accusations, but really, they have no hold on you. Your shame and guilt have been paid for; you are free from them, indeed. *The Lord rebukes Satan from your life, so why do you keep inviting him back?* The battle is over. Christ won your freedom through His blood on a cross. Believe it, and rejoice in that victory today.

Day 350

Aim to Please

A Good Soldier of Christ: You then, my child,
be strengthened by the grace that is in Christ Jesus,
and what you have heard from me in the presence of many witnesses
entrust to faithful men, who will be able to teach others also.
Share in suffering as a good soldier of Christ Jesus.
No soldier gets entangled in civilian pursuits,
since his aim is to please the one who enlisted him.
An athlete is not crowned unless he competes according to the rules.
It is the hard-working farmer who ought to have
the first share of the crops.
Think over what I say,
for the Lord will give you understanding in everything.
2 Timothy 2:1-7 (ESV)

An effective soldier does not get entangled in civilian pursuits. In the same way, as soldiers for Christ, we are made for Heaven, not for this world. We have a deep desire within our being for the perfect world that is to come. But while here on earth, we must stay focused on the teachings of Christ in order to be certain we are facing the battles God intends for us to face. In other words, not all battles are ours to face, for God wants His people to have balance in their lives. With the exception of God, too much of anything is a bad idea. You can even spend too much time at church. God wants His people to be home sometimes so they can influence and help the people there. So, what does that mean to your ministry? Your ministry outside the home might not be fully blessed until you have a ministry at home first. God is calling you to be a witness for Him everywhere you go. Your battle is to win souls for Christ, and your aim is to please Him in the process.

Are you seeking God's understanding and perspective in your battles of winning souls? God will give you the understanding you need, at the perfect moment, when you learn to be strengthened by the grace found in Christ. One of the fruits of the Spirit is self-control. God wants you to tap into His strength, and then you can find the self-control you need to live a balanced life.

Day 351

Blessings in the War

The LORD will grant that the enemies who rise up against you
will be defeated before you.
They will come at you from one direction but flee from you in seven.
The LORD will send a blessing on your barns
and on everything you put your hand to.
The LORD your God will bless you in the land He is giving you.
The LORD will establish you as His holy people,
as He promised you on oath,
if you keep the commands of the LORD your God and walk in His ways.
Deuteronomy 28:7-8 (NIV)

How comfortable are you asking God for His blessings over the battles in your life? God wants to be commander-in-chief over every hard situation you face. He also wants to establish you in His ever-present grace and mercy by teaching you how to walk in His ways. He wants to fill you with His goodness every day, not just the hard days. He wants to have authority over your days of blessing and your days of war.

Are you getting ahead of yourself? Is your mind racing at the thought of how much more you need to do before you can see your battles won? You can't outrun the grace of God, but you can make a mess of things if you don't slow down and listen for God's whispers. Let the adversary be afraid when you shout the battle cry armed with faith that God will come through and do all He promised you. Only because you fear the trumpet call may your victory seem far off. God is calling to get you moving. He wants you to face the things blocking you from taking hold of your spiritual weapons, and He will bless you for your obedience to His will. His will is for you to be completely healed from your brokenness; to face your battles and stand up to the people that oppress you; and to be established in the foundation of Christ, wearing the full armor of God. Satan likes to send you enemies you think you can't handle. Yet, when you fight your battles while obedient to the Word, you can claim victory. Do life God's Way, and claim your blessings.

Day 352

Bring Unity

And when news of wars and troubled times comes to your ear,
have no fear; for these things have to be, but the end will not be now.
Luke 21:9 (BBE)

Where does chaos reign in your life? What is still confusing you?
Who in your life is acting unpredictably and erratically? God has
warned us that in this world we will have trouble, but take heart: He
has overcome the world (John 16:33), and we have peace through
Jesus Christ. Every day as we battle Satan, he wants to steal your
peace by bringing chaos. Yet, God pours out His blessing of wisdom
when you trust that He will expose the areas that have you confused.
Satan's chaos works through behaviors that are unpredictable and
cause confusion, but God does the exact opposite. Our world is
chaotic, and the only way to experience God's peace is to live out the
truth of His Word. Every single battle you face is an opportunity for
you to bring unity or division onto the battlefield. God is telling you
not to fear the troubled times, the chaotic times. So, you have a choice
in how you handle the chaos. You can respond in fear and choose to
forgo the blessing of God's peace, or you can trust that Jesus has the
answer to how you should handle your troubles, and through that, you
will find your peace. He has already given you the freedom to live out
your peace found in Him.

Christians are a community of peace in a chaotic world; yet, we
are not called to stand by, doing nothing about the chaos. Some
battles bring peace because the chaos is exposed and the truth is
known. God wants you to fight the good fight by not tolerating the
sins of the people around you. Being personally connected with Jesus
over your whole day will bring you to a better understanding of what
battles you should face, or what ways you can bring in God's shalom.

Day 353

The Perfect Solution

But the Lord said to me, "Do not fear him,
for I have given him and all his people and his land into your hands.
Deuteronomy 3:2 (ESV)

Do you feel like you try and try, but still face a brick wall over and over again, and you just don't know how you can ever stop running into the walls and break free? Perhaps you are fighting battles God did not intend for you to fight. Not all battles are yours. Many battles are won when you trust these words of the LORD: "Do not fear him, for I have given him and all his people into your hands." Satan wants you to give in and quit, but God wants to reassure you that His way is the best way.

Faith is built when you actively watch God fulfill His promise of fighting off your opponents. When God decides you will win certain battles, you will win. Nothing can stop Him from giving you the victory, and He won't change His mind. *Are you making things harder than needed because you think your way is the only way to accomplish the mission?* God designed some battles in your life as examples for you to remember; He will bring you peace when you let Him fight your battles. God wants you to remember what He did in the past because then you will know that He can do it again. Learn to live by trusting that God is on your side and that His holy mindset is the perfect solution every time. God wants you to bring all that you battle to His feet. He can give you the knowledge you need to know whether you should take the hands-off approach and trust Him with the outcome, or if you should seek His guidance on how to attack the problem you face. Either way, you are trusting God, continuing to build your faith, and showing others what true faith in God looks like. You will see your fear dissipate and your confidence in the Lord blossom. And that, my friend, is a beautiful thing to see.

Day 354

A Vessel to Share Christ

The following night the Lord stood by him (Paul) and said,
"Take courage, for as you have testified
to the facts about Me in Jerusalem, so you must testify in Rome."
Acts 23:11 (ESV)

God had a battle He wanted Paul to fight, the same battle that God expects each of us to keep on fighting. We are told that by the words of our testimony, people will be saved (Revelation 12:11). We are to go into all the world and make disciples (Matthew 28:19). God is telling you to take courage and testify to the work of Christ in your daily life. Nothing in your life is a coincidence. You have faced each battle that God predestined for you. In your free will, you may be losing some battles because you are not taking charge, with God's courage, to win them over.

Are you living out the Word of God during your battles? Your testimony is your proof of God in your life. *Are you letting Satan tarnish your testimony by choosing to fear telling people what God has done in your life?* The more you recognize God working in your life, the more you want to talk about it. Paul recognized Christ's work so much so that he wrote, "To live is Christ, and to die is to gain" (Philippians 2:21). He counted his life as only a vessel to share the knowledge of Jesus. Paul was not flashy, but simple and humble. Sending Paul to Rome was a death sentence, but in the few years it took for Paul to get there, he influenced multitudes of people. He wrote letters to churches, some of which ended up in the Bible we read today. He shared the Gospel message with officials, and he had enough freedom for people to come and see him in prison. He spoke unashamedly of the Gospel message of Jesus, regardless of his surroundings. God placed Paul before government officials, men of the law, Jews and Gentiles, and he told them about the saving truth of Jesus. He spoke in palaces, churches, people's homes, on the streets, and in prison. The only thing that mattered was the one soul who needed to know the redemption of Jesus Christ.

Day 355

Position Yourself

*Do not be afraid and do not be dismayed at this great horde,
for the battle is not yours but God's.*
2 Chronicles 20:15 (ESV)

As the king of Judah, Jehoshaphat was afraid and set his face to seek the Lord (2 Chronicles 20:3). He stood in the sanctuary and prayed to God with a sincere heart, and the Lord's response is our verse of today. Christians have the Holy Spirit with us everywhere we go, but back then the presence of God was in the Temple. The Jewish people would prepare themselves to go to the Temple, mindful they need to be purified and recognizing that God could place Himself anywhere, but in the Temple they could meet Him. And Jehoshaphat, needing reassurance and God's help, positioned himself to be in God's presence.

Somehow over time, society has forgotten the beauty of preparing oneself to meet with God in His presence. Yet, what was true then remains true now. If we prepare ourselves to meet with God, we purify ourselves by being honest about the sin in our lives. We seek God's direction on how He can redirect our thoughts and actions. And we humbly position ourselves to receive a Word from God. We position ourselves to be quiet with God, stripping away the doubt, the heaviness, and need to control our battles. God's glory can shine on our countless battle fields. *God wants to fight your battles, but are you taking them to Him in prayer, admitting you lack the ability to win a war without Him?* Do so today, asking Him to fight for you as the only way to win the battles and ultimately the war that rages around you.

Day 356

On the Verge

"When you go out to battle against your enemies,
and see horses and chariots and people more numerous than you,
do not be afraid of them; for the LORD your God is with you,
who brought you up from the land of Egypt.
So it shall be, when you are on the verge of battle,
that the priest shall approach and speak to the people.
And he shall say to them, 'Hear, O Israel:
Today you are on the verge of battle with your enemies.
Do not let your heart faint, do not be afraid,
and do not tremble or be terrified because of them;
for the LORD your God is He who goes with you,
to fight for you against your enemies, to save you.'"
Deuteronomy 20:1-4 (NKJV)

Too many people don't want to read the Law, but God has some amazing promises to those who faithfully believe His Word. Every word of the Bible has amazing value. Deuteronomy is a book of law, and although Jesus Christ came to earth to save us from the penalty of our sins, we still need to understand the Law. God did not change His idea of what is holy and perfect just because sin entered the world and corrupted His perfect plan. God's instructions and laws for us don't change because Jesus went to the cross. In fact, because Jesus paid our penalty for sin, we ought to know all the ways we have sinned against God.

Do you repent of sins when you don't know what they are? So, knowing His Word holds great value. And His Law stands yesterday, today, and forever. Although we no longer follow all the blood sacrifices, we still need to understand God's perfect instructions so we can live as pure a life as possible. Know that today's verse is God's instructions for handling your battles. You can claim victory because Jesus is on your side, even when the battle seems unwinnable. Remember, God took you out of slavery when you accepted Christ. And although Satan loves to remind you of your past, Jesus says, "Do not let your heart be faint, I AM fighting for you." Enjoy your victory!

Day 357

Dwell Secure

"There is no one like the God of Jeshurun,
who rides across the heavens to help you
and on the clouds in His majesty. The eternal God is your refuge,
and underneath are the everlasting arms.
He will drive out your enemies before you, saying, 'Destroy them!'
So Israel will live in safety; Jacob will dwell secure
in a land of grain and new wine, where the heavens drop dew.
Blessed are you, Israel! Who is like you, a people saved by the LORD?
He is your shield and helper and your glorious sword.
Your enemies will cower before you,
and you will trample down their high places."
Deuteronomy 33:26-29 (NIV)

You are almost to the end of this devotional. I want to congratulate you for deciding to work your way through your fears with God. You have plenty of days ahead when your courage to claim the victory in Christ will be tested. *Are you nervous for the next phase? Do you feel equipped with new knowledge on how to fight your battles with God on your side? Do you have an action plan for the next time you feel the confrontation building between you and someone else?*

Today's passage records some of Moses' last words—words to encourage the people that they will have the victory because God is on their side. Certainly, they could have feared what lay ahead, but Moses was a leader who listened to God's Word, with full respect for His holiness. Moses allowed God's words to hold weight on the scales of his judgments. The people knew God would direct Moses' decisions, but Moses wanted to build them up so they could find their own courage in God. While Moses was going to die, he left an example to live by. He knew if the people followed God's instructions, they would be successful. "Who is like you, a people saved by the LORD?" The term "Jeshurun" signified endearment for Israel, meaning "the dear upright people," and God is speaking words of endearment over your life. You will step into heaven, the Promised Land, claiming Christ's victory, but today as you look in the direction God wants you to go, remember all He taught you this last year. One by one, God will destroy your enemies.

Day 358

Down to the Core

Fear not, nor be afraid; have I not told you from of old and declared it?
And you are My witnesses! Is there a God beside Me?
There is no Rock; I know not any.
Isaiah 44:8 (ESV)

Are you positioning yourself to live in the freedom of Christ? Are you positioning yourself to be near the Rock of your salvation? Are you positioning yourself to be a witness to His victory that blesses you? You can live with your heart in a position of victory because Jesus set you there. Anytime God places you in a position, you can be certain it's a sure foundation. From the top of your head to the bottom of your feet, the Rock of all ages encapsulates you with His attributes. God gives you the helmet of salvation, renewing your mind. He gives you ears to hear and understand His Word. He makes your eyes pure and bright. God's outstretched arms protect you, holding your right hand. He has created your body as a holy temple, with the Holy Spirit dwelling within. He has given you a breastplate of righteousness, faith, and love, with an armor of Light. It was God who made you as surefooted as a mountain goat, walking the narrow path with your feet steady in the Gospel of peace. Both physically and spiritually, no angle of your being lies uncovered by God's Word. Every part of you is being renewed in the love of Christ. When you give your spiritual health over to God, He nourishes you down to the marrow. His Word is so deep, it exposes our thoughts and intentions down to our core.

God will equip you for victory. He alone can continue to bring victory to the souls scarred by the works done in the dark. You exist to demonstrate your victory in Christ. Your testimony of Jesus Christ is victory over the enemy, now and forever. Live in the position of victory. Victory feels good. Victories are celebrated. Enjoy being victorious through Christ.

Day 359

Compete for Glory

For He has delivered me from every trouble,
and my eye has looked in triumph on my enemies.
Psalm 54:7 (ESV)

Do you like challenges, or do they frustrate you? What obstacles are you facing that seem so strange you feel nothing good can come from them? God is challenging you to find your victory in today's verse. Look back over your life. Remember how He delivered you. Be challenged to strategize against the future schemes of the Devil.

Many people like competition, but we should not be mean-spirited about winning. God wants us to try our best and congratulate someone when they win the prize you were competing for. In God's economy, we humbly accept that God blessed someone a little differently than us. God's glory shines through each person differently, at different times. We can put our hope in winning the next time. God's victory is often found in His peace. When you learn to live in the victory of Jesus, you have a peace in your soul that will keep you even tempered. When you are calm and level-headed, His peace keeps you out of trouble. God's blessings keep on coming when you learn to live in Christ's victory.

What if we took that competitiveness and directed it toward Satan? Satan wants to steal God's glory, but we don't let him do so. Through the power of the Holy Spirit, we battle against him, and we shine God's glory, His goodness and love, with brightness and strength. God gives us a peace that transcends the circumstances that look dark and daunting. If we allow the darkness to scare us, then we let Satan win, stealing some of God's glory. And you who has the Light of Jesus burning bright in your soul have a right to get mad, fighting hard against Satan's schemes. *So why not decide today to battle in God's strength and be zealous for Him?* Take hold of your victory!

Day 360

Faithfully Equipped

*It shall come to pass in the day the LORD gives you rest
from your sorrow, and from your fear and the hard bondage
in which you were made to serve.*
Isaiah 14:3 (NKJV)

Can you process the notion that you were created to serve God in hard bondage? Can you find comfort and peace in God, knowing He designed you to live a life defeating the enemy time and time again? God did not create you as a wimp, nor does He call His people to war so they will face defeat, but rather so we can see that our victory comes from Him alone. God wants you not to live in fear of failure but to learn to do things His way. The flesh is ever present, and in your flesh, you may doubt that victory is at hand, but Hebrew 11 reminds us that "faith is the assurance of things hoped for, the conviction of things not seen." It's important to build your spiritual muscles, and seeing God give you victory develops those muscles that strengthen in faith. Without faith that God will bring victory to your battles, you will miss the blessing of increased faith when the battle is won. His will prevails, but don't miss seeing God work in your life and the amazing joy that results.

Regardless of the difficulty of God's assignment for you, nothing is too hard for Him. It's an honor when God asks you to do difficult work as He has confidence you can do it. Be assured that God is for you and by faith you can have the victory. Then others will see God's hand in the battle, your testimony will go forth, and the faith of many may be ignited—and then not only will many people around you rejoice but all the angels in heaven as well.

Day 361

Seek Jesus

In Me you may have peace. In the world you will have tribulation.
But take heart I have overcome the world.
John 16:33 (ESV)

How concerned are you with your comfort level? How much effort do you put into seeking the things of this world? God knows what we need, like food, clothes, and shelter, but He has instructed us not to go after the world's things but to seek Him first (Matthew 6:31-33). You cannot have peace if you keep wanting more. You won't have victory if your heart is set on *things*. A heart fully devoted to God is the key that unlocks the ability to overcome the world. Two of God's most blessed prophets wore clothes made not of fabric, which was costly, but made of leather (2 Kings 1:8; Matthew 3:4). These clothes represented a lowly status in the community, but spiritually they represented humility and aversion to people's earthly ways.

Always remember who you are *in Christ*, who gives you all good things. Nothing good comes from following a crowd of worldly folks. If you want a good husband, find a man who seeks Jesus first. If you want friendships that build you up, find friends who seek Jesus first. If you want a job you love, seek a place of employment that honors the laws of the Lord, not of the world. No greater benefit exists than working for a godly purpose. God designed you to fit into the fabric of life with other believers, calling you as a light in the darkness, but it's a place of ministry. God has not called you to comfort but to be fearless toward the world because He has tasks for you here. He will bring you to a place of discomfort, where people oppose what you try to set right, but God wants you to fight the good fight of faith and bring others into His grace. He wants to fill the void in your life, which can happen only if you stop seeking more stuff and start seeking God. You can have victory when you lay down your desires of what money can buy and start saving for your future in heaven. All you get to take into heaven are the souls you win for Christ. Only eternal love lasts from this side of heaven into eternity. Lay down your greed, and make your victories count.

Day 362

Abundant Peace

We are more than conquerors through Him that loved us.
Romans 8:37 (ESV)

Are you still feeling defeated by a situation you cannot get under control? Do you feel defeated when you try to break up fights and arguments around you? Do you feel like you just don't have the right words to settle a dispute? God wants to give you victory over these tough situations through humility and peace. He wants you to remain calm when others argue.

You have victory in Jesus! Your heart already holds the prize. God has given you every spiritual gift you will ever need to do His will (1 Corinthians 1:6-7). Recognize that Jesus is alive in you, and be confident in your spiritual gifts. Remember, spiritual gifts are many, and no one has them all. So, don't be jealous of what someone else has. God equipped you for the work He planned for you. We are all the body of Christ, and He is our Head. God is about relationships, and we need each other. We stand even more victorious when we choose to work together with other believers to complete a large task. Usually, no one person builds a house; it takes a team. Most houses have lots of builders working together, specializing in their talents and trades. *Why would God's desires be any different for His people?* When we stop arguing and work together, we are better. *Do you always have to be right?* Maybe your stubbornness is keeping you from seeing things with God's eyes. You are not the only one hearing God's voice. God speaks to all His children, and sometimes people hear God's voice but other times they don't but feel certain they do. God gave you a mind to discern the difference, but He does not permit you to force your opinion. The pride of trying to be right all the time can put a wedge between you and the people you love. God has called you to have victory through peace. Victory is not won when you walk away more frustrated than when you started. I pray that you find the courage to live peacefully in the victory God has given you.

Day 363

Willing and Able

God spoke to Israel in visions of the night and said, "Jacob, Jacob."
And he said, "Here I am."
Then He said, "I AM God, the God of your father.
Do not be afraid to go down to Egypt,
from there I will make you into a great nation.
I Myself will go down with you to Egypt,
and I will also bring you up again
and Joseph's hand will close your eyes."
Genesis 46:2-4 (ESV)

Can you trust that God will allow you to face future difficulties that will reshape who you are and where you go? Can you trust that God will go the distance with you? Do not be afraid to go. Do not be afraid to go into your Egypt. God is with you always, wherever you go. If you stay on the path of God's will, or if you falter and stumble back to your old ways, God is with you. You can go up high or go down low, but you cannot escape the omnipresent God. You are sealed into the family of God by the blood of Jesus. Your bond through Christ keeps you forever connected to God, wherever you travel. The only place you cannot go is hell; in every other place, you will be found in the presence of God and His angels. Yes, God is sending you on a hard journey, but He promises He will bring you out of the difficulties. You will not be stuck in a tough place forever. If you will seek Him first, setting you mind on His righteousness, you will succeed because He goes with you. The impossible is possible with God.

Satan wants to distract you and keep you doubting that anything good could result from the trauma you endured. God does not enjoy His people being wounded. Satan brought evil into the world, but God can masterfully use your scars to exhibit His glory. God knows the future days, and He is fighting for you. God comes close to those who choose to turn to Him in distress. The Great I AM is with you. He already made you the promise, so claim it! Trust God's path, and He will go with you. He will protect you. God's promises remain *always* true.

Day 364

Show Off His Glory

Jesus met them and said, "Good morning!"
They came up, took hold of His feet, and worshipped Him.
Then Jesus told them, "Do not be afraid.
Go and tell My brothers to leave for Galilee
and they will see Me there."
Matthew 28:9-10 (HCSB)

The living God designed everything to show off His glory on the earth. *Are you joining with creation and all believers to do so as well? Or you are trying to show off yourself?* God designed you specifically to shine His glory in a way no one else ever will. You can go with Christ's plan and design, or you can go your own way. If you want to have humility, go show off God's glory by staying in the moment with Christ. Show off all He has done through you. Do not be embarrassed to receive someone's compliments, but humbly deflect any praise, knowing it's only because Jesus is alive in you that you can do any good in your body.

It's an honor when God has confidence in you to do the hard work, but He does not want you deflated by the task of healing completely. He wants you to bravely go in the name of Christ, sharing all about your healing. Literally stand up and call it out: "I was (fill in the blank), and God is working with me on my healing by_____." Go tell of the work He is doing in your life by the work of the cross, and give someone else the confidence he or she needs to face the torment of fears inside. Only because you serve a Living God can you be alive, made new, in your brokenness. Jesus does not want you to fear tomorrow, but focus on what He is doing in your life. You have influence, so use it wisely. When you meditate on God's goodness, you will be brought to your knees for Him. In time, you will find your heart most content when you fall at Jesus' feet and worship Him in Spirit and truth. So, go tell the world. Soon, you will see Him face to face, and oh, what a joy that will be.

Day 365

Bold Honesty

Do not fear and do not be dismayed.
Take all the fighting men with you, and arise, go.
Joshua 8:1 (ESV)

Who are your "fighting men" that you want to have standing behind you? Who will walk beside you, "doing life" with you, and have your back as they pray with you and for you? God's fighting men for Joshua saw God hold back the waters when they crossed the Jordan (Joshua 3:17), and they marched around Jericho for seven days, seeing God tear down Jericho's walls (Joshua 6:20). They had been circumcised and consecrated to the Lord, and they knew God was to be obeyed and sin needed purging.

God wanted Joshua to call on those with integrity. Today is no different; God is calling His people, telling you to arise and go with the same bold honesty. God does not want you to be dismayed, worried, agitated, shocked, startled, distressed, unsettled, or fearful. God wants you to arise and go with the power of Christ and the people with whom you fellowship. Our weapon of warfare is prayer, one of the most powerful forces that reaches from our world into the spiritual realm. Your Christian brothers and sisters can be your greatest strategy against your enemy.

Joshua had faith that God would do exactly as He promised. When Joshua put his trust in God, talked with Him, and obeyed Him fully, he led Israel right into the Promised Land. So now, in the name of Jesus, go and pray for the people you love. Pray for their salvation and contentment. Pray for their fallen child, their abusive relationship, their broken marriage, their need for money. God wants you to arise and go pray for the lost and broken; you don't have to look far. Don't worry about what to pray or how elegant it sounds; pray with an open heart to receive the Holy Spirit's leading, and worship with your fighting prayer warriors as you see God work His miracles. Your bold journey with Christ continues. *Arise, go*, in faith and love! Do not fear or be dismayed. You will *always* have Jesus, your Redeemer and Friend, at your side.

Acknowledgments

Thank you, Jesus, for the desire to intensely study fear in a simple, biblical way. Once blinded by my own fears, I experienced You opening my eyes to see how to live courageously for Your good and gracious will.

I am extremely grateful to my husband, Brian. Next to Jesus, he is my favorite. My healing journey has been so fruitful because of him. Thank you, Brian, for supporting all my efforts to bring healing to other women who have been shattered from abuse.

Dearest Donna Skell at Roaring Lambs Ministries, my deepest gratitude goes to you for repeatedly encouraging me to write a book, my "glory story." Thank you for all the opportunities you have given me to share my testimony. Your ability to help others articulate their testimony so they can effectively share their hope in Jesus Christ is a gift from God. You are a Roaring Lamb!

God also gave me the perfect editor when He choose Karen Steinmann! I cannot say enough about how awesome she has been to work with. Karen, I appreciate all that you poured into this book. People will never know how blessed they are that you toned down and softened my harsh words and sought clarity in every thought throughout this devotional.

Everyone needs a person on her team who will teach her to be the best she can be and inspire her when she feels worn out. I am extremely honored to have Mrs. Linda Perry on my team. Thank you for "grading" (proof-reading) all my devotions. You gave me the confidence to keep going. I am indebted to you.

From the bottom heart, I want to thank every one of my Bible study "sistahs." I think each of you may find a little piece of yourself in the pages of this book. Iron sharpens iron, and thank God, we have each other to stay sharp. I love doing life together with my sistahs!

To my sister Kimberly, thanks for your willingness to always listen to me process life. Anyone who knows me knows how long-winded I can be. And, thanks to my Mama Sherry, I continually seek to be a God-fearing woman, though I often fall short. To my precious daughter, Zoey, I treasure the sweetness that resides in you. You can light up a room. My dearest son, Alex, you have no idea how much you impact my life. Thank you for being true to who God created you to be; you absolutely amaze me. Skylar, my little grand-Lovie, thank God for the fun of being your Grammy. I started this book when you were born. Seven years later, it is complete. One reason I wrote this book was to help your generation find their courage, in the name of Jesus. Thank you for your simple faith. Jesus will bring revival.

Cheers to all the broken people hurt by Satan's schemes but willing to tap into the power of the Holy Spirit.

About the Author

Stefanie Jane is a singer, speaker, and writer who speaks truthfully from the heart. Her passion, she states, lies in sharing her hope in healing through Jesus Christ—a hope borne from personal experience and conviction. As a trained advocate for sexual abuse survivors, she seeks God's leading and prayerfully uses her many talents to open doors of communication with those who find themselves in hard, painful places.

In 2009, she released her album *See Me Change?* which walks listeners through her own path of healing. Now seeking to help others remove the shame of past abuse and brokenness, Stefanie says she speaks boldly for the broken-hearted "because healing can be found when we hear we're not the only ones."

In the Light of Jesus, she remains confident that all darkness exposed can be healed. Stefanie Jane also enjoys leading Bible studies in the Dallas area, where she resides with her husband, Brian.

You may contact Stefanie at StefanieJane.com or Stefanie@stefaniejane.com

Topical Index

Topic	Day	Topic	Day	Topic	Day	Topic	Day
Identity		Identity		Peace		Promise	
	18		265		197		91
	19		266		288		92
	93		310		289		230
	94		311		290		231
	95		312		291		232
	96		313		292		233
	97		314		293		234
	98		315	Praise			235
	99		316		108	Protection	
	100		317		109		101
	157		318		110		102
	158		319		111		103
	159	Obedient			112		104
	160		74		113		105
	161		75	Prayer			106
	162		76		47		107
	163		77		48		198
	164		78		49		199
	212		79		50		200
	213		80		51		201
	214		190		52		202
	215		191		53		203
	216		192		170		204
	217		193		171		326
	218		267		172		327
	219		268		173		328
	257		269		174		329
	258		270		175		330
	259		271		176		331
	260		272	Promise			332
	261	Peace			87	Redeemed	
	262		194		88		147
	263		195		89		148
	264		196		90		149

Topic	Day	Topic	Day	Topic	Day	Topic	Day
Redeemed		Sovereign		Stand Firm		Trust	
	150		42		181		188
	151		43		182		189
	341		44				294
	342		45	The Light			295
	343		46		134		296
	344		120		135		297
	345		121		136		298
	346		122		137		299
	347		123		138		300
	348		124		139		301
Rescue			125		140	Victory	
	54		126	The Word			165
	55		249		20		166
Rescue			250		21		167
	56		251		22		168
	57		252		220		169
	58		253		221		356
	59		254		222		357
	60		255		223		358
	242		256		224		359
	243		333		225		360
	244		334	Trust			361
	245		335		61		362
	246		336		62		
	247		337		63		
	248		338		64		
Satan			339		65		
	226		340		66		
	227	Stand Firm			67		
	228		177		183		
	229		178		184		
Sovereign			179		185		
	40		180		186		
	41				187		

Scripture Index

John:	DAY
John 14:1-4	87
John 14:1-6	145
John 14:27	195
John 15:1-11	146
John 16:13	361
John 16:33	220
John 17:17	22
John 19:30	9

Acts:

Acts 1:8	232
Acts 18:9-10	268
Acts 23:11	354
Acts 27:24-25	188

Romans:

Rom. 4:20-21	152
Rom. 5:1-5	115
Rom. 8:14-16	15
Rom. 8:28	121
Rom. 8:31,34	96
Rom. 8:37	362
Rom. 12:1-2	163
Rom.12:17-21	123
Rom.12:21	253
Rom.13:3	271
Rom.14:23	153
Rom.15:13	119

1 Corinthians:

1 Cor. 2:2-5	325
1 Cor. 10:13	230
1 Cor. 16:13-14	181

2 Corinthians:

2 Cor. 1:3-5	261
2 Cor. 1:20-22	88
2 Cor. 3:16-18	12
2 Cor. 4:6	137
2 Cor. 7:5-7	187
2 Cor. 9:6-8	309
2 Cor. 10:5	160
2 Cor. 11:3	226

Galatians:

Gal. 5:1	182

Ephesians:

Eph. 3:14-21	48
Eph. 4:1-3	19
Eph. 4:26-27	229
Eph. 4:29-32	162
Eph. 5:8-14	135
Eph. 6:10-18	81

Philippians:

Phil. 1:6	308
Phil. 1:12-14	287
Phil. 1:28-29	213
Phil. 2:12-16	265
Phil. 4:4-7	170
Phil. 4:8	159
Phil. 4:13	91

Colossians:

Col. 1:9-14	47
Col. 1:15-20	129
Col. 2:6-15	110
Col. 3:1-5	157
Col. 3:15-16	196

1 Thessalonians:

1 Thess. 2:13	222
1 Thess. 5:23-24	316

2 Thessalonians:

2 Thess.1:6-7	122
2 Thess.2:13-17	178
2 Thess.3:2-5	104

1 Timothy:

1 Tim. 6:11-12	156

2 Timothy:

2 Tim. 1:7	94
2 Tim. 2:1-7	350
2 Tim. 3:11-14	242
2 Tim. 3:16-17	20
2 Tim. 4:16-18	201

Titus:	DAY
Titus 1:2	227
Titus 2:11-14	345

Philemon:

Philem. 6	214

Hebrews:

Heb. 2:14-17	11
Heb .4:15-16	32
Heb. 6:17-19	116
Heb. 11:6	36
Heb. 11:23-28	274
Heb. 12:3-7	211
Heb. 13:5-6	260

James:

James 1:5-8	92
James 1:13-18	134
James 3:13-18	97
James 4:7-8	34

1 Peter:

1 Pet. 3:6	192
1 Pet. 3:8-15	99
1 Pet. 4:1-2	298
1 Pet. 5:7	28

2 Peter:

2 Pet. 2:9	57
2 Pet. 3:17-18	76

1 John:

1 John 1:5-7	136
1 John 2:14	33
1 John 2:27	283
1 John 4:18	93
1 John 5:3-5	166

2 John

2 John 8-9	193
3 John 11	98

Jude:

Jude: 20-21	155

Revelation:

Rev. 1:17	132
Rev. 2:10-11	168

Made in the USA
Monee, IL
02 July 2022